Richard Josiah Hinton

English radical Leaders

Richard Josiah Hinton

English radical Leaders

ISBN/EAN: 9783742847249

Manufactured in Europe, USA, Canada, Australia, Japa

Cover: Foto ©ninafisch / pixelio.de

Manufactured and distributed by brebook publishing software
(www.brebook.com)

Richard Josiah Hinton

English radical Leaders

BRIEF BIOGRAPHIES

OF

EUROPEAN PUBLIC MEN.

EDITED BY

THOMAS WENTWORTH HIGGINSON.

RECENTLY PUBLISHED:
BRIEF BIOGRAPHIES.

Vol. I.—ENGLISH STATESMEN.
BY THOS. WENTWORTH HIGGINSON. $1.50.

TO FOLLOW IMMEDIATELY

Vol. III.—FRENCH LEADERS.
BY EDWARD KING. $1.50.

G. P. PUTNAM'S SONS, . . . NEW YORK.

BRIEF BIOGRAPHIES

ENGLISH RADICAL LEADERS

By

R. J. HINTON.

NEW YORK
G. P. PUTNAM'S SONS
FOURTH AVE. AND 23D ST.
1875.

PREFACE.

THE preparation of this little volume has been a pleasant task. It has afforded an opportunity to delineate not only some of the most influential of living Englishmen, but also the popular agitations and reforms through which their influence has been exerted. For this purpose it has been necessary to carry the reader into a domain little known to Americans, even to those Americans who have personally visited the mother country. English governing influences are in a great measure social, rather than political; and American travellers usually see little of the life of the English people, and often know less than they see. Bearing in mind this fact, I have tried in each case to link the man and his work together, pointing out not merely the personal qualities of the individual, but his importance as the representative of some principle or popular movement.

Few of those described in this volume are distinguished for social position, wealth, or literary culture; but they all have sincerity, earnestness, experience and the power to make their influence felt among the people. It has seemed to me—an Englishman born and reared, an American by choice, service, and loyal belief in the republic,—that the story of these lives was worth telling, if only to illustrate the manner in which democratic principles are gradually penetrating and re-moulding the institutions of Great Britain.

RICHARD J. HINTON.

CONTENTS.

PART I.

THE INDEPENDENT MEMBERS.

	PAGE
I.—Professor Fawcett	11
II.—Sir Charles W. Dilke	25
III.—Peter A. Taylor	55
IV.—Sir John Lubbock	71
V.—Joseph Cowan	77
VI.—Robert Meek Carter	86

PART II.

THE LABOR AGITATION AND ITS FRIENDS.

VII.—Thomas Hughes	99
VIII.—Anthony J. Mundella	121
IX.—Alexander Macdonald	142
X.—Thomas Brassey	161
XI.—Samuel Morley	178

PART III.

PARLIAMENTARY AGITATORS.

XII.—Samuel Plimsoll	189
XIII.—Sir Wilfred Lawson	209
XIV.—Edward Miall	222
XV.—Henry Richards	239

CONTENTS.

PART IV.

POPULAR LEADERS.

XVI.—GEORGE JACOB HOLYOAKE........................ 255
XVII.—JOSEPH ARCH............................ 275
XVIII.—CHARLES BRADLAUGH............................. 305
XIX.—GEORGE ODGER..................................... 326
XX.—JOSEPH CHAMBERLAIN............................. 347

PART I.
THE INDEPENDENT MEMBERS.

Professor Fawcett.

 BLIND scholar is not so unusual a phenomenon in the history of intellect and culture as to excite marked attention, but a blind statesman or successful politician is so uncommon a character as to arouse extraordinary interest. In the case of Professor Fawcett there is ample justification for this feeling. In spite of all the drawbacks which his infirmity creates, there are not a half a dozen public men in Great Britain more likely than the member for Hackney to become, at a day not very distant, the Prime Minister of that great empire. While the Professor cannot be, in any way, considered a Republican, except in the same sense as are all advanced Liberals in England, yet were it possible to now organize a Republic there, Professor Fawcett's name would be among the foremost of those advanced for the executive leadership thereof. He is esteemed so universally a man of such wisdom and equitable intention, as to have thoroughly won public confidence. A friendly writer says:—

"The visitor to the House of Commons, waiting at the door of the Strangers' Gallery, and watching the members of Parliament as they file in by the main entrance, will no doubt have his eye particularly arrested by a tall, fair-haired young man, evidently blind, led up to the door by a youthful, petite lady with sparkling eyes and blooming cheeks. She will reluctantly leave him at the door. The British Constitution would be quite upset were a woman to invade the floor of the House of Commons after the chaplain's incantation has been heard, even so far as to conduct her blind husband to his seat, so she has to consign him to a youth who stands waiting to lead the blind member to his place. As she turns away, many a friendly face will smile, and many a pleasant word attend her as she trips lightly up the stairway leading to the Ladies' Cage, near the roof of the House. The whispers pass around, 'One day, perhaps not far off, she will take her seat beside her husband and remain there.' And certain it is that when ladies have the suffrage, the first female member of Parliament will be the lady of whom I write—Mrs. Fawcett. Not one-half of the members of that body are so competent as she to think deeply and speak finely on matters of public policy, while not the daintiest live doll moving about London drawing-rooms surpasses her in care of her household, her husband, and her child. The two whom I have mentioned are as well-known figures as any who approach the sacred precincts of the legislature. The policemen bow low as they pass; the crowd in the lobby make a path; the door-keeper, Mr. White, the most amiable Cerberus who ever guarded an entrance, utters his friendly welcome. The strangers ask 'Who is that?' and a dozen by-standers respond, 'Professor Fawcett.' No one can look upon him but he will see on his face the characters of courage, frankness, and intelligence. He is six feet two inches in height, very blonde, his light hair and complexion and his smooth beardless face giving him something of the air of a boy. His features are at once strongly marked and regular. He narrowly escaped being handsome, and his expression is very winning. His countenance is habitually serene, and no cloud or frown ever passes over it. His smile is gentle and winning. It is probable that no blind man has ever before been able to enter upon so important a political career as Professor Fawcett, who, yet under forty years of age, is the most influential of the independent Liberals in Parliament. From the moment that he took his seat in that body he has been able—and this is unusual—to command the close attention of the House. He has a clear fine voice, speaks with the utmost fluency, has none of the university intonation, and none of the hesitation or uneasy attitudes of the average Parliamentary speaker. He scorns all subterfuges, speaks honestly his whole mind, and comes to the point. At times he is eloquent, and he is always interesting. He is known to be a man of convictions. The usual English political theory that you need not prove a thing right in principle if you can show that it for the time works without disaster, is one which Professor Fawcett ignores. He defends the right against the wrong, with little respect to consequences." *

Naturally such a character has had to encounter the opposition of the ordinary English Philistine in politics.

---

* Moncure D. Conway, in *Harper's Monthly*, February, 1875.

The author of "Men and Manner in Parliament," declares that the House of Commons "will not brook a lecture or advice from a member whose face and figure are not so familiar that they seem to have become as much a portion of the chamber as the clock over the gangway or the canopy over the Speaker's chair." *

After referring to the election of Mr. Fawcett, in 1865, to represent Brighton, the same author adds that "at a period when the nation seemed to be awakening to the desirability of having culture as well as cotton represented in Parliament, Mr. Fawcett, like John Stuart Mill, excited in the public mind a lively expectation of great things. He strove valiantly to justify this expectation by continually pronouncing an opinion upon all questions that cropped up." This course tired the House, and besides, "Mr. Fawcett labored under the additional disadvantage of new membership."

"But," continues this lively writer, "he is not a man who may be smothered in the folds of a wet blanket. I have seen him stand for fifteen minutes by the clock over the bar endeavoring to finish a sentence which the House protested it would not hear. It happened during the debate on the Education Bill. The Ministry had coalesced with the Conservatives in the enterprise of passing a clause which was as wormwood and gall to hon. members below the gangway. Mr. Fawcett was declaiming in a strain of fervid eloquence against the spirit which, he said, had unaccountably taken possession of the Liberal Ministry. Mr. Lowe, in his customary trenchant style, had, earlier in

---

* "Men and Manner in Parliament," pp. 180, 181.

the debate, protested against the unyielding hostility of the Irreconcilables, likening them to a herd of cattle which, having given to them a broad pasture whereon to browse, discovered in one corner a bed of nettles, and, forgetting the sweet pasture to be found elsewhere, stood bellowing their discontent around this little patch. 'The right hon. gentleman has likened us to a herd of cattle,' said Mr. Fawcett. 'Let me remind him and the Ministry, of which he is a distinguished member, of the fate that befel another herd into which evil spirits had entered, and which, running violently down a steep place into the sea,—' At this moment the House caught the bold allusion, and broke into a roar of laughter, cheers, and cries of 'Divide!' Mr. Fawcett waited patiently till the storm appeared to have subsided, and then speaking in exactly the same tone, began again: 'Which, running violently down a steep place—' Once more the roar drowned the speaker's voice, and Mr. Fawcett stopped, beginning again at exactly the same word when a lull in the storm seemed to offer an opportunity, being once more overpowered, only to start afresh when an opening presented itself. The contest raged for a quarter of an hour, but in the end Mr. Fawcett triumphed, and continuing at the word he had originally returned to, proceeded, 'Which, running violently down a steep place into the sea, perished in the waters.'"*

Mr. Fawcett is declared to be, "for strength of character, political integrity, inflexibility of purpose, and power in debate," the "model independent member of the House

---

* "Men and Manner in Parliament," pp. 141-5.

of Commons," yet, it is acknowledged, that having become a power there, he has conducted himself with "rare moderation and dignity." In 1873, he compelled the Gladstone Ministry, after some ungracious treatment, to accept as their own, a bill he had introduced relative to Irish University Education. His moderate course in that moment of triumph gave him a marked popularity in the House, which he has retained and enlarged.

At a subsequent debate this was made manifest "in a remarkable manner," when the Professor, having separated himself from those who supported the policy of which Mr. George Dixon, Member for Birmingham and President of the "National Education League," is regarded as the Parliamentary leader, declared for the Government measure. Opinion ran high for and against the bill, and Mr. Forster's policy was especially and severely condemned by the Nonconformists' votes, headed by Mr. Miall, who declared that the Liberal Ministry had "brought them through the Valley of Humiliation," and who, with Mr. Dixon and his associates, almost regarded Professor Fawcett's action as a betrayal of public faith. The issue involved was as to the continuance of support, by the Government, of denominational schools — the radical opposition wanting to allow only voluntary religious schools, and secular instruction only in those of a public character.

It has been said of this event that occasions are rare in Parliamentary history when a crowded House has been so absolutely swayed by the eloquence of a private member as it was on the night when Mr. Fawcett made clear his intentions in this matter. Mr. Bright has frequently had great oratorical triumphs, speaking from the bench behind that at which the sightless Professor stood. But the applause which Mr. Bright's eloquence was accustomed to call forth came chiefly from one side of the House, whereas Mr. Fawcett drew alternately and at will enthusiastic cheers alike from the Conservative as from the Liberal ranks. Mr. Gladstone himself was quite excited, leaning forward with hands clasped over his knees, watching the words as they fell from the speaker's lips, while Mr. Forster lost no time in declaring that "amid the numerous very powerful speeches delivered by the hon. member for Brighton, this assuredly was the most moving."*

Of his manner of speech, a critic, not so partial as Mr. Conway, says that the Professor "suffers much as a speaker from a habit of pitching his magnificent voice at too level a monotony of height and in 'mouthing' his words when he desires to be specially emphatic. His speeches," he continues, "are rather professorial exercitations than statesman-like orations." It is added, with a dry air of witty patronage, that after having overcome the Puritan in him, that "there are no bounds to the possible heights he might reach in the state if his acceptance of office were conceivable."

Mr. Conway believes that Professor Fawcett's "mind has the instinct of leadership; it is able to bring out every thought in a circle of minds. He has also a rare humor, enriched by imagination, and has a large repertoire of good stories with which to enliven his altogether extraordinary conversation. He must be regarded," continued his ad-

---

* "Men and Manner in Parliament," p. 147.

miring friend, "as a type of 'the coming Liberal' as dis
tinguished from the democrat of that familiar description
which approaches demagogueism. All men have faith in
the fundamental honesty of the masses. The most rigid
Tory, walking in a lonely place after midnight, may feel
a qualm of apprehension if he discern a single individual
approaching; but if there are a dozen he will feel safe.
He knows that security, so far as good intent is concerned,
is with the many. That feeling is the basis of democracy."
And it is this idea and feeling that Mr. Fawcett seeks to
embody in his political life. In some respects, says Mr.
Conway, he "is the most radical man in Parliament, yet
no man is less servile to the many, none more normally in
the minority."

"Henry Fawcett belongs to a county family of the
Midland Counties, of ancient descent and high character.
Born in 1835, he is now forty years of age, and his superb
physique promises as many more years of useful life.
Fortunately the accident by which he was deprived of
sight, did not occur until he had graduated at Cambridge,
which University he entered as a scholar of Trinity Hall.
His graduation, with the highest mathematical honors, oc-
cured in 1856. He then studied law and was admitted as
a bencher of the Middle Temple in 1862. But blindness
has necessarily prevented him from pursuing his profession. That misfortune was the result of an accidental
discharge of his father's gun, soon after the son's graduation, while both were out shooting. Part of the charge
entered the young man's face, putting out both eyes, but
leaving him otherwise undisfigured." Mr. Conway says:
"The father who had looked forward to a distinguished

career for his son, was almost inconsolable, and it was for a time feared he would not survive the event. I have heard from Professor Fawcett's intimate friends at Cambridge touching accounts of how the blind boy sat beside the father, who felt the affliction more keenly than himself, assuring him that the accident should make no difference whatever in the career to which they both had looked forward. 'The accident,' he would say, 'did not happen until I had received at the University the basis of my education, and fortunately we have the means to secure aid from the eyes of others for practical needs. Rejoice with me that my health is unimpaired, my purpose still strong, and my spirit as cheerful as ever.' He has lived to make good the hope he thus held out to his father."

Henry Fawcett turned his attention to the study of Economic Science, and to literary pursuits in connection therewith. As a writer on these topics, he ranks with Thorold Rogers, and for ability and vigor stands but a step below Prof. Cairns. As a teacher, his influence is great and his success remarkable. He soon became a Fellow of his College and then Professor of Political Economy in the University, a position he still holds. The Manual of Political Economy which he has published has become the standard work of his school. Other volumes on the Agricultural Laborer Question, Pauperism, and kindred topics, prove his thorough mastery of the massive materials, which go to make up what Thomas Carlyle has designated as the "dismal science." At Cambridge the Fawcetts are great favorites, and the Professor's rooms are crowded when the duties of his position and the adjournments of Parliament bring him the opportunity to pursue the congenial work of his Professorship. His lecture-room is always crowded.

Though Professor Fawcett is classed among the "irreconcilables," and has always assumed the position of an "Independent Member," it must not be supposed that his Radicalism is necessarily of the aggressive, "root and branch" order, or has in it any of the iconoclast spirit. It is based on moral order and convictions; does not seek to pull down, but conserving the good, aims to re-create his country without disorder or dangerous excitement. A disciple of the strictest school of Economists, he does not support all the measures of an ameliorative character which are pressed on the British Parliament. Mr. Fawcett has several times opposed such propositions,—the most notable case being that of the Factory Health Act of 1874, by which the hours of labor for women and children were still further restricted. On this subject and that of pauperism, Mr. Fawcett (whose economic views on population, etc., are largely tinged with Malthusian ideas) is not in accord with the active labor agitators and their friends, in and out of Parliament. Yet his frankness and honesty have saved his popularity with the masses, though there is a bitter hostility to the cold and theoretical way in which, it is charged, he has dealt with this question. Mr. Conway, in the sketch from which so much has been quoted, pithily states the sentimental side of the economic argument which the member for Hackney gave inside the House, and his wife, Mrs. Fawcett, talked outside. "It is not often," he says, "that one has to charge large masses of the working classes with a deliberate scheme of injustice or oppression. But I fear that under the terrible struggle for existence in this country, the workingmen have at length begun to show signs that their instincts have become impaired. From them appears to have proceeded a demand for a measure which, under the pretence of a desire to protect women and children from overwork by restricting the hours per day in which they can labor, can only result in rendering women unable to compete with men even in the few employments now open to them, and so crippling that sex still further in the struggle for life. The excess in the numbers of women over men in Great Britain is nearing a million."

It is, Mr. Conway writes, speaking in review of Professor Fawcett's position, certain that the pressure in the market for manual labor (women being denied access to the customary professions and many lucrative employments) "has induced the workingmen to take this mean way of handicapping women in the competition, disabling them from selling their time on the same terms as man sells his."

The argument of Professor Fawcett against the measure also rested on another ground than that quoted from Mr. Conway's sketch. That was undoubtedly the argument of his brilliant wife, who is one of the foremost leaders in the women's suffrage agitation, and is also a capable writer on Political Economy. In the House, the Member for Hackney urged that the measure would largely decrease both production and wages.

"Manufacturers," he said, "showed an increasing tendency to establish concerns on the continent, where they were free from such restrictions as were imposed in this country. In Switzerland and Germany legislative restrictions were confined to children, and our working men could not too carefully remember that capital was year by year emigrating to other lands.

"The Home Secretary had based this legislation on the ground that women were not free agents. If the women of Yorkshire were not free agents, how could it be said that the women of Dorsetshire and Cambridgeshire were so? If women had to wade up to their middle in agricultural work, could they be called free agents? Let this kind of legislation be carried out with regard to factories, and the women of London must be included in it, and Parliament must decide at what hour domestic servants should retire to rest. The Home Secretary said women were forced to work too long through the pressure of want, or of their employers. If they accepted the first alternative it resulted that want was worse than work; if they accepted the second the conclusion was that employers were tyrannical. He ventured to say that this legislation, when it was understood, would be hurled back with contempt, and working men would tell the house that it had no right to accuse them of forcing their wives and daughters to work against their will."

The Trades Unions' Organs and their representatives and friends in the House were strongly in opposition to the Professor. Mr. Mundella, a large employer of female labor, declared it would not derange production, reduce wages, or lessen profits, while it was essential to the physical and moral well-being of the population to protect those unable to protect themselves. Mr Joseph Owen, member for Newcastle, Alderman Carter, member for Leeds, Mr. Samuel Morley, who sits for Bristol, Messrs. Stanhope, Baxter, Tennant and other large employers of labor, supported the bill. Mr.

Joseph Chamberlain recently headed a deputation to the Home Secretary, Mr. Cross, on this subject and emphatically represented the same views. Of course the members who were elected as the representatives of working men, Messrs. Macdonald and Burt, were strong in opposition to the economic view urged by Mr. Fawcett, and quite bitter in replying to the charges of selfish motives applied to their clients—the Trades Unions. This debate indicates an important fact in the political policy and purposes by and for which Mr. Fawcett is governed and acts. It partially places him among the "administrative Nihilists," as Prof. Huxley has described the philosophy of which Herbert Spencer in theoretical polity, and "the Manchester School" in practical politics, are the representatives.

In other matters Mr. Fawcett's position is in the vanguard. He has supported, at considerable risk of popularity among his present constituents, the opening on the Sabbath of the public museums, picture galleries, &c.,—a subject greatly agitated in England. He is persistent and consistent in advocating the redressing of political, economic and educational wrongs that bear hard on the agricultural population—tenant farmers and laborers alike. His thorough knowledge of law and history comes in good stead, when bills for the enclosure of commons, or other measures of land monopoly are on the docket. The extension of the suffrage to the counties meet his cordial support. This measure, a compulsory Tenant Rights act, and one providing for laborers' allotments and holdings in the Crown and common lands of Great Britain, are propositions, with one for better educational opportunities, which Professor Fawcett fully sustains, and which, if ever carried and put into practical effect, will mark a wide sweep of ameliorative and constructive radicalism. In a speech to his constituents at Hackney, Mr. Fawcett thus pertinently expressed his opinion on the enfranchisment of the laborer:

"When a population for centuries had been sunk in a position of dependence, there was no chance of improving their condition unless one could inspire in them the sentiments of self-respect and self-reliance. In order to do this it was necessary to make them see that they were citizens in a free state, not serfs of the soil, nor the clients of powerful patrons."

There is one other great question in England, in which the statesman-like grasp of the blind member must be acknowledged. His position on the disestablishment and disendowment of the Established Church illustrates the many-sidedness of his judgment. In his speech at Hackney at the General Election, accepting the Liberal nomination, Mr. Fawcett gave free expression to the general course he should pursue on the leading issues of English politics. Among these, of course, was that of the Church. The *Examiner*, the literary representative of radical opinion and criticism, said that Mr. Fawcett gave utterance to some "peculiarly wise words" on this question. Summarizing and quoting his language, it writes:—

"Nothing in English politics," he declared, was more remarkable than the new way in which most people now look at the connection between the Church and the State. 'Twelve months ago, Disestablishment was spoken of as the distant dream of a few enthusiastic fanatics; but now even moderate politicians speak of it as a change certain to come, and the only question is by whom and in what form it should be done.' To all men who see how the currents of the age are running it has long been clear that Disestablishment is not only inevitable, but near. Mr. Fawcett anticipates that Mr. Disraeli will do unto the Church as he did unto the Ten-pound franchise. We are happy to record the prediction that the Conservative chief, who, above all things, wishes to be considered an extraordinary man, will end his career by earning the epitaph—He was a Tory Minister, who enfranchised the Democracy and disestablished the Church."

" Mr. Fawcett fears, indeed, that the day of Disestablishment may come too soon ; and his words of warning on that subject were by far the most important part of his speech. There must, of course, be Disendowment as well as Disestablishment, and the appropriation of the funds will be incomparably the more important process of the two. Now, Mr. Fawcett gives clear warning that, much as he would like to see the Church separated from the State, he would not vote for such a change if funds were to be left to it in the same lavish way as they were left to the Irish Church."

After referring to the extent of these funds, and especially the manner in which, by the cessation of the tithe rent charge the ecclesiatical revenues will all fall into the landowner's hand, the *Examiner* says, " Some members, it is true, had too much common sense to let so preposterous a scheme of spoilation be sanctioned without offering an emphatic protest ; and by far the most energetic protest came from Mr. Fawcett himself."

In concluding its comments, the *Examiner* says :—The English Church is immensely richer than the Irish was in what were called 'private endowments,' and it may be left in possession of perhaps ninety millions of money, if the disendowment should be effected in accordance with the existing precedent. Now, it would be positive madness to arm any body of clergy with ninety millions. It would be hardly less insane than to arm garroters with Martini-Henry rifles and disband the police. A body of men who think that they are priests, that they can work invisible miracles, that they are armed with infallible truth, and that all their foes must be the servants of the devil, may be nice amiable gentlemen so long they are held down by the impartial scepticism of the State ; but they become dangerous indeed if the State stuffs their pockets with money, and leaves them free to do what they like. Hence Mr. Fawcett does quite right to warn us that we must prepare a scheme of Disendowment very different from that which was applied to the Irish Church. The work will be so difficult, the prize at stake is so vast, and the day for action may be so near, that the Radical party cannot too soon begin to prepare such a scheme of Disendowment as will make it safe to disestablish the Church."

The future political career of Professor Henry Fawcett is well indicated by the road he has so far travelled. He will be found radical in all measures that look to the improvement of the masses, while at the same time he will be conservative in opposing what may be regarded as personal politics. Able, wise and disinterested as he is, Great Britain is fortunate in the presence of such a public man.

Professor Fawcett is the second son of William Fawcett, Esq., of Longford, Wiltshire, and of Mary, daughter of William Cooper, Esq., of Salisbury. He was born in 1833, and married, in 1867, Millicent, daughter of N. Garrett, Esq., by whom he has several children. He has published, jointly with Mrs. Fawcett, a volume of essays.

II.

SIR CHARLES W. DILKE.

GREAT BRITAIN received, socially and politically speaking, a decided sensation, three years since. A young, wealthy, cultivated and titled gentleman, —one whose father had been the companion of princes, and whose name is linked with the fairest aspects of later English history—rose in the House of Commons and delivered a carefully prepared, moderately-toned speech, very level and direct in its argument, and aimed at the extravagant cost of the Royal Establishment. The act was a daring one, and it raised a howl of anger and indignation. No other word expresses the feeling which was aroused among that portion of the English people to whom the newspapers chiefly cater, and who are generally meant, when the "British Public" is referred to in ponderous terms.

What made this passion so ungovernable, was the fact that the radical baronet, seeing the antagonism which his motion to enquire into the "Civil List" expenditures was sure to arouse, had stepped from St. Stephen's and appealed to the *vox populi* in advance. The motion was entered in 1871; the speech in support was made at the session of 1872. Mr. Gladstone had gone out of his way, in the speech annually made by or for the Prime Minister, at the Lord Mayor's banquet in London, to criticise Sir Charles W. Dilke's proposed action. The latter responded by canvassing the country. A radical conference was held at Birmingham, at which Dilke, Bradlaugh, Taylor and others were present. Three resolutions or declarations were adopted: 1st, Opposition to Hereditary Legislators and to a second chamber: 2d, That the people are the final authority, and that some means must be speedily devised to make that effective: 3d, Opposition to the Bishops as legislators. Sir Charles Dilke held meetings at Birmingham, Bolton, Bristol, Sheffield, Manchester, Leeds, Newcastle, and other large cities. At nearly all of them he was met by organized mobs. The supporters of his views and the authorities,—though these last were often lukewarm, and, in a few instances, openly indifferent to the principle of Free Speech—were always strong enough to protect the baronet. At a meeting held December 7, 1871, at Bolton, while Dilke was speaking, a concerted and murderous assault was made, and William Schofield, a peaceful working-man, was killed. This violence defeated its own object and aroused the liberal element to the danger. An American unacquainted with English affairs would be surprised at the mildness of the speeches which aroused such bitterness. Sir Charles Dilke's speech at Newcastle, on the 6th of November, 1871, where he was welcomed by an immense meeting, was probably the boldest of all his efforts. Yet no more aggressive language can be found in it than is contained in such extracts as these. Replying to some remark of Mr. Disraeli, about the power of the Crown, the speaker said that "the Queen's political conscience is of such a character as to admit of her fully approving of everything"—the Prime Minister does. His review of the costly anachronisms in the Royal Household, was caustic enough, but there was no word in it that transcended even the limits of Parliamentary debate. He made amusing reference to the fact that the Royal medical staff consisted of thirty-two persons; that the Queen's private household, numbered twelve persons, as Secretary, Librarian, etc.; that the Lord Steward's staff embraced one hundred and fifty-four officials; the Lord Chamberlain's, four hundred and thirty; the Master of Horse twenty-six, and that the Household Brigade, consisting of Life Guards (cavalry) and Grenadiers (infantry) were maintained near the Royal person, as a privileged corps, at a great cost. He pointed out the fact that the Queen's "Pages of Honor" are the only persons allowed to enter the army without an examination. He charged that privileged corps were demoralizing and unprofitable in armies; alluded to the claim that had been made relative to the abolition of certain sinecures, and asked if the cost of these officers had gone to swell her Majesty's Privy purse, as they had not been deducted from the annual estimates. What seems to have most thoroughly angered his antagonists, was the fact that he proclaimed himself a republican, though only remotely so. At Bristol, November 20th, 1870, he said: "I make no concealment of the fact that I am a republican myself." Again at Newcastle, he said: "There is a wide-spread belief that a republic here is only a matter of education and time. It is said some day a commonwealth will be our government. * * * Well, if you can show me a fair chance that a republic here will be free from the political corruption that hangs about a monarchy, I say for my part—and I believe the middle classes in general, will say—let it come!" It is very difficult to portray the rage which such expressions created. The governing classes seem to rest in fancied security when such men as Bradlaugh are undermining their power, but a Dilke brought name, culture, and wealth, to popularize a dangerous cause.

The London *Standard*, the acknowledged leader and organ of ultra Toryism, gave unreasoning expression to its vehement anger at such audacity, while the mild and unreflecting *Spectator* could find no defence other than an apology and excuse for what Sir Charles Dilke criticised. The *Standard* declared that—

"The respect and attachment of Englishmen for the Royal Family, and their contempt and aversion for libellers and traitors, will not be silenced by the ruffianism of a metropolitan mob. The former finds utterance in every newspaper, in every club room, in every home, in every act and movement of national life; the latter may take an unpleasantly practical form if Sir Charles Dilke should ever insult a party of gentlemen by repeating in their presence calumnies such as he was permitted to utter with impunity before the roughs of Newcastle."

The *Spectator* could only show, while mildly reflecting on Sir Charles Dilke, that in 1738, the Royal Household numbered one hundred and ninety-seven officials more than at present, saying—"We are strongly inclined to believe that—assuming the pageantry of a court to be still kept up—a judicious weeding out of superfluous officers would be practicable, and would probably bring relief, in many ways, to the Sovereign herself. But there is one element of singular unfairness in Sir Charles Dilke's mode of dealing with the subject. To judge from his speech one would think that the Household had been hitherto treated as a sacrosanct ark, on which no hand had ever been laid. It would be easy to show that this is by no means the case, and that the Sovereign's House, in 1871, however superfluously ample it may yet appear to many, is yet of far scantier dimensions than it was, say, a century and a half ago." But the radical orator had the facts on his side. The "Civil List" formerly embraced the whole of the national expenditure other than those for military and naval purposes. Prior to Cromwell's day it did not exist at all. The king was supposed to provide for all national expenditure out of his land and hereditary revenues, and any extra war expenditure was contributed by the various feudal lords, under the conditions of their several tenures. Deficiencies were made up, sometimes by forced loans, sometimes by parliamentary grants, which, however, were by no means voted as a matter of course. The resistance to this method of collecting the revenues needed, led to the Commonwealth. The subsequent development of Parliamentary government led, after the House of Brunswick came to the British Throne, to the more or less distinct separation of the Royal Household expenditures, from those which properly belong to the Government of the Realm itself. In the contests arising over the development of this separation, which, like English affairs, has been very gradual indeed, the Royal Family have driven close bargains with "their Faithful Commons." George the Second received £800,000 per annum in all, or about $4,000,000. The "Civil Lists" of the two following Georges, especially that of George the Fourth, were swelled by all sorts of devices, the records of which do not form an encouraging chapter in the history of ministerial responsibility, and parliamentary government. The annual total for George the Fourth was $5,000,000. In addition to this he received as Regent and King, gratuities amounting to $16,000,000, and a large sum was voted to cancel his debts. Under William the Fourth and the reigning Queen, the Civil List was nominally reduced to £385,000, or $1,925,000, per annum. Its expenditures are directly confined to the maintenance of the Royal Establishment.

Sir Charles W. Dilke arraigned the current estimates as not being confined even to this large sum. He showed, with a merciless array of figures, that the income of the Duchy of Lancaster, £42,000 net, is added to this total, making the Crown income equal to $2,035,000. Besides this large sum, however, the nation maintained at its own cost, all the Royal residences, Buckingham, St. James, Hampton and Kew Palaces, Windsor Castle, and some minor places. Balmoral and Osborne House, in Scotland and the Isle of Wight, are private property. The Royal family are also a charge on the Civil List, and their total incomes amount annually to £219,515, or about $1,097,575. This sum swells the total of the direct Civil List to $3,254,515. Other sums more than equal in amount have been expended on the Heir-apparent alone—to pay his debts and defray the expenses of his various State tours. The cold and careful presentation of this costly show, is what aroused the anger which has been described. Mr. Smalley, the very capable London correspondent of the New York *Tribune*, under date of December, 1871, says, "In the mere fact that a young and able, and liberal M. P. has made a public criticism on the Royal Household, there is nothing to explain all this outcry. No single politician in a single speech can shake the Throne, or convert popular loyalty into popular discontent. It is the *restless* sentiment behind the orator which makes him formidable."

The excitement in and out of Parliament, which attended and followed Sir Charles Dilke's motion of inquiry into the "Civil List," is a vivid illustration of one of the most prevailing superstitions that exists as to public affairs in Great Britain. Mr. Mundella put it in one form when he recently protested against a "pinchbeck and tinsel" monarchy, and the venturesome baronet aroused its more pugnacious manifestations. At the very time the Conservatives were inciting mobs to break up the meetings called by Sir Charles Dilke, and the press of London were indulging in more or less violent criticism of his position, the habitués of the clubs and of West End social circles, might have heard daily the most scandalous stories of the Prince of Wales, with many hints of a nature not complimentary to his Royal Mother. It was about this time, that Matt. Morgan, the artist, made a reputation by cartoons in the *Tomahawk*, which for their graphic boldness have hardly been surpassed. The *Tomahawk* was not a Radical, but a Conservative satirist. Yet it gave to the

British world, without exciting rebuke or anything more than a sarcastic smile, designs like the one which, in the attitude of the Queen's well-known attendant, John Brown, designedly lent wings to the contemptible club slanders that were then circulated; or like another, far more powerful and expressive, as described by Justin McCarthy, in which the Prince of Wales, dressed as Hamlet, was represented as breaking away from the restraining arms of John Bull as Horatio, and public opinion as Marcellus, and rushing after a ghost which bore the form and features of George IV., while underneath were inscribed the words, "Lead on; I'll follow thee!"

Sir Charles Dilke's mode of attack excited anger because it was practical. It reached home to the English pocket, and though the criticism was couched in the most respectful language, it laid bare only the more effectually the absurd anomalies for the maintenance of which Englishmen were taxed. The scene that occurred in the early days of the session of 1872, when the young Baronet rose to speak to the motion he had given notice of at the session of 1871, is thus described by the author of "Men and Manner in Parliament:" — "The scene was led up to, as most memorable outbreaks in the House of Commons are, in the most unexpected and unpremeditated manner. The eager throng that crowded the galleries allotted to the public looked for something startling when Sir Charles Dilke should rise to speak. It had been rumored, and the sequel showed that the statement was not without foundation, that the Conservatives intended to meet the motion by rising *en masse*, and leaving Sir Charles to talk to such Liberals as thought the subject of an inquiry into the Civil List one not absolutely forbidden to the representatives of the people. But the count-out was a card held for playing, if necessary, at a later stage of the game, and after Lord Bury had succeeded in his constant endeavour of putting himself *en évidence* on every possible occasion, Sir Charles began his speech to a crowded and attentive House, which, whilst freezingly deprecatory, remained politely attentive till the hon. Bart. had brought his monologue to a conclusion. Mr. Gladstone, anxious to make an end of the matter, followed ; and it was taken for granted that the incident was closed, and the strangers who had come to see "a scene" remained to mutter their disappointment. Sir Charles Dilke had made his motion, the Prime Minister had replied, both sides of the question were before the public, and to let the matter rest, was the evident wish of the House. But it was not to be. As Mr. Gladstone sat down, Mr. Auberon Herbert, who, it was well known, desired to advocate the motion, leaped up from his seat beside Sir Charles Dilke, and found himself face to face with such a storm as has rarely beaten against the roof of Saint Stephen's. The country gentlemen, famed in parliamentary annals for ability to assist the progress of legislation by the utterance of unearthly noises, excelled their historic efforts of the eras of the Reform Bill and the debates on the Corn Laws. They roared and yelled and even hissed, lashing themselves into fury as Mr. Herbert stood shouting out something at the top of a voice that was utterly lost in the storm. But even country gentlemen cannot bellow "Divide, Divide!" for more than five minutes at a stretch, and Mr. Herbert, taking cognizance of this fact, husbanded his resources accordingly; and when something, which might by comparison be termed a lull, occurred, he looked up to the press gallery, and, by a superhuman effort shouted out two or three words that seemed to reach the reporters. Then the Conservatives brought up their reserve forces and a sustained yell drowned the speaker's voice. A few minutes more and the hon. member, perceiving signs of renewed exhaustion in the Opposition benches, continued his speech at the very words at which he had left off; whereupon the Conservatives came back with a deafening roar, and Mr. Herbert resigned the innings to them. But it became clear that he was winning the game by strategy. No human lungs were equal to the prolongation over an hour of such an effort as the country gentlemen were then making, and whilst even in the full tide of their vigor, Mr. Herbert was getting out his speech by piecemeal, it was too evident that when they had shouted themselves hoarse he would come up smiling and say all the horrible things he had at heart. Accordingly a change of tactics was decided upon, and the count-out card was dealt. But it requires two to play at the game, and as Mr. Gladstone and his colleagues would not lend themselves to the effort to stop free discussion by these means, the count-out, thrice essayed, thrice failed, Mr. Herbert, profiting by these brief pauses to gain fresh breath and renewed vigor. Thoroughly beaten, the Conservatives finally resorted to the expedient of clearing the House of strangers, with the intention of preventing Mr. Herbert's interjections from being reported. But this proceeding did not in the slightest degree affect the hon. member's purpose, and amid a babel of sounds, through which the shrill crowing of the cock could alone be distinguished, he continued his speech for ten minutes more, when apparently reaching the end, he sat down and the ferment subsided as quickly as it had arisen."

As a speaker, Sir Charles does not appear to have captivated the critics of the press gallery. The writer in *Fraser*, who discourses pleasantly on the House of Commons "Its *personnel*, and its oratory," says that in "Sir Charles Dilke, the visitor to the House of Commons will see the influence of Mr. Disraeli's periods and phrases," * * " he contents himself with copying the more *bizarre* of Mr. Disraeli's alliterations, as when he told the House—as he told the Ancient Order of Foresters at Hammersmith last month —that the publicans were perplexed, the parsons persecuted, and the Dissenters disgusted."

A more soberly stated, if slightly satirical, view of his parliamentary appearance and manner, is given in the following:

"Sir Charles Dilke does not owe any of the Parliamentary fame he may possess to the manifestation of gifts of oratory. The hon. Baronet is, to tell the truth, a very wearisome speaker, and if he had not, as a rule, something to say that was worth listening to, he would never find an audience. If in any future edition of Mr. Robert Montgomery's poems a metaphorical illustration were required for the famous stream that

'Meandered level with its fount,'

the publisher could not do better that procure a *carte-de-visite* portrait of the hon. member for Chelsea as he appears when addressing the House of Commons. Sir Charles usually sits on the second or third seat on the front bench below the gangway, but when he rises to make a set speech he invariably stands partly in the gangway itself with his back turned to his personal friends. The note upon which he begins his oration is marvellously preserved throughout its full length, and as he monotonously turns his body from left to right, as if he were fixed on a pivot, the impression he leaves on the mind of the beholder is that the reservoir of his speech is ingeniously located in his boots, and that he is pumping it up. For an hour at a time the level stream, unrelieved by a single coruscation of wit, imagination, fancy, or humor, flows out upon the House of Commons. But the House, nevertheless, attentively listens, as far as human endurance can withstand the more than mortal monotony, for Sir Charles Dilke generally has something notable to say, and he has a fearless way of saying it which, to those who have souls capable of being stirred by the fire of political Knight-errantry, covers a multitude of sins of manner." *

Sir Charles Wentworth Dilke, the second baronet of his name, is the son of a well known public man, and the grandson of a literary critic of large reputation. The present baronet, like his father and grandfather, is the active editor of the *Athenæum.* His only brother, Austin Dilke, is now the proprietor and editor of the London *Weekly Dispatch*, a paper which he has restored to more than its original popularity and circulation. Thirty years ago the *Dispatch* was the most influential journal in Great Britain. W. J. Fox, the member for Oldham, and pastor of the famous South Place (Finsbury) Chapel, contributed regular-

---

* "Men and Manner in Parliament."

ly over the signature of "Publicola;" other well known writers also contributed to its columns. It then passed under a cloud. Its former editor, Sydney Smith, a London barister, was identified with the opposition to Trades Unionism, and became the leading critic thereof. This destroyed the popularity of the *Dispatch*, which Mr. Austin Dilke is said to have raised to a remarkable circulation. He is the author of a brilliant book on Russia, now being published, and is considered by all odds the best informed living Englishman on Russian affairs. He speaks the language fluently. His brother in the witty *brochure* "Prince Florestan," which he issued anonymously in 1874, describes him as—"Mr. Dilke of Trinity Hall, Sir Charles Dilke's brother—but a man of more real talent than his brother, although, if possible, a more lugubrious speaker."

Charles Wentworth Dilke, the grandfather, was born in 1789, of a county family in moderate circumstances. He graduated at Cambridge, and receiving an appointment in the Naval Pay office, remained there for twenty years. During this time he was a frequent contributor to the *Westminster* and *Retrospective Review*, as also to "*Notes and Queries*," In 1830 he became editor of the *Athenæum*. In 1846, he transfered its editorship to Thomas Keble Hervey, in order to take charge of the *Daily News*, which he retired from in 1849. His son was born in 1810. He became editorially connected with the *Athenæum* soon after leaving the University. He married Mary, daughter of Captain William Chatfield, and their eldest son, the present member for Chelsea, was born in London in 1843. He is therefore in the thirty-second year of his life. The father was among the earliest promoters of that movement for artistic and technical education which has already borne such remarkable fruits in Great Britain. In 1844 he urged upon the Society of Arts, of which he was Vice-President,—in connection with the late Mr. Cole, of the Kensington Museum, and Scott Russell, the engineer,—a plan for the Exhibition of the Useful Arts and Industries. This was the first outline presented of the plan on which the London Universal Exhibition of 1851 was subsequently based. In 1846, with the encouragement given by Prince Albert, the Society of Arts gave its first exhibition. Mr. Dilke was one of the active Commissioners at that, the first, Exhibition. He also visited New York as English Commissioner to the American Exposition, and served on that held in England in 1862. He several times declined Knighthood, but was created a baronet after the last named service. He died in 1869, after his son had entered Parliament.

The latter received his early education under a private tutor, and entered at Trinity Hall, Cambridge, in 1862, graduating with the degree of LL.B., in 1866. He sailed almost immediately thereafter for the United States, on the interesting "round the world" journey, which added his attractive volumes, "Greater Britain," to the literature of the times. The theory, or purpose of the journey the book narrates, is in itself a very attractive one, and the manner in which it began was quite original. Mr. Dilke illustrates the growth of the Anglo-Saxon stock by the spirited account he gives of the great communities it has founded. He landed at Norfolk, Virginia, soon after the close of our civil war, and proceeded through the South, judging wisely that he would thus obtain a better idea of the real condition of affairs in the States over which war had swept like a fierce wind. The chapters in which the South is described, constitute one of the fairest and clearest statements yet given of its permanent characteristics and of the conditions then existing. His general sympathy with the national cause is not disguised, but it does not color his judgment of existing facts. He came from the South by the Mississippi River, and made his way into the Northern States *via* St. Louis. His judgment is fair and keen, his descriptions are generally accurate, his insight is good and his style graphic and lively. One of the best proofs of this is to be found in his reference to the American plan of protection. Unlike most English observers and writers, his mind has a continental outlook, and he does not merely seek to use his observations as a string on which to hang opinions preconceived and settled. He evidently seeks to find out why the American people have, as a rule, so largely favored a protective policy. The reasons which he finds given he also finds to prevail in the great English Colonies, both in America and on the Australian Continent. He speaks of it in these words:—"It is a common doctrine in the Colonies of England that a Nation cannot be called independent, if it has to cry out to another for supplies of necessities; that true national existence is first attained when the country becomes capable of supplying to its own citizens those goods without which they cannot exist in the state of comfort they have already reached."

Mr. Dilke conveys the idea that the future holds both the possibility and probability of a federation of the English-speaking communities, which now belt the world with two hundred millions of population. He indicates quite clearly that the American Republic must be the organizing centre of such a movement; and that the federal plan on which it is constructed must be, with modifications, that of the union of English-speaking communities, which, it is argued must yet be framed in the interest of civilization. At the time of Mr. Dilke's journey there was a good deal of speculation on such themes. The immense growth of the Anglo-American offshoots, as well as the rapidly rising importance of the Anglo-Indian and Australian Colonies and dependencies, make a problem of importance of the question:—What are to be the future relations of the Mother-country to these children of hers? Alfred H. Louis, formerly editor of the London *Spectator*, and now a resident of Boston, has long advocated the idea of an Anglo-Saxon federation, belting the world with its international comradeship. Our brilliant young publicist had doubtless been influenced by the largeness of the idea, as he has also, it is evident, by the comprehensive criticisms which have been made from the "Positivist" standpoint, on the Asiatic policy of Great Britain. The observations of the baronet, as expressed in "Greater Britain," and more recently manifested by his motions and questions in Parliament, show that he has carefully studied the average Anglo-Chinese and Indo-Imperial view of affairs, coming to the conclusion that they have heretofore "been weighed in the balance, and found wanting."

The good feeling for, and admiration of, the United States, which Sir Charles Dilke expresses in his book, has found expression in more than one instance on the floor of the House of Commons. At the opening of the session of 1870, the member for Chelsea was selected to second the address in response to the Queen's Speech. This is a duty usually devolving on some younger member of the party in power, this representative being selected by the Ministry. The choice of Sir Charles Dilke was regarded as significant of both a radical policy and a conciliatory manner towards the radicals, on the part of Mr. Gladstone. During Sir Charles' speech he made the following kindly and graceful reference to the United States : " With one foreign power, if the word 'foreign' be strictly applicable to a people whose tongue and whose thought are ours, relations are returning to something better than their former state. Time and the sympathies of race are too strong for politicians and for governments. As the days roll by, bitter words are forgotten, and men begin to wonder where the angry feelings of the past can have had their rise, when they note the calmness of the reasoning with which former subjects of dispute are now approached on either side of the great seas. We are told in the Speech that we are soon to deal with the Naturalization matter. No declaration could give more pleasure to the millions of persons, now citizens of the United States, who were born on British soil, and there is reason to believe that the settlement that has been reached conflicts with no sentiment of English dignity, and with no principle of modern English law, but that it will prove even more satisfactory to the Americans than the arrangements they have made with the Prussians."*

Sir Charles Dilke's parliamentary record shows him to be both an industrious and practical member. Though his ultra views have rendered him somewhat unpopular as a politician in the House itself, his acknowledged freedom

---

* " Hansard's Debates," Feb. 8, 1870.

from affectation of superior knowledge; his readiness for hard work; his fund of extensive and accurate information; and the genuine manliness and courage with which he has met the opposition, have secured him personal respect and close attention. A wider experience and recent sorrow have naturally given tone and depth to the character of one who has assuredly won a right to be esteemed as among the foremost of the younger generation of English public men. He has, more recently, too, shown his possession of a humor for which he had not received credit, turning the tables on his critics by good-naturedly and pointedly holding up a mirror to himself in "Prince Florestan." "Dod's" manual records Sir Charles Dilke as "A Radical; in favor of further distribution of seats and the assimilation of county franchise to that of the boroughs, the abolition of the income tax and sugar duties." There is nothing in this of the "Red Spectre," with which at one time many English people associated the name of Dilke.

He was re-elected in 1874, at the head of the poll, in spite of the fact that many of his votes had run counter to the prejudices, and perhaps to the interests, of a large number of his constituents. Chelsea, like Lambeth and Hackney, is a borough largely made up of the trading or shopkeeping class. On economic questions the baronet generally finds himself in accord with Professor Fawcett, while on education, he follows, as a member of the Executive Committee of the Birmingham League, the lead of Mr. George Dixon. He is a warm advocate of a compulsory system, under the direction of the State itself. Opposed of course to denominational control, he does not concentrate himself on that point or the demand for secular direction, so much as he does on that of compulsion. He brings to this discussion, as his speeches show, a comprehensive knowledge of the condition of education in various countries, and this trait is equally characteristic of his mind in other matters. Sir Charles Dilke has strenuously advocated the extension of suffrage to women, especially urging the rights of the unmarried, who are also the possessors of property, as a logical application of the idea on which the franchise rests to a larger extent than on anything else in Great Britain. Addressing the House, May 8th, 1870, he said :—" If you make property the absolute test, without exception or disqualification of any kind, you have for the first time an intelligent basis on which you may rest your suffrage, and upon which you can withstand the demand for universal suffrage." He did not indorse the limitation as equitable or wise ; he only argued its logical character as relating itself to the measure then pending— a bill according the vote to unmarried women who were freeholders and ratepayers in their own right.

The measures on which Sir Charles Dilke has widely rested his usefulness in the House, since the outburst against him over the Civil List inquiry, relate chiefly to the Franchise, and the more equitable adjustment of population and representation. He voted with Mr. Trevelyan for the extension to counties of the Borough Franchise, thus aiding the Agricultural Laborers' movement, but his own measure for re-distribution of seats necessarily underlies any real readjustment. The bill was introduced into the last Parliament, and received the support of but a comparatively small portion of the Liberal vote,—the Prime Minister himself opposing. At the last division, in the session of 1875, Mr. Gladstone voted for it, with a greater portion of those who were in his Ministry. The motion to proceed to a second reading was defeated by a vote of 190 to 120, a majority of 30. This is regarded as a great gain. The consideration, too, with which the *Times* especially, as well as all the London papers, treated its advocate, shows the great gain Sir Charles Dilke has made within the past three years.

In his last speech he advocated the equality of franchise through the re-distribution of seats, nearly, though not entirely, on the basis of population; and he also urged the representation of minorities. As to inequality of the franchise' he showed that members were seated at the last general election who had not one-twentieth or even one-sixtieth the number of votes required to elect elsewhere some other member. Thus some voters are favored unduly. A Parliamentary document printed on motion of Sir Charles Dilke, shows that the constituencies in England and Wales number 2,301,206, of whom 840,360 are electors in counties, 1,448,779 in boroughs, and 12,067 in universities. In Ireland, the Parliamentary electors number 230,436—175,414 in counties, and 55,022 in boroughs. In Scotland, there are 289,789 electors, of whom 84,752 are in counties, 195,176 in burghs, and 9,861 in universities. This makes a total for the United Kingdom and Ireland of 3,021,431 electors. The total number of inhabitants is, in Great Britain alone, 31,457,331, the number of electors, 2,680,680; the number of unrepresented adult persons is stated at 14,388,335. The Electoral Reform Association, a body formed to support Sir Charles Dilke's efforts, offer in a striking petition, which the senior member for Chelsea presented, the facts whereon the new demand is based. They say :

"That the borough and county constituencies of the United Kingdom, with less than 100,000 inhabitants each, had a total population in 1871 of 10,346,667 and are represented in the House of Commons by 402 members; while the constituencies with more than 100,000 inhabitants had a total population of 21,113,655, and are represented by only 241 members. The constituencies which, as regards population, are in a minority of 10,766,988, have a majority of 161 representatives in the House of Commons.

"That the number of electors upon the register now in force, in boroughs which in 1871 had a population of less than 10,000, is 67,257, returning 77 representatives, while the number of electors in the boroughs which in 1871 had above 100,000 inhabitants is 910,073, returning 68 representatives. The former class of constituencies have one member for every 873 electors, while the latter have only one member for every 13,383; the electors of the small boroughs have fifteen times the weight in Parliament of the large cities and towns.

* * * * * *

There are 45 of these boroughs; in 1871 they had an aggregate population of 497,962 and 68,281 electors, returning 52 members.

"That the evils of the existing distribution of seats become daily more aggravated with the increase of population in the large towns. The electors in the boroughs with less than 10,000 population were 64,092 in 1871, and are 67,257 on the present register, showing an increase of only 3,165, while in the boroughs with more than 100,000 population, the electors were 776,755 in 1871 and are now 910,073, an increase of 133,318, or within 1,196 of double the whole amount of electors in the small boroughs.

"That the returns of the last census show that the town population of England and Wales in 1871 was 12,900,297, and the rural population 9,803,811, the former occupying 3,287,151 and the latter 34,037,732 acres of land; while the population of the Parliamentary boroughs was only 10,652,423, showing a town population of 2,247,874 which is deprived of borough representation.

"That the population of London within the limits of the Metropolis Local Management Act was 3,266,987, in 1871, while the population of its Parliamentary boroughs was only 3,022,066, showing that, within its limits, a town population of 244,921 has no distinctive representation in the House of Commons, although as fully qualified, in every respect, as the inhabitants of the small constituencies which have now a preponderating influence in Parliament.

. "That the metropolitan boroughs with their population of 3,022,066 have only 22 representatives, while the counties of Buckingham and Wiltshire, with an aggregate population of 433,056, have 23. The metropolis has 13 per cent. of the population of England and Wales, but only 4½ per cent. of the representation. Its claims to a fair share of political power are ignored in favor of small boroughs whose main qualification appears to consist in the fact that they are the means whereby the "landed interest" maintains its predominance in the House of Commons.

"That the existing distribution of political power fails to secure a fair representation of the electoral body, a fact which is evidenced by the returns for the contested constituencies of the county of Lancaster. The number of members returned by those constituencies at the last general election was 22 Conservative, and 6 Liberal; whereas the strength of the two parties, taking the highest polls on each side as the test, was 105,441 Conservative, and 95,345 Liberal votes. Under an equitable arrangement of representation the numbers returned would have been Conservative, 15; Liberal, 13.

"That the number of English county constituencies in which

political life is becoming extinct, and large classes of electors are being deprived of any opportunity of recording their convictions at the polling booth, is a serious evil, which demands the early consideration of Parliament, as it is very undesirable that large constituencies should exist for the sole purpose of registering the edicts of a small but dominant fraction of the population. In 1868 there were no contests in thirty-eight, and in 1874 none in fifty-four, county constituencies.

"That the limitation of voting power in constituencies returning more than two members, introduced by the Reform Act of 1867, is a very unsatisfactory attempt to provide for the representation of minorities; that it is partially and unjustly applied, the constituencies selected having been the largest in boroughs and the smallest in counties; that it is an aggravation of the existing inequality of representation, and tends to perpetuate a system under which the minority of electors have a large preponderance of representation.

" That the true problem to be solved in connection with this question is that of securing the effective and proportionate representation of the whole community, so that both the aggregate majority and minority in the constituencies shall each have a representation proportionate to their numerical strength, and that individual electors may have the widest possible area of choice."

The petititioners asked for a Royal Commission of Inquiry. Among the best points made by Sir Charles Dilke, in a speech conceded to be unusually effective from its moderate tone and ample acquaintance with the theme, was the reading of an advertisement clipped from the *Times*, in which a landed property was offered for sale, including among other advantages, that of a seat in the House of Commons. He showed also that the small towns were decreasing and the larger ones increasing in the number of inhabitants. Any one ward in Chelsea was larger than twenty-four of the small boroughs he named.

Sir Charles Dilke is a man of good proportions, middle stature and a handsome, open countenance, thoughtful in expression, and of a decidedly English look. Prosperity and honors have, in his case, been accompanied by a full share of public and private sorrows. The death of his father shortly after the son's entry into public life, the fierce arraignment of his motives which followed his action in 1870, and the early death of his young wife, have left their influence on his character, strengthening his convictions while moderating their manifestations. The early death of Lady Dilke, who is generally spoken of and written about as a lady of uncommon brilliancy of talents and wit, was widely commented on; owing to the fact that at her own request her remains were submitted to the process of cremation. Lady Dilke was the daughter of the late Arthur Gore Sheil, Esq., was married to Sir Charles in 1872, and died in 1874.

The London correspondent of the New York *Tribune*, writing of Sir Charles Dilke's second voyage "round the world," says, that "the chief object of this journey is Japan, which he will explore as thoroughly as time and circumstances permit. Neither in New York nor anywhere in the Eastern States does he propose to stop, but may renew his acquaintance with Brigham Young and the Mormons, who seem to be an unfailing attraction to every class of Englishmen. Whether Sir Charles means to write another book, I cannot say. Perhaps he himself cannot say. I suppose his tour is undertaken partly to satisfy the restlessness which at one time or another always resumes its hold on a man who has traveled much and rapidly ; partly to judge for himself something of an extraordinary people whose relations to Europe, and particularly to England, are growing yearly more intimate. There is a great field for a rising English politician in Oriental questions. Few Englishmen study them, except from a commercial point of view, a mistake Sir Charles Dilke will not commit. He is able to master a subject, and has lately shown more cleverness than he at first did in the use he makes of the knowledge he accumulates. Once unpopular in the House —for purely political reasons—he is now popular, having taken the sure way to regain its confidence—constant attendance, infrequent speaking, and steadily speaking better. When a man has abilities and industry, with some tact, he need not wait long to get a share of the confidence and good will of the House."

He will probably be as fortunate in this tour as he was in his first visit to the United States. Then, he saw the earliest phases of Southern reconstruction ; now, he will witness the reception of the Prince of Wales by the Indian population and princes, as well as learn of the remarkable changes both in conditions and policies, which are in progress in the East. These experiences cannot but be of great value to an English statesman, with prospects before him as notable as those of Sir Charles Dilke. It is by no means among the improbabilities that he may become at some not over distant day, the actual ruler of that great empire, whether it shall be as Prime Minister, under the system of liberalized monarchy which has been described as an "hereditary presidency," or as the elected President of a Constitutional Republic. There is a good deal of that confidence felt in him, which George Odger expressed when, in 1871, he said, "I look upon Sir Charles Dilke as the future leader of the republicans. He has everything necessary to fit him for the position. Whatever he does, he does well, he speaks well; he works well; he studies well; he thinks well; he is a republican through and through from conviction and from choice, and he associates with republicans, for he really likes their society, and it is because he is one himself."

Yet this statement will give, if unqualified, an erroneous impression of Sir Charles Dilke's position. He himself has so good-humoredly indicated it in "Prince Florestan," that it will be worth while to quote there-from This clever volume, which excited a great deal of discussion and comment on its appearance, was sent in manuscript to Messrs. Macmillan for publication, without anything to indicate the authorship. At first they declined the book, because it was construed by them to be a satire on Sir Charles Dilke. On their being satisfied as to this matter it was issued. It is entitled "The Fall of Prince Florestan of Monaco," and purports to be the history of a princeling educated in England and imbued with the theoretical republicanism of the Cambridge school. Monaco is the tiny principality on the coast of the the Gulf of Nice, which was known as the principal public gambling place in Europe, after the Kursaal, at Baden and elsewhere in Germany, had been suppressed. Prince Florestan is suddenly called to rule over his pocket principality, and on arrival proceeds to lay down his philosophy and carry out his reform without much regard to actual conditions. The story is but a sketch, but it is cleverly done. Of course it ends in his being driven out of Monaco. Everybody in England versed in politics, Cambridge affairs, and the radical cliques generally, was much amused at the incisive but not unkindly satire with which these matters were treated. Dilke himself was the best lampooned figure in the group. The "Prince" says: "Fired with the enthusisam of my party and my age, I had subscribed to the Woman's Suffrage Association, to Mr. Bradlaugh's election expenses, to the Anti-Game-Law Association and to the Education League. My reading was less one-sided than my politics, and my republicanism was tempered by an unwavering worship of 'Lothair.' Mr. Disraeli was my admiration as a public man —a Bismarck without his physique and his opportunities —but then in politics one always prefers one's opponents to one's friends. As a republican, I had a cordial aversion to Sir Charles Dilke, a clever writer, but an awfully dull speaker, who imagines that his forte is public speaking, and who, having been brought up in a set of strong prejudices, positively makes a merit of never having got over them. This he calls 'never changing his opinions.' For Mr. Gladstone I had the ordinary undergraduate detestation. There are no liberals at Cambridge, we were all rank republicans or champions of right divine."

After an amusing account of his efforts as Prince of Monaco, "Florestan" says: "The only later views that I have to record is a letter from my friend Gambetta, promising that when he becomes President of France I shall be Préfet of the Department of the Alpes Maritimes, which includes my ex-dominions, on condition that I am very moderate."

This amusing *jeu d'esprit* ended of course, with a reference to the reception in England of the news of the "Prince's" downfall; and the little satire winds up by the following apt reflections on English affairs, illustrative of the different conditions that prevailed in Monaco:

"In England you have a divided Church; an increasing and active though still little numerous Catholic body; a materialistic world of fashion which goes alternately to Mr. Wilkinson and Canon Liddon, Mr. Haweis and Mr. Stopford Brooke, and does not believe a word that any of them says—unless it is Mr. Haweis; but then, doctrinally speaking, he says nothing. You have the old non-conformist bodies, able and powerful still, though less powerful than before 1868; and you have the Wesleyans, pulpy and rich. Outside of them all you have people who believe, two-thirds of them, in the Bible pure and simple, but with prominence given in their mind to the communistic side of the New Testament; and one-third in nothing unless it is Mr. Charles Watts, Mr. Austin Holyoke, and Mr. Bradlaugh. The most flourishing publications in your country are *Zadkiel's Almanac* and *Reynolds' Newspaper*, belonging to the opposite poles, but equally at war with all that is most powerful and rich and respectable in society."

This holding up the mirror to society so amused the English club and political circles that when it became known that Sir Charles was himself the author, it put everybody in such good humor as to take the personal sting out of his ultraism. It was felt that a man so thoroughly in harmony with himself as to be able to laugh at and with the incongruous elements in his position, was a man of much more weight and metal, than he had heretofore obtained credit for.

III.

Peter A. Taylor.

POLITICAL principles are often inherited in England, like landed property. Nor is this peculiarity confined to the country gentlemen and the scions of the great families— Whig or Tory. The denominational relations of a household will shape the future political positions of the young men growing around the hearth-stone, just as they did those of their father. This is quite often true of the wealthier middle-class families—commercial or manufacturing—who are usually the lay leaders of the non-conforming sects. The further removed these are from the Church Establishment, the more radical, as a rule, are the politics; the closer too the communion among themselves. This even extends to matrimonial relations, so that the larger portion of whole congregations may be often found distantly related to each other. The member for Leicester is the head of one of the most noted Unitarian families, and comes naturally by the talents and radicalism which make him a marked man in the House of Commons.

Peter A. Taylor was born in London, in 1819, and is now in his 56th year. His father was a very well known silk manufacturer, of the firm of Courtauld, Taylor & Courtauld. Their sons are still in the same business. The elder partners, Samuel Courtauld and Peter A. Taylor, Sen., were well known Unitarians and Liberals in their day, as their sons are at this time. Mr. Taylor, Sen., was one of the most prominent and active members of the Corn Law League, but not being a popular speaker, his reputation is not as widely known as that of others. It was a period of intense agitation, of deep and abiding utility in the work performed. The Corn Law League discussion, in its origin and progress, embraced some of the finest talent of England, as it certainly did by its earnestness arouse the enthusiasm of nearly all classes, a result which can hardly be said to prove the economic theories which have grown in the shadow of its triumph. The "Manchester School,"—as the hard, dry measurers of human lives and human society, by the rule of "supply and demand" are now termed,—evoke no sympathetic feeling, arouse no admiration or regard, whatever they may compel by their ability, logic and success.

The *Westminster Review*, under the proprietorship of Col. T. Perronet Thompson, was the pioneer in the Corn Law agitation, and the papers which that veteran radical wrote for its pages and has since republished in his collected writings,* were among the most valuable of all that were written to call attention to the monopoly. Then came the Corn Law Rhymer, Ebenezer Elliott, whose powerful

---

* "Political Exercises." 6 Vols.

and melodious lyrics were first published in Tait's *Edinburgh Magazine*, of which W. E. Hickson, wholesale ironmonger, was the proprietor. Mr. Hickson owned the *Westminster Review* after Col. Thompson retired. It was then the *Liberal Quarterly*, par excellence. Then came Mr. W. J. Fox, known as an eloquent Unitarian divine and pulpit orator, but more widely as the " Norwich Weaver Boy," of the Anti-Corn Law League's organ ; as the " Publicola" of the London *Weekly Dispatch*, and also as the Member for Oldham,—a cotton mill borough in Lancashire, where great studies are now being made towards solving the problem of Labor and Capital, through the increasing ownership by the former of the latter, by the application of the joint stock and limited liability ideas to the ownership of cotton and other factories.

Mr. Fox published and edited the *Monthly Repository*, and in its pages many of Elliott's Corn Law and Reform lyrics appeared, as did those of Sarah Flower Adams, wife of William Brydges Adams, who, with John Stuart Mill, Mazzini, Mr. Hickson himself, and others, wrote for the great quarterly. The Cambridgeshire *Intelligencer*, edited by Mr. Flower, father of Mrs. Adams, was the first really liberal paper in England. With all these persons and their associates, the father of Peter A. Taylor, an able and modest man, was actively engaged, in the Anti-Corn Law, Church Rates and Reform agitations. His sons were brought up in the atmosphere thus generated, and the eldest, now a member of Parliament and the " dean " of the extreme or Radical wing of the Liberal party, has established his rightful heirship to the opinions and policies it naturally engendered.

When Mr. Taylor himself entered public life nearly

thirty years since, English politics were in state of ferment amounting almost to turbulence. The Chartist movement represented one wing of that activity, and the more popular or radical one; while the calmer and more thoughtful phase of current discussion found expression through a small but influential body of political writers and thinkers known as the "Philosophical Radicals." This school was deeply influenced by the teachings of Joseph Mazzini, whose politics were always kept true to a high ideal by a lofty sense of duty. Those who belonged to the school were intimately acquainted with European affairs, and endeavored heartily to aid the Italian leader in his chosen work by creating a favorable public opinion in Great Britain. They understood also that long preparation is necessary to make Republicans, and in seeking to set in operation principles of government, believed that in the end forms would necessarily become harmoniously adjusted to these. Among the better known of those who belonged to this class of thinkers was the member for Leicester—then a young man, rich and popular. Others may be mentioned, as Thornton Hunt, son of the graceful poet and critic; William J. Linton, the artist; George Jacob Holyoke, whose articles on the American abolition movement over the signature of "Ion," obtained from Wendell Phillips in reply, one of the most notable orations of his life; Mr. Stansfield, afterwards in Parliament; Goodwyn Barmby; Doctor, afterwards Sir John Bowring; W. H. Ashurst; Mr. Asher, (now solicitor to the General Post Office); Thomas Cooper; W. J. Fox;—these with others were members of the class which founded the *Leader* and left through that and other channels a distinct impression on British affairs.

Peter A. Taylor has been consistent to his earlier convictions. That fact, combined with his courtesy and moral worth, has won for him, during his fifteen years of continued parliamentary service, the respect of all who associated with him, however much they may be hostile to his opinion. In Dod's Parliamentary Guide, he is now recorded as "a Liberal," favoring extension of the suffrage, an extensive re-distribution of seats, abolition of the rate-paying qualification, the total abolition of the game laws, and it might be added of the unpaid magistracy of England, and of all grants beyond the Civil List to members of the Royal family. Mr. Taylor long antedates Sir Charles Dilke in his antagonism to the last grants, and has never failed to speak and vote against them, even though he has gone into the lobby alone, when the House divided on his motion. The London correspondent of a leading New York paper pays Mr. Taylor this sarcastic compliment, when referring to his vote on appropriating $250,000 for the expenses of the trip to India made by the Prince of Wales—that among others, it was opposed "by Mr. P. A. Taylor, a sentimental revolutionist, whose mission in life is to save ruffianly wife beaters and kickers from the lash, and to get the royal family cashiered."

Mr. Taylor's connection with the South Place Chapel —which stands to Unitarianism in England somewhat as Theodore Parker and his congregation did to the same denomination in New England, has helped to make him the representative of the liberal thought that gathered around such men as the famous W. J. Fox, known when living as one of the most eloquent orators in England. He has always been an ardent advocate of disestablishment for the State Church, and of Public Schools supported by taxation, with secular and compulsory education for the children. Mr. Taylor is the proprietor of the *Examiner*, a weekly journal and review that has been long known for its identity with radical reform in English politics and affairs. Under his proprietorship it is reassuming the leading place it maintained when it was contributed to or edited by men like Leigh Hunt, Grote, Place and others of that day. Its boldness and plain-speaking verges on the trenchant order. It has handled the Heir Apparent without gloves, at the risk, if its estimates of that work be true, of having its own hands soiled. "The Greville Memoirs" afforded a fair excuse for this freedom of discussion. The examiner reviewed the Life of the late Prince Consort, and did it in a style of singular candor, considering how everything but adulation is tabooed on that theme. "While the popular judgment of the Prince during his lifetime was far from erring as gravely on the side of exaggeration as his own opinion of himself, or the laudation of a little clique about the court, his memory for the last fourteen years has been unrelentingly pursued by posthumous adulation. He was merely a commonplace, plodding person, with fair natural capacities carefully trained, and not a gleam of the warmer imaginative fires of the intellect. In its well-tilled flatness his mind resembled those Flemish farms where a hillock or a hedge is resented as a loss of valuable ground." These criticisms indicate the general direction of Mr. Taylor's course in relation to royal grants, and similar measures, for which course he inevitably receives the severest criticisms. Yet the senior member for Leicester makes no pretensions of favoring republicanism. He simply exercises, as he claims, his right to see that the executive is not more extravagantly or ostentatiously dealt with than are the other officers of the Kingdom. He has made himself the representative of this view and has undoubtedly won the respect of the House by his courtesy, consistency, and unwavering courage.

A notable incident in the earlier political life of Mr. Taylor was his connection with the agitation led by Mr. Thomas S. Duncombe, so long member for Finsbury, on account of Sir James Graham's action while Postmaster-General during Sir Robert Peel's last administration, in opening for the benefit of the Austrian Government the letters of Mazzini and other Italian revolutionists, then living in England as political refugees. The fact of the opening was acknowledged by Sir James Graham before a secret committee of the House of Commons. In the outdoor discussion and agitation Mr. Taylor, then quite a young man, took an active part. He became identified soon after with the "People's International League," which was founded in 1856-7, and enrolled among its sympathizers or active advocates such names as Grote, Place, Hume, Dr. Bowring, Barmby, Henry Vincent, Dr. Epps, James Watson, Mr. Solly (since known as the organizer of the Workingmen's Clubs in England), Thornton Hunt, Linton and the Messrs. Taylor, father and son. The object of the League was stated to be the enlightenment of the "British Public as to the Political Conditions and Relations of Foreign Countries; to Disseminate the Principles of National Freedom and Progress; to embody and manifest an efficient public opinion in favor of the right of every people to self government and the maintenance of their own Nationality; to promote a good understanding between the people of all countries." In an address full of warm appeal and genuine fire, it was urged that the Unity of Humanity, which expresses the law of individual intercourse, also includes the law of the inter-communication of nations. * * * As no man will reach heaven who seeks to reach it alone, so no nation will ever develop the highest and most enduring forms of national life, while it is contented to remain the passive and uninterested spectator of the onward and upward struggles of kindred peoples. Multiplication in unity is the law or type of National progression. May not a calm and peaceful evolution avert the threatened strife? Why can not these Nationalities be recognized—as each proves the justice of its claim,—be set free to develop each its own peculiar growth, to fulfil each its own special mission, so to work out God's providential plan? For, if this is not God's plan, languages, tendencies, traditions, geographical characteristics, have no meaning. When a people is struggling to embody its inner life in new forms of outward institution, why not hail the event, and assist instead of hindering its ascent to the dignity and capacity of a nation?

"The League was formed," continues the address, "in the interests of peace, as based on civilization and human progress, and to that end seeks to know the conditions and circumstances of all nations.

"With political questions," it declares "except this question of Nationality, we, as a League, have nothing to do. With forms of government, with contests between Democracy and Privilege, we, as a League, cannot interfere."

Mr. Taylor at the first public meeting of the League

made a speech, in which he declared that every nation must decide its own form of government, "by the national tendencies, the state of education and enlightenment of each and every people."

During the secession war, Mr. Taylor was from the beginning to the close, an active friend of the Union cause in Great Britain. In conjunction with the member for Rochdale, Mr. Potter, John Bright, Mr. Thomas Hughes, and other gentlemen, he gave his money and his labors ungrudgingly to promote English sympathy in favor of the Federal struggle. How much of the former was spent by Mr. Taylor, Mr. Bazley Potter, and other friends, will probably never be known. There was a period in the progress of the civil war, when the intervention of Great Britain seemed imminent. It would certainly have been disastrous. It was during the latter part of 1862, when the Confederate agents in England spent money freely in the efforts to induce the working class organizations, leader and organs, to pronounce in favor of their government's raising the blockade of the Southern ports by force, under the pretext of obtaining cotton, and so ending what is known as the "cotton famine." Messrs. Lindsay, Laird & Co., who were in parliament, hard at work endeavoring to obtain a recognition of the Southern Confederacy, were aided by the efforts made to arouse the masses. But, it must be borne in mind that the Radical leaders and their followers, with the populations in those centres from which their strength is derived, never for a day wavered in their support of the Union cause, or faltered in their apprehension of the motives which led so large a proportion of the land-governing, commercial and trading classes to side with the South. In London, Liverpool, and Glasgow alone of the great cities of that country, was there either a marked hostility or coldness on the part of the working men. In Liverpool, the close relations of its leading interests with the Cotton States, accounted for this in large degree. Glasgow was the centre for the blockade runners. London was cold because her workmen were not as compactly united, and could not be reached as well as was the case with the same class in the manufacturing towns. In fact where the war caused the most suffering, there was shown the most fidelity to principles, and an outspoken faith in the American Republic, which contrasted strongly with the lukewarmness exhibited in some quarters at home.

In speaking of this, Mr. Taylor's active aid to the work cannot be overlooked. His purse-strings were unloosened, and his money was freely given for the publication of documents, the expenses of meetings, and to enable leading workingmen like Odger, Howell, and others, to devote themselves to the task of organizing and animating their associates. Mr. Taylor spoke whenever his voice was of service, in or out of the House, and subsequently when the Alabama discussion again aroused hostile feeling, he remained unshaken by the excitement involved by Senator Sumner's severe arraignment of English policy. Speaking on the escape of the confederate cruisers, Mr. Taylor addressing his constituency in 1868, said that "The Alabama went forth freighted with something worse than guns and men, to fire upon American commerce; it bore a heavy freight of jealousy, ill-will and suspicion." The course pursued, he declared, was only calculated to "promote discord between the two greatest and freest peoples in the world." Alluding to the Reform league agitation, and the Hyde Park demonstrations, he said that Russia was sometimes spoken of "as a despotism tempered with assassination," but Great Britain might be considered "as a class government modified by Hyde Park railings." Refering to complaints of the Irish people, and the growth of the "Home Rule" movement, the "Irreconcilable" member said: "We cannot afford to part with you. We have a common battle to fight. You are no longer oppressed as you were fifty years ago; you suffer now under an apprehension which Englishmen also feel. You are overlaid with the landed power, so are we; and were it not that our manufactures act as a set off to the evil we endure under the remains of the feudal system, all England would be (as Norfolk and Wiltshire indeed are) like Munster."

That Mr. Taylor possesses the entire confidence of his constituency, is evident from the bold and independent policy he pursues. When taunted on one occasion that he would not be supported for opposing a royal grant—that of the marriage portion or gift to the Duke of Edinburgh, Mr. Taylor replied by visiting Leicester, and before a large meeting—ten thousand persons being present—he made a statement of his action. He then asked for a vote in approval or disapproval, and received an unanimous endorsement. Mr. G. W. Smalley, the London correspondent of the New York Tribune, said in a letter "Mr. Taylor indeed, can afford to be as radical as he likes, and has a constituency which respects him for his frankness and ability."

But his chief public labors have been directed towards the abolition of the game laws and of the unpaid magistracy. Few persons, without a personal knowledge of English affairs, or accurate information from close study, can comprehend the character of these two abuses, or the tenacity with which reform in these directions is resisted. The game laws have long been, and are yet an infamous adjunct of the land monopoly, and are sustained simply for the amusement of a limited class. It should be however borne in mind, that an English Premier who should fail to get through the public business, or adjourn Parliament in time for the August grouse shooting, or at latest the beginning of September, would stand very little chance of preserving the friendship of his followers, and would in fact have committed as serious a blow at time-honored customs, as if he had assailed the crown, or worse still, the law of primogeniture itself. Capt. Maxse, a well known radical, who however differs somewhat from Mr. Taylor on this question, speaking of the stringent trespass laws that have been passed in connection with the preservation of game, says:

"In most districts in England no lawful highways now exist beyond the dusty or miry road, and yet there is scarcely a piece of land which may not during some portion—frequently a long one—of the year be traversed without damage."

He urges that laws against trespass are necessary, and thinks the member for Leicester has failed in presenting them while demanding the repeal of the game laws. He says:

"I have a very high opinion of Mr. Peter A. Taylor, but I hold that he has misdirected public opinion upon the subject of the game grievance. He has very properly aroused indignation against it, but he has not known how to formulate this indignation into a just demand, and his habit of comparing the hare to a Bengal tiger brings the whole subject into ridicule. It is true, Mr. Taylor says a 'new Trespass Law might be passed,' but in the same breath he invites the 'slayer of wild animals' 'into the field.' The result of this can only be constant broil and tumult. I am of Mr. Mill's opinion upon the matter, namely, 'that wild animals should belong to those at whose expense they have been fed, the nearest approach to which is that they should belong to the occupier of the land on which they are taken or killed.' If they are found upon the highway or public ground they should belong to the public."

How much the efforts of Mr. Taylor, and those associated with him now, or who preceded him in the agitation, have accomplished, may be judged by some words of Mr. Fowell Buxton, uttered in 1821, urging the modification of the animal laws he said: "Kill your father, or a rabbit in a warren, the penalty is the same;—destroy these kingdoms, or a hop vine, the penalty is the same;—meet a gipsy on the high road, keep company with him or kill him, the penalty by law is the same,—that penalty being, death."

The unpaid justices of the peace, are wholly taken from the land owning class. In fact such a commission can only be given to a person possessed of a certain freehold in fee simple. It is therefore practically a class tribunal of considerable importance. To defending those who have been unjustly convicted for poaching, trespass, breach of labor contracts, etc., and otherwise exposing the incompetency of such magistrates, Mr. Taylor has devoted the greater part of his Parliamentary efforts. Like Mr. Plimsoll, he never yields; but unlike his excitable friend, he never loses his temper. He has at last obtained the ear of the House, and when rising in his place he calls its attention to some such matter, he is sure of respectful attention from the Government benches as well as from the Opposition.

The session of 1875 presented a notable case of this, in the person of Luke Hill, a farm laborer hired as a carter by one Captain Hyde, a farmer and land owner in Sussex. The laborer was convicted for breach of contract under the "Master and Servant Act." Capt. Hyde claimed that the man had hired himself for one year, and on his leaving some time after hiring, had him arrested and taken before a Bench of County justices, who convicted him and fined him £5 as damage. Capt. Hyde estimated his loss at £9, but only claimed the smaller sum. The man was allowed a fortnight to procure the money and was then sent to prison for three months for non-payment. The conviction created a great deal of indignation. The "Laborers Union" took it up and agitated boldly. It was claimed on Hill's part that he had made no such contract, and that having given the lawful notice of twelve days, he was entitled to leave. No contract was produced, other than a memorandum in Capt. Hyde's pocket book, which he stated was made at the time of the hiring and shown to Hill. At any rate, it was easy to prove how disproportioned the punishment was to the offence. Mr. Taylor in calling attention to the case said it reminded him "in its high-handed justice, of the stories we have read in Smollett and Fielding of the magistracy of their day."

The Home Secretary, Mr. Cross, said it was beyond his power to release or remit the fine, in such a case. The amount was raised and Hill was set free after a month's imprisonment. The case assumed considerable importance to the Agricultural Laborers' agitation, and quite a large demonstration occurred on the day of his discharge. Mr. Taylor spoke briefly, saying they met to welcome Luke Hill and assure him "in their name, that the disgrace which attached to a gaol-bird did not attach to him; that, in their opinion, he left the prison without a taint upon his character, and that the disgrace which usually attached to such a punishment attached to those who sent him there. This was not a slight case. As he stated in the House of Commons, it was one in which a man, with a long honest record behind him, without the slightest offence or any misdeed attaching to him, had been ruined, so far as it lay in the hands of his judges to do so. It was only because his case was so flagrant that it had been exposed to the world: he feared that there were scores of cases of which they had never heard, and in which the ruin of persons followed sentences such as Hill's." Mr. Taylor declared that not only was the conviction unjust, but illegal. He believed that, by the Statute of Frauds, no agreement which was not for a period within a year was legal, unless regularly signed and stamped. In this case that was not done, and therefore he considered that the sentence was a distinctly illegal one. He charged also that the injustice was done knowingly, as there was not that legal proof of contracts the law required; and in closing he urged the necessity of the laborers obtaining the franchise. This, he said, was not merely as a general principle of abstract justice, that all men should be represented who are taxed, but that all those who are called upon to obey laws should have a share in making them through their representatives.

Mr. Taylor is socially a great favorite, and his London residence, Aubrey House, is the centre of a delightful society. His wife is a most accomplished lady, whom he knew first as the governess of his sisters; and she, like Mrs. Fawcett, is an active leader in all public movements relating to the condition of woman. They have no children, but their cultivation and literary tastes draw round them a large circle of those whose names are best known in literature and art. One of the most attractive private clubs in London, the "Pen and Pencil," held for a long time its meetings at their house.

IV.

SIR JOHN LUBBOCK, BARONET.

AT the annual meeting, in 1867, of the British association for the advancement of science, a generous and well-deserved compliment was paid by the distinguished savant whose name heads this page, while he presided over one of the sections of that learned body, to a gentleman sitting in the gathering but not of it, a journalist reporting the proceedings for the *New York Tribune*. The correspondent was George Jacob Holyoake, and Sir John Lubbock, in speaking of him, referred to the service he had rendered the cause of free inquiry by his fearless assertion of the right, and his unyielding endurance of persecution in consequence. Mr. Holyoake is the founder of the secularist movement in Great Britian; and was the last man imprisoned there for what the law termed blasphemy, but which in reality in his case was no more so than the studies and the discussions consequent thereupon, which have since made renowned the names of Huxley, Darwin, Tyndall, Lubbock, and Spencer. The baronet declared, that but for the labors of Mr. Holyoake, it might not have been possible for them, the *savans*, to speak as freely as they do in these days.

The incident is characteristic of the liberal member for Maidstone. A gentleman uniting in himself the broadest reputation for scholarship and science; great aptitude for his business as a banker, and a wise, firm radicalism in politics, which makes him deservedly popular with the people; while of him, as of Prof. Fawcett, it may well be said, "The true liberal is more and more felt to be he who, while trusting the heart of the people, does not bow to their superstitions or their prejudices, and, while serving them, does not suffer their dictation as to the way in which the service shall be rendered."*

Sir John Lubbock was born in 1834. He is the son of Sir John William Lubbock, of Mitcham Grove, Surrey, and High Elms, Down, Kent, eminent as a mathematician and astronomer, and of Harriet his wife, daughter of Lieutenant-Colonel George Hotham. The baronetcy was created in 1806, in favor of the great great uncle of the present Baronet, who succeeded to it in 1865, and resides at High Elms, near Farnborough, in Kent, on an estate of some thirteen hundred acres, purchased by his grandfather. Sir John is a partner in the London bank with which his family has been connected for several generations, the business having been commenced in 1772.

He was initiated into his business career at the age of fourteen, leaving Eton in 1848, and being taken into the banking-house, where his father had no working partner. At the age of twenty-two he married Miss Ellen Frances

---

* Mr. Conway in *Harper's Monthly*, February, 1875.

Horden, daughter of a clergyman, and has had six children, three sons and three daughters. At the time of his marriage he was already eminent as a banker, not only by virtue of his inheritance but by the unmistakeable business talent he brought to its discharge. He has written on finance with the same clear insight, power of investigation and comprehension of details, which are characteristic of his scientific inquiries and writings. He has been for some years honorary secretary of the London Bankers' Association, and is the author of many improvements, chief among which is that of the "Country Clearing" system, whereby provincial transactions are greatly facilitated.

He also organized a method of examinations for clerks, conducted by the City of London College, for the bankers, merchants, and joint-stock companies, in the same manner as those instituted by the Government under the Civil Service Commissioners. Instances might be named in which boys of very humble parentage, educated in a simple English School, have been enabled, by this means, to obtain employment in the bank of Sir John Lubbock himself.

Sir John Lubbock's reputation as a banker and a politician, though eminent, is still circumscribed; but his position as a man of science belongs to the civilized world. In America he is known chiefly as the author of "Prehistoric Times," of the " Origin of Civilization," and of other important works in the same direction. These books have been translated into several languages, the first named being now published in French, German, Swedish, Danish and Russian. Others have been widely issued in the same way, besides running through several editions in England itself. Sir John Lubbock has done valuable work as a scientific specialist, having written for the Ray Society, important papers on the "Origin and Metamorphoses of Insects," and on the curious genera named "Thysanura" and "Collembola;" while other scientific memoirs have been contributed by him to the Transactions of the Royal Society, the Linnean, and other philosophical associations of which he is a prominent member. Of several he has been President, the Entomological Society, the Ethnological Society, and the Anthropological Institute; besides being Vice-President of the British Association, the Royal Society, and other learned bodies, both British and foreign.

His active political career begun in 1865, when he first stood as a Liberal candidate for the Western Division of the County of Kent, in which he resides. Defeated by a small majority, he stood again in 1868, with Mr. Angerstein, against Sir Charles Mills and Mr. John Y. Talbot, to be once more unsuccessful, though defeated by only 50 majority. He was soon afterwards elected to represent the borough of Maidstone, and was re-elected in 1874. In 1868 he was asked to stand for the University of London, an honor of a high character, which he felt compelled to decline, because of promises made to his friends in Kent. He is now Vice-Chancellor of that University, having been elected to succeed George Grote,—banker, historian, and philosophical republican.

In the House of Commons Sir John Lubbock's career has been of great usefulness. Classed properly among the "Independent" members, he cannot be counted as an "Irreconcilable." His largest work has been in the direction of education, and other matters in which he might properly be deemed of great service.

He has given loyal and earnest service to the work of perfecting the Elementary School Laws, but the best part of his efforts in this field have been in connection with the Endowed Schools and the Royal Commission on Public Schools, of which, and of the Commission for the Advancement of Science, Sir John Lubbock was a prominent member. He was also active in promoting various reforms in connection with national universities. The student of English affairs will readily bear in mind the great abuses which, it has been shown, had crept into the great public and endowed schools of England. Originally designed, in almost every instance, to be accessible to the poorest boy in the realm, they had grown to be largely viewed as instrumentalities for cheapening education to the favored classes, or sinecures for well-paid teachers. The report made by Sir John Lubbock's commission has largely exposed these abuses, and in preparing the way for their correction, has also indicated a radical change in policy. Even under present conditions a generation will hardly elapse before these schools, in many instances so consolidated as to make stronger those that remain, will form, as they were intended to do, a complete collegiate link between the more elementary and preparatory schools and the great universities, and will be as accessible to the studious poor as but recently they were to the fortunate rich or those whom they patronized and aided.

In other work, such as the Bank Holidays Acts, the International Coinage Commission, the Act for the Protection of Ancient Monuments, as well as in the support of those measures of political reform and economic legislation which have come up during his parliamentary career, Sir John Lubbock has been active and prominent. He has usually voted with the most advanced wing of the Liberal party, though not following the smaller minority in opposition to all Royal grants and similar measures.

In person Sir John Lubbock is of middle height, rather slender figure, with fair Anglo-Saxon face, features and complexion. As a speaker he is easy and fluent in manner and words, while as to matter he is direct and weighty—speaking from a full mind always. His political career bids fair to bring returns worthy of high ambition, and is certain to be full of honorable service. He is prominent among an increasing class in British politics—men of wealth, at least of independent means, of high culture, good birth, and eminent intellectual ability—a class comprising such men as Fawcett, Dr. Lyon Playfair, Huxley, Frederic Harrison, Thorold Rogers, Chamberlain, Auberon Herbert, Cowen, Sir Charles Dilke, and others too numerous now to name in these pages;—a class of men who seem destined to lead their nation through the peaceful ways of ameliorative reforms, into the larger liberties and ordered equities of a practically democratic future.

V.

JOSEPH COWEN.

THIS gentleman represents his native borough, a distinction not often attained in the British House of Commons. Newcastle is an ancient burg, filled with a sturdy and industrious constituency, who have never willingly brooked harsh authority, and have always been apt at asserting themselves and their rights. Founded by King William Rufus or the Red, —though its river had long before been a landing-place for the Romans, the Picts and the harrying Danes with whom Alfred the Great effected peace by dividing England with them,—it afterwards became known for its coal mines. Now, its shipping, commerce and manufactures are second only to its mining interests. They hold together one of the most thoroughly homogeneous communities, in a political sense, that can be found in England. It has always been Radical—often turbulent, seldom inconsistent. Mr. Cowen is not only "native, and to the manner born," identified with all the activities of the place, but, as the proprietor and political director of the Newcastle *Chronicle*, is in a notable sense its representative. The fact of this proprietorship gives him a more than personal importance. Within a few years past, the country or "provincial" press of Great Britain has become a great power, both as to enterprise and political importance. Mr. Gladstone recognized this fact three or four years ago in a speech made to his Greenwich constituency. The Newcastle *Chronicle* is one of the most influential of this class, and is especially so in its attitude towards all advanced politics. Its tone has always been aggressively Radical, as much so when, one hundred years since, the American colonies and their action were the chief topic of discussion, as at the present time when the extension of the suffrage to the Agricultural Laborers, and the visit of the Prince of Wales to India, constitute the principal themes of debate.

Joseph Cowen is the son of Sir Joseph Cowen, Knight. He was born near Newcastle at Blayden Burn in 1831, and is, therefore, in his forty-fourth year. His father, who represented the same borough for many years, began life as an artisan, but when the discovery of gas was being utilized, he made a number of ingenious inventions which greatly facilitated the manufacture. He soon grew to be a rich and influential citizen, and was known for liberal views and public spirit, as well as quaint ways and homely wit. His eldest son, the present member, was carefully educated near his birth place, and then entered Edinburgh University, graduating with honor as a classical and general scholar. This University has always had a wide reputation for the debating societies connected therewith, and at these Mr. Cowen took a leading place, being distinguished for readiness in debate and facility as a public speaker. With the exception of having acquired during his (twenty years,) later mingling with the Northumbrian people, something of their deep and not unmusical pronunciation, Mr. Cowen has already shown in the House that his ability as a debater has not diminished by comparative disuse.

A friendly writer and evidently an admirer, thus writes of Mr. Cowen's political life :—

"In 1848 Mr. Cowen began to distinguish himself in connection with those public movements which sought that extension of the franchise Pitt meditated towards the close of the last century. In this course he followed faithfully the footsteps of his father, who had been a Radical in days when Radicalism involved something bordering on social proscription. Sir Joseph Cowen formed one of the intrepid band of North country reformers who met on Newcastle Moor to protest against the Peterloo massacre. To the enthusiasm of the idealist, Mr. Cowen unites a sagacious common sense which the sternest realist might envy. This combination of faculties gives to his nature that equipoise which is necessary for practical statesmanship. With the deepest sympathy, and the most generous consideration for erratic politicians, Mr. Cowen has never shared their illusions. When the Crimean war arose, the member for Newcastle was not led astray by the sentiment with which so many of our countrymen regarded that tragic episode in the history of Europe. On the contrary, he belonged to a school of politicians who conceived the war a mistake. The Foreign Affairs Committee, with which he was conspicuously associated, did what it could to unveil the diplomatic intrigue by which we had drifted into that inglorious, even if triumphant, campaign. Almost contemporaneous with the close of the conflict, the Northern Reform Union was called into existence, and of that union Mr. Cowen became the treasurer. The work done by this association was enormous, and of that work Mr. Cowen was the animating spirit. At once by tongue, and pen, and purse, he contributed to arouse the North from the political indifference into which the country had unhappily sunk. The success which this devotion achieved was attested by the political enthusiasm it evoked. When the Reform agitation—so long the mere stalking-horse of official statesmen—had reality breathed into it in governmental circles by the earnestness of Mr. Gladstone, nowhere was that earnestness more powerfully seconded than in Northumberland. The political demonstrations of 1866 and 1867 which took place in Newcastle are among the most memorable events in the public history of that epoch. The important part Mr. Cowen's energy and organizing power played in these demonstrations is known to all who know Northumbrian politics. At the present moment the member for Newcastle is president of a League which is directing its energies to securing that assimilation of the county and borough franchise and equalization of electoral districts, of which the late Earl Durham was so conspicuous an advocate. As a member of the Council of the Anti-State-Church Association, and of the Executive of the Birmingham League, Mr. Cowen has done good service to the causes represented by these organizations.

"Some time ago Mr. Disraeli said our position would be improved by 'a little less activity at home and a little more activity abroad.' We doubt if, in the sense the Premier meant these words to be understood, Mr. Cowen would endorse either proposition. His activity at home is known and read of all men, and he is not the friend of that intermeddling foreign policy which has so often rendered England odious to Continental Europe. Nevertheless, no man has been more distinguished for the operative sympathy which he has shown for the leaders in the great struggles that have done so much to transform the political institutions of the Continent. To Poland, to Hungary, to Italy, he has been one of the most important friends these countries ever found in England. With Kossuth, with Mazzini, with Garibaldi, Mr. Cowen was on terms of the closest intimacy, and towards the illustrious triumvirate he has ever entertained an appreciation worthy of their characters. The last letter Mazzini wrote was written to Mr. Cowen, and one of the first in which Garibaldi broached his scheme for the regeneration of the Campagna came to the member for Newcastle."

Mr. Cowen possesses a character so calm and generous, that his friends are enthusiasts over him, and the feelings he arouses are attachments, not admirations only. When General Garibaldi was in England just before the British Legion was formed, he was the guest of Mr. Cowen, who also presented him with a sword of honor subscribed for by his admirers. The crowning friendship of this period, Mr. Cowen considers to be his intimate and affectionate relations with Joseph Mazzini. The Italian publicist and republican has left behind him a small but influential body of Englishmen, over whose intellectual lives and opinions his own views were almost paramount. Peter A. Taylor,

Mr. Stansfield, Joseph Cowen, William J. Linton, the well-known wood engraver and writer (for forty years the foremost republican worker and thinker in England), are among the better known of this school. These associations give the Member for Newcastle a knowledge of European politics from the stand-point of republican endeavor which is rare in Parliament at present, and is only equalled by that possessed by Peter A. Taylor, the member for Leicester.

Mr. Cowen has served for several years as a member of the Newcastle Town Council, and, as may be inferred, has taken an active part in all local movements of a worthy character. "Previous to entering the House of Commons, he was repeatedly solicited to allow himself to be nominated as a candidate for Parliamentary honors. These solicitations, however, were invariably declined; but on the death of his father, which occurred rather suddenly towards the close of 1873, he was practically compelled to stand for Newcastle. Scarcely had he been elected as the successor of his sire in the representation of that ancient town ere the dissolution of Parliament took place, and Mr. Cowen was again plunged into all the turmoil of a contested election." In this contest his energy and eloquence were so marked and exercised so large an influence, as to attract national attention to his canvass. Long before, political managers on all sides had been compelled to take note of the movements of the great mining population, of which Newcastle is the centre. A community which could gather at short notice and in peaceful order, demonstrations numbering from twenty-five thousand to double that number, was one not to be lightly left unregarded by a governing class or classes, whose leaders make it the study of their political lives to ascertain how little they can give and how much they may withhold. Mr. Cowen has already shown himself to possess a commanding influence with this population. This gives him in the House an important position. Of his oratorical capacity, the "Beehive" biographer thus writes :—

"It is said of one of the most accomplished of English actresses—a lady with quite a genius for her profession—that when satisfied of thoroughly comprehending what she meant to act, she never troubled herself further, assured that all else might be left to natural and spontaneous impulse. Something akin to this feeling is at the root of Mr. Cowen's oratorical success. A perfect comprehension of great political questions by an earnest and capable man unlocks the fountains of sensibility, and exercises over an audience that mesmeric influence which constitutes the triumph of eloquence. Few men have entered the House of Commons in recent years who possess a more thorough comprehension alike of English and European politics, who have greater capacity for work, greater sympathy for the people, or a more intelligent appreciation of those industrial and political problems with the just solution of which the weal of England is indissolubly associated. Prediction is proverbially dangerous, but with the vigor of earlier years restored, there is really no political position to which, should the emergency arise, Mr. Cowen may not only adequately but honorably fill. His parliamentary career has been yet too brief fully to disclose his powers. During the greater portion of last session he was laid aside from duty by illness, precipitated by overwork. The moment, however, that he had sufficiently recovered, he devoted himself to Parliamentary duty with characteristic assiduity. Throughout the present session his attendance has been unflagging, his name appearing in nearly every division. To all questions connected with the social welfare of the people he has given the closest attention. His speech on the Friendly Societies Bill was, in many respects, the best delivered on the subject; and as a vindication of the people from charges too frequently hurled against them, it was pre-eminently successful. As a business man, Mr. Cowen's skill, integrity, and sagacity are universally recognized. The importance of this fact can scarcely be overrated in a country where it is almost impossible to achieve the highest political success without a practical knowledge of commercial questions. Mr. Cowen married early. His wife is the daughter of John Thomson, Esq., Fatfield. His family consists of a daughter and son."

During the session of 1875, Mr. Cowen participated in several debates—relating to the County Suffrage Extension, the act relating to Labor combinations and disputes, the proposition to pay the expenses of the royal trip to India, and that arising from Mr. Plimsoll's bill and agitation for the better protection of seamen. In the latter discussion, as the representative of a great shipping mart, his vote and words were influential. It is clear that Mr. Joseph Cowen's public career, so fairly begun, with ample background of preparation behind it, has a long foreground over which to advance with increasing usefulness. He has a happy home, two fine children, and that guarantee of happiness which lies in the confidence of friends and neighbors. His exertions have not been confined to political efforts only, but in all movements, such as co-operation, arbitration, temperance, education, he has been a friendly counsellor and active advocate. The same admiring writer closes the sketch, before quoted, with words which those who know Mr. Cowen best do not regard as overdrawn: "Though yet only in the meridian of life, he has crowded into that life an amount of work which very many who have reached the allotted span of existence have failed to achieve. With ample resources Mr. Cowen shuns the pleasures of sense, having early learned to 'scorn delights and live laborious days.' Alike in purity, elevation, and devotion of character, and breadth of sympathy, Joseph Cowen is an example to the age in which his lot is cast."

VI.

ROBERT MEEK CARTER.

AMONG the eighteen members of the House of Commons who voted against the recent appropriation of £60,000 from the Imperial treasury towards defraying the larger portion of the expenses of the East Indian journey of His Royal Highness the Prince of Wales, was the senior member for the important borough of Leeds, Yorkshire. In English politics that vote probably places Mr. Carter among the "Irreconcilables"—certainly it ranks him with those who are classified as "Independents." It required a considerable amount of political devotion, or the courage which comes from the consciousness of having behind the vote a constituency who will not only sustain the member but endorse the act. Such a vote requires almost as much moral force or "fanaticism" on the part of the British member, as it did ten years before the secession civil war for a northern representative to vote against the Fugitive Slave Law in an Amercan Congress. The vote and the popular excitement attending it marks one of the steps in English politics, from which in the future the critic, student and statesman will date marked results. Moncure D. Conway writes as follows in relation to these demonstrations, and especially that held in Hyde Park, which seems to have been most formidable :

"All the bright sunshine—which some authorities have suggested was diabolically manufactured—and the luxuriant verdure of the park could not make the scene idyllic. It is the most angry, and at the same time the most calm and orderly popular demonstration which has occurred in London during the fourteen years in which I have resided here. Strange to say, the Provincial papers are coming in bringing telegrams sent to them from London on Sunday night, saying that the Hyde Park meeting had ended in a riot, and that the military had been called out. These distant journals passed the London papers on their way, which will make them aware that they have been hoaxed. * * * The simple truth is that it was the very largest meeting ever held in London. No one wishing to state the truth could possibly estimate it less than a hundred thousand people, and my own belief is that there were at least one hundred and fifty thousand present. The papers attempt to convey the impression that even the numbers, as diminished by them, were made up to a large extent by the habitual loungers in the park ; but the brightest Sunday does not usually show in the park a thousand people." * * * * *

"There was a considerable number of peers, and also of members of the House of Commons, standing in the crowd, within easy ear-shot of the speaker, and they have certainly not heard any speech in either of their Houses this session so eloquent as that of Bradlaugh on the present occasion."

"The multitude," continued Mr. Conway, "cheered

only the boldest portions of the orator's utterances. One of those manifestations occurred when Bradlaugh cried, 'This Prince of Wales, for whom our money is spent, is no Prince of ours; he is Prince of the wealthy classes.' The other instance was when he said. 'If these great popular meetings, and their protests against the diversions of public moneys to Princes, continue to be despised by Parliament, on the next occasion when a grant is proposed to a Prince, we will carry our petition and our protest ourselves into Westminster Hall.' This was followed by several minutes of uproarious unanimous approval. While Bradlaugh was speaking, six telegrams were brought at different times and handed to him by official messengers. Each was addressed to 'Charles Bradlaugh, Esq., Hyde Park.' Each was from some large city, where a similar mass meeting was being held at the same hour, and they announced the passing in the six cities of resolutions protesting against the grant to the Prince. In one week there have been held in the country forty vast meetings of the same character. It had been announced that a meeting of the Durham miners, who are in the habit of carrying to their meetings the portraits of popular leaders as flags, the portrait of John Bright—who has kindled great displeasure by even his qualified approval of the grant to the Prince—was carried in procession hung with crape. Bradlaugh having mentioned Bright's name, some present were inclined to hiss, but the orator quickly raised his hand to hush such, and said solemnly, 'His name is now to be received with regret, but not with anger; he has done the people great services; and no crape is so mournful as that speech with which he himself has obscured an honored name.'"

When the meeting closed,—which it did, writes Mr. Conway, without disorder,—the orator, escorted by the marshals and their deputies, went through the Park and left in a cab, driving away amid loud cheers. Mr. Conway writes—

"And so ended a meeting whose significance I have certainly not overestimated. Royalty in England cannot stand many more such gatherings of indignation: and I am confidant that the chances of future appropriations of the people's money by the 'Ring' of princelings which has so long fed on the English Exchequer have been considerably diminished by the proceedings of Sunday last."*

These facts show the importance to be attached to the opposition indicated by the eighteen noes, and the out of doors demonstrations. The men who hold them are all voters and can make themselves felt. Mr. Carter's vote was endorsed by a very large meeting in his own borough, attended by about 150,000 persons and presided over by a prominent alderman of the place.

This vote is in full sympathy with the opinions of a gentleman who is recognised as one of the strongest among the provincial radical leaders in Great Britain; as well as a practical and careful business member and citizen. Robert Meek Carter was born poor, the son of a peasant, and is now wealthy. Unlike many others whose lives can be summed up in the same way, the opinions of his earlier manhood, formed when struggling in sympathy with his conditions and associates, have matured and grown with his prosperity, animating his public career and shaping its actions. His life is one of marked activities and great usefulness.

* Cincinnati *Commercial's* London Letter, July 20, 1875.

Mr. Carter is now in his sixty-first year, having been born in 1814 at the hamlet of Sheffling, near Spun Head in the East Riding of Yorkshire. His father was at that time successfully cultivating a small farm, but became involved at the close of the European war and was compelled to abandon his occupation. For five or six years he worked as a laborer, and then recommenced business as a common carrier, between the Yorkshire towns of Hull and Burlington. At an early age Robert accompanied and assisted his father, living two nights of each week in the carrier's cart. He was often compelled at night and in the winter time, to walk the distance between the two towns. At eight years of age he went to reside with his uncle, a farmer. Here he had the privilege of attending school during the three winter months, walking four miles daily to and from the school house. His mother died when he was ten years old, and, at twelve, Robert began his active life as a farm hand. He remained with his uncle till he was sixteen and then removed to Leeds (in 1830) where he obtained work in a cloth mill. A younger brother had preceded him there.

The borough of Leeds is the chief seat of the woolen cloth manufactory in England, and its operative population are regarded as among the best and most intelligent of their class. Leeds is the seat of one of the largest and most profitable co-operative societies, and of the most successful Building and Loan Associations ; and is the centre of the "Yorkshire Association of Mechanics' Institutes," of which it has one of the largest, with excellent classes, lectures, library and well appointed collection of models, etc., for technical and industrial art, applied science, philosophy and mechanics. The bright and active boy, who now as a man represents this great constituency, took up his residence there just when the first impetus was being given to the movements which during the past forty years have wrought such great and beneficial changes in the condition of the laboring people of Great Britain.

Robert Meek Carter's first employment was in working "a gig" for raising the nap of cloth. He and his brother roomed together, and on their earnings (fourteen shillings, about $3.36 per week) managed to live quite comfortably. Robert attended night school, subscribed to a library, and also connected himself with a famous local Sunday school in Wortley, a suburb of Leeds, which was held in a blacksmith's shop. It still exists, and is known as the Zion School. The *Beehive* says:

"When only nineteen years old, he was placed at the 'man side' of the 'gig' and received a man's wages, viz., 22s. per week. Continuing to show aptitude for his work, he was raised to the position of foreman three years afterwards, and held two or three different situations in this capacity. In 1844 the cloth trade of Leeds was in a very depressed state, and work was scarce. This compelled Mr. Carter to seek for some other occupation. He was successful in obtaining a position * * * as weighman. After a few years, Mr. Carter conceived the idea of beginning business on his own account as a coal merchant, and he was bold enough to rent a yard in the Calls. Perseverance and attention soon brought him custom, and very soon he was in a position to purchase the coal-yard which he holds to this day, in addition to others.

"Mr. Carter now took up his residence in the heart of

Leeds, and his business tact being noticed by some members of the Board of Highway Surveyors and others, he was asked to join the Board, which he did. His honorary labors here, and also in connection with Zion Sunday School (which had now become a flourishing institution), brought him into prominence, and in the year 1850 he was invited by a number of ratepayers in Holbeck to become a candidate in the Radical interest for a seat in the Town Council, and was returned unopposed."*

His active public life was now fairly begun. While serving for three years in the town council he became a prominent member of the various societies already referred, to, and of other associations for Political and Social Reform. He developed ready talent as a speaker, was pithy and direct, but was most formidable as an organizer. A vigorous opposition was made by the Whigs to his re-election as a Town Councillor, but he was successful, polling the largest vote that had been cast up to that date, (1853). He was re-elected for four terms, serving in the Council for twelve years. He was then elected as alderman and served until November 1874, when he resigned on account of the pressure of his parliamentary duties. During all these years of municipal service, he came to be recognized as the leading Radical of both his town and section. He participated actively in the Chartist agitation, though opposing the physical force demonstrations, which ended so disastrously for many of the most sincere leaders. During the interest

---

* *Beehive* "Portrait Gallery," 2d series, London, 1875.

aroused in Garibaldi's efforts for the liberation of Italy, he aided by purse and personal exertions. His name is prominent in the coöperative and other social-economic and ameliorative reforms, which have taken such deep root in the portion of England of which he is a resident. Leeds possesses two notable provincial papers, the *Mercury* and the *Express*, and of the latter Mr. Carter is the chief proprietor. It is widely circulated and very influential, ranking in that regard next to the Newcastle *Chronicle*, owned by Mr. Joseph Cowen, M. P. for that ancient burgh. A marked tribute to the increasing power of the country press of Great Britain, is the pecuniary interest which ambitious politicians are obtaining in their proprietorships. Mr. Carter's interest in the *Express* began early, however, when it was struggling and required outlay, being then the organ of new and somewhat unpopular ideas. The Leeds *Mercury* is better known in the United States, owing to the fact that its proprietor and editor, Edward Baines, Esq., was prominent in the West India Emancipation agitation, and since then as an active member of the British Anti-Slavery Society. He wrote profusely and effectively against American slavery, and many of his papers were republished on this side of the Atlantic. Both papers and their proprietors were the active friends of the Union cause and materially assisted in keeping the public sentiment of their important section in that direction. Mr. Baines represented Leeds in more than one Parliament.

Mr. Carter long since became, with all this activity, a recognized leader of the Radical party, and at the beginning of the last Reform agitation he was made the President of the "Radical Reform League" of his section. With all these public activities, he did then and still does conduct large business enterprises. He is still largely engaged in the coal business, has large interests in two collieries, and owns and conducts a cloth finishing mill, which finishes one-third of all the cloth exported to China from Great Britain.

A biographical sketch says of his later political career, that:—" In the year 1866, this League got up one of the grandest political demonstrations that ever took place in the country. It was held on Woodhouse Moor, and was attended by about 250,000 persons. There were numerous platforms erected, and the whole proceedings were admirably carried out under Mr. Carter's direction. In the evening a great meeting was held in the Town Hall, under Mr. Carter's chairmanship. The demonstration was attended by Mr. John Bright, Mr. W. E. Forster, Mr. Leatham, Mr. Beales, Mr. Ernest Jones, Mr. George Potter, and others.

"In 1868, the Leeds Radical Reform League selected Mr. Carter as their candidate for the general election then ensuing. He was accepted, along with Mr. Edward Baines, at a meeting of the entire Liberal party, and was returned M.P. for Leeds, receiving upwards of 15,000 votes. In the House of Commons, Mr. Carter has pursued a straightforward, consistent course, endeavoring to make himself a practically useful member, rather than a fussy, talkative one. At the last general election, Mr. Carter was again selected by the Liberal party along with Mr. Baines. The latter, however, in consequence of his sectarian education views and other reasons, was defeated; but Mr. Carter was returned at the head of the poll, receiving no fewer than 15,390 votes." *

In the House of Commons, though not a frequent speaker, he is one always listened to, because that practical assembly recognizes in Mr. Carter the fact that he has always something to say when he rises to speak, and that he draws from wide knowledge and a large personal experience in presenting his reasons and stating the conclusion he has reached.

In the current movements of the day, Mr. Carter's position is logically related to his past agitation. His votes, as shown by Hansard's reports, have supported Sir Charles Dilke's propositions with regard to the re-distribution of seats, Mr. Dixon's bills for a National system of undenominational education, and Mr. Trevelyan's measure for the Agricultural Franchise. He has voted with Macdonald, Burt and Mundella, on labor questions, and with Mr. Peter A. Taylor, in opposition to Royal grants.

The *Beehive* writer says of him—that

"Mr. Carter's success may be taken as a lesson by every workingman, and by all who desire to raise themselves in the social scale. The positions of trust and of honor which he has filled, and now fills, have come to him, not because he sought them, but because he was worthy to occupy them. His industry has been great, and his honorary labors extraordinary. Yet he never appeared in a fuss nor in a hurry. His private virtues, like his public ones, are of the highest kind. Strict integrity and purity of life are his strong characteristics; and to his

---

* *Beehive* "Portrait Gallery."

sound advice in matters of business and of finance many a man in Leeds and elsewhere owes much. In his political conduct, Mr. Carter acts fairly and openly with his opponents. This view of his action was once represented by one of the most respected of Leeds vicars, who said of him :—'I like Mr. Carter as an opponent, for he always hits straight out from the shoulder.'"

PART II.
THE LABOR AGITATION AND ITS FRIENDS.

PART II

THE LABOR AGITATION AND ITS FRIENDS

VII.

THOMAS HUGHES.

IN tracing the progress of the various movements which have during the last forty-five years exercised so marked an influence on English affairs, and especially on the condition, political and social, of the working masses, the decade embraced between 1850 and 1860 is worthy of especial notice. So far as political agitation was concerned, that ten years appeared to pass with but little more than a ripple on the surface of feeling. Yet two remarkable forces were at work, organizing the social and economic side of that Democratic growth, which is now so energetically re-occupying the political arena. The forces or movements referred to are in a large generalization, resolved into but one—and a writer in *Blackwood's Magazine** thus indicates its character: "A new power has been introduced into our political system, new forces are at work within the pale of the Constitution. The Government has become national in the fullest sense

---

* "The State, the Poor, and the Country." April, 1870.

of the word; and with the change a new breath of life is stirring society. New views are also rapidly forming; new hopes and inspirations are entering into the hearts of the masses." The rule of the middle-class, adds this writer, "has come to an end, and the doctrines which regulated the legislation of that period are now being tested and considered from a different, indeed opposition principle. * * * For nearly forty years the prime object of our legislation has been the interests of the consumers; now, we shall soon have the masses advocating their own interests as producers."

Mr. Thomas Hughes has had a large share in the direction of one of the two forces that have tended to bring into prominence the interests of Production—especially of its most important factor, Labor. His connection with Co-operation and its organization in Great Britain, is his highest title to that general esteem to which he may now fairly lay claim. In 1850, the European reaction was attended by a subsidence of radical agitation in England. The defeat of the State-help movement in France, as illustrated by the failure of the national workshops, as well as of that of the various Labor societies, that had received aid from the French Republic in 1848-9, was followed in Great Britain by a remarkable increase of Trades' Union strength, and an equally vigorous growth of self-help in the form of Co-operative Distribution or Stores. Among the very earliest movements in the direction of Co-operation was that of the society known as "Christian Socialists," of which the late Canon Kingsley,—whose "Alton Locke" had become the inspiration of every aspiring youth in the ranks of Labor, and had attracted the minds of many others to its condition;

—the Rev. Frederick Denison Maurice, Vansittart Neale, Mr. Ludlow, the present "Registrar of Friendly Societies,"* the Chevalier St. André, and others, more or less widely known, with Mr. Hughes, were members of the Co-operative stores of Yorkshire and Lancashire, which have since become so famous as illustrating the advantages of Co-operation. Many were already in successful operation, but they had not attracted more than local and class attention. One of the first efforts of the "Christian Socialists" was the organization of a "Co-operative Tailors Society," which continued in existence for a few years. Not long before this period, Thomas Hood's mournful "Song of a Shirt" had awakened a new interest in the condition of those who were poverty-cursed; that interest received intelligent direction from the investigations conducted by the Brothers Mayhew, — first as the London *Chronicle's* "Commissioners," and afterwards on their own responsibility—observations which have since been gathered in their remarkable volumes—"London Labor and the London Poor." Hence it was natural that the coterie of philanthropists and thinkers among whom Mr. Hughes was a leader should endeavor to aid the handicraft which these investigations showed to be in especially bad condition. Another and even more useful effort was the organization of the "Working-Men's College," of which Mr. Hughes is now President, and over

---

* Mr. Ludlow is the present Registrar of Friendly and Benefit Societies, Building and Loan Associations, Co-operation Societies, and Trades Unions, all of which are now brought under laws enacted for their protection and encouragement, and are therefore required to register at his office and render regular statements of their business and standing.

which the Rev. Frederick Denison Maurice* was so long the animating soul—the master spirit. It still flourishes and works very beneficially, quietly and without cant, to the end sought—that of helping laboring men to help themselves to liberal education, by an arrangement of hours, fees, tuition, studies, etc., adapted to their circumstances. Mr. Hughes graduated in this school to the larger usefulness of place and sphere which he now fills. It is this work which places him among the genuine radical leaders of England, though in many respects, as the term is commonly used, he might be regarded as a moderate or even Conservative-Liberal.

Thomas Hughes is the second son of a country gentle-

---

* The friendship between Messrs. Maurice and Hughes is illustrated by the following graceful tribute to the former, written to the Co-operative Congress of 1872, by the President.

BROWNLOW FOLD MILLS, BOLTON, April 2, 1872.

Dear Mr. Pare:—When I got home last night I heard of the death of Mr. Maurice. I feel that I should be quite useless, even if I forced myself to take part in the conference to-day and in the public meeting. I am therefore going back home, and must ask you to make my excuses to the Congress. They will remember that Mr. Maurice was the president, 24 years ago, of the Society for Promoting Working Men's Associations, in which I learnt my first lessons of Co-operation. In this, as in all other good work of the last 40 years, he was a foremost thinker and doer. The first time I was ever in Bolton was with him, and Mr. Neale, and other gentlemen, at a social gathering to forward the Co-operative movement. I am sure the Congress will sympathize with me, even if they do not feel as I do that that the best and wisest Englishman I have ever known has left us. Pray say for me, that if they like to elect me again to serve on the London Section of the Board I will gladly serve.—Ever yours, most truly,

THOS. HUGHES.

man, John Hughes, Esq., of Donnington Priory, near Newbern, Berkshire. He was born October 23d, 1823, and is therefore in his fifty-second year. At an early age he was sent to Rugby, then under the Mastership of the famous Dr. Arnold, whose reputation is somewhat merged for the rising generation in that of his son, Matthew Arnold, well known as a scholar and poet, whose writings have had a not less marked influence, though less robust, than that his famous father exercised. Dr. Arnold was the founder of the Broad Church movement, of which Dr. Stanley, the Dean of Westminster, and Dr. Temple, Bishop of Exeter, are now the leading clerical representatives, and Mr. Hughes, himself, one of the foremost lay adherents. Mentally and spiritually, Dr. Arnold's career marks an epoch. From Rugby, Thomas Hughes entered as an undergraduate at Oriel College, Oxford. In 1841, he graduted with high honors and the degree of Bachelor of Arts. His Alma Mater has since conferred on him that of Master. His residence at the University was coincident with the more advanced stages of the Tractarian movement, under the leadership of the now venerable Dr. Pusey. Mr. Hughes belonged by right of temperament and early training to the liberal wing. He has remained an earnest churchman, differing in this respect from the majority of those with whom he has been closely associated in politics and in social agitations. He entered Lincoln's Inn in 1845, and was admitted to the Bar in 1848. He was not known publicly at the time, though his pen had already become active, training the fine literary talent which has since been utilized in his valuable and manly books. "Tom Brown's School-days" was published in 1856; its companion volume, "Scouring the White Horse," in 1858; a third volume, "Tom Brown at Oxford," appeared some years after; and an admirable history of "Alfred the Great," in 1870. He is at present engaged on a work relating to the English Church. Mr. Hughes prefaces his history of "Alfred the Great" by an essay which is notable for the incisive statement it gives of his own views of "Kingship," "Democracy," and other questions which are the problems of present English politics. His definition of "What does Democracy mean" to the English, "in these years," is—"Simply an equal chance for all; a fair field for the best men, let them start where they will, to get to the front; a clearance out of sham governors, and of unjust privilege, in every department of human affairs. It cannot be too often repeated that they who suppose the bulk of our people want less government or fear the man who can rule and dare not lie, know little of them. * * * They *will* go for compulsory education, the organization of labor (including therein the sharp extinction of able-bodied pauperism), the utilization of public lands, and other reforms of an equally decided character. That for these purposes they desire more government, not less; will support with enthusiasm measures, the very thought of which takes away the breath and loosens the knees of ordinary politicians: will rally with loyalty and trustfulness to men who will undertake these things with courage and singleness of purpose." Mr. Hughes proceeds to argue that true kingship must possess the function of "sympathy with the masses." He is Carlyleian in his view, *plus* a deep and earnest faith in the people. He argues that—"This is no age in which shams or untruths, whether old or new, are likely to have a quiet time or a long life of it. In all departments of human affairs, religious, political, social—we are travelling fast * * * and under the hand and guidance, be sure, of Him who made the world, and is willing and able to take care of it. * * Individualism no doubt, has its noble side, and 'every man for himself,' is a law which works wonders; but we cannot shut our eyes to the fact that under their action English life has become more and more disjointed, threatening in some directions altogether to fall to pieces." In the closing chapter Mr. Hughes looks the political future of England full in the face and says:—" All the signs of our time tell us that the day of the earthly kings has gone by, and the advent of the power of the great body of the people, those who live by labor, is at hand. Already a considerable percentage of them are as intelligent as the classes above them, and as capable of conducting affairs, and administrating large interests successfully. * * In another generation that number will have increased tenfold, and the sovereignty of the country will virtually pass into their hands. * * * It is vain to blink the fact that democracy is upon us, that 'new order of society which is to be founded by labor for labor,' and the only thing for wise men to do is to look it in the face, and see how the short intervening years may be used to the best advantage." He adds that the task has been begun and the soundest and best of English thinkers are "engaged upon the great and inevitable change, whether they dread or exult in the prospect. Thus far, too, they all agree that the great danger lies in that very readiness of the people to act in great masses, and to get rid of individual and personal responsibility, which is the characteristic of the organizations by which they have gained and secured their present positions." This is to be met, Mr. Hughes argues, by developing the sense which he has indicated as now lacking—that "of personal and individual responsibility."

Mr. Hughes does not accept the extreme views of the "supply and demand" school of political economists, especially as applied to the relations of employers and employed. His advocacy of co-operation has led him a long way from the teachings of the "competitive" theory—that which regards the human family as divided into three classes,—those who make and produce; those who buy and consume; and those who pocket the profits arising from the management of these operations. Mr. Hughes has a decided leaning in the opposite direction, his mental habit being tinged with socialism. He has spoken and written at length on these matters, though he has managed also to keep in the van of practical ameliorative efforts. Besides the works named, Mr. Hughes published, in 1873, a memoir of his brother, then deceased, of whom he writes with great tenderness. He has been for years an occasional correspondent of the New York *Tribune*, and some of his letters, written during the early Fenian excitement and the Alabama negotiations, as well as his very admirable descriptions of the great University boat races on the Thames, are among the best contributions that England has furnished for the American press. He was an active friend of the North during the civil war, but felt very keenly and resented rather sharply, the severe arraignment of Great Britain made by Mr. Sumner in the American Senate, during the session of 1866.

Mr. Hughes failed to secure a re-election to the present Parliament, after serving in three preceding ones. He was twice elected from Lambeth, one of the Metropolitan boroughs, and afterwards from that of Frome, a considerable market town,—with some small manufacturing interests, principally blankets and cloth,—situated in the loveliest part of Somersetshire. The little borough has always been of a radical tone in politics, probably in contrast with the Tory views of the county electors. Mr. Hughes was an active supporter of the Reform League movement, and entered Parliament as one of its leading friends. His defeat at Lambeth affords a striking illustration of the independence of his character. The borough is a densely populated division of the Metropolis, on the south side of the Thames. It begins at Westminster Bridge, and the first object that strikes the eye, turning from the Parliament Houses, with their wide front of ornate gothic, to look across the river, is a venerable pile, standing amid its own grounds, and with the dinginess of centuries gathered on its walls. This is Lambeth Palace, the London residence of the English Primate, the Archbishop of Canterbury. The upper portion of the superb Thames Embankment runs in front of the Palace, and of the dingy collection of pottery works and wharves which stretch above it to Vauxhall Bridge. Lambeth proper comprises probably the largest division of small householders and stores to be found in the great city. There are some large railroad works, and shops, but it is in general an aggregation of suburbs. inhabited by the mechanic and poorer trading classes. " Public houses " abound. The retailers are in great force. Mr. Hughes, a doctrinaire on co-operation, which the storekeepers regard as their bane,—a vigorous reformer in the matter of false weights and measures, the interference with which was a pet grievance,—zealous also as to adulteration of food, etc., and a warm supporter of early closing and permissive liquor bills,—was not at all likely to maintain his popularity, after the success of the reform bill had worn the edge off the enfranchised householders' suffrage. Another count against him was his absolute refusal to defray anything but the necessary election expenses. Hence it was not surprising that he had to abandon his second candidacy, retiring before a wealthy city man, to Frome, as has been before stated.

His return to the House of Commons is sincerely desired by all the advanced liberals, and as soon as an opening occurs it is probable that he will allow his name to be again presented. His capacity for work must be very great, as he not only conducts a large and profitable chancery practice, but is a laborious and faithful worker on the central co-operative board, and a frequent speaker at co-operative and other meetings ; while as a writer his pen is always actively engaged. He is now President of the College already mentioned, and is one of Mr. Plimsoll's strongest supporters, being Vice President of the "Plimsoll and Seaman's defence fund," which was raised to defray the expenses arising from the agitation over unseaworthy ships. Mr. Hughes is a busy member of the Social Science Association. He is also President of the Sydenham Crystal Palace Company, and is actively engaged as stockholder and director of many co-operative enterprises—the scope of which is now notably enlarging, until banks, coal mines, cotton mills, founderies, machine shops and land-owning are embraced by their energies. He is also Colonel of the 19th Regiment Middlesex Rifle Volunteers, one of the best drilled organizations of its class in the Metropolitan County. In addition to these labors, professional, personal and public, he is frequently called upon to act as arbitrator or umpire in disputes between employer and employed. In this capacity he is much respected. Since he has become actively engaged in political life, Mr. Hughes has twice served as a member of Royal Commissions—one being appointed to enquire into the Sheffield outrages, and the character and practices of Trades Unions in general, while the other, a later body, is known as the "Labor Laws Commission." Their duty was to inquire into the working of the "Master and Servants act (1867); the Criminal law amendment act (1871), and finally, the law of conspiracy." The commission consisted, besides Mr. Hughes, of Lord Chief Justice Cockburn, known to Americans from his connection with the Geneva Arbitration; Mr. Russell Gurney, Recorder of London (also one of the Mixed Commission which sat in Washington for over a year, to adjudicate British claims growing out of our civil war), Mr. Justice Smith, Lord Romilly, Messrs. Bouverie, Roebuck, Goldney, and Macdonald. The legislation into which it inquired has recently been swept away almost entirely by an act passed during the session of 1875, which nearly abolishes the distinction between offences committed by workmen as such and those perpetrated by other parties.

Mr. Hughes voted for the dis-establishment of the Irish Church, and with the Gladstone ministry in 1870 and 1872 in support of the Elementary Education acts. He is a member of the Manchester Education Union, which differs from the Birmingham League in consenting to denominational or "voluntary" schools. During his earlier Parliamentary life he presented a bill embodying a sweeping proposition in relation to the Irish Land question. This measure and the speech he made thereon were sharply criticised by the London Times and the Pall Mall Gazette. Mr. Hughes in a brief reply illustrated the tendency of his thoughts on this subject, when he wrote: "You cannot argue as to the land as though it were any kind of personal property. Absolute ownership may exist in all kinds of personal property." How absolute this may be, he illustrated by supposing that a man may throw unchallenged a bag containing one thousand guineas into the Thames. "But," he continues "I and all the owners of land * * * have not made it, and cannot destroy it; could neither have added to it nor lessened it * * *. All that has been done since has been to put value upon it, and it is this value we speak of as 'real property,'—'landed property.'" Opinions such as these make him a consistent opponent of the Commons Enclosure Acts, by which the "common," or it might be said the "public," land, has for a number of years past been gradually encroached upon, fenced in, and made private property. This system of monopolization has been going on very steadily and creates great discontent. The English common lands "are the remaining proofs of the old British and Saxon *commune* or common ownership. The feudal system which the Norman Conquest perfected, if not introduced, placed the land in the hands of a comparatively few families. The commons were however numerous up to the close of the last century. The people—laborers and freeholders, lords of the manor and the farmers, with the parish clergymen, all possess certain rights, such as that of pasturing cows, etc., on these commons.

The laborer's rights are often a sham and are now fast becoming a fiction. The enclosure acts, generally divided the land among the abutting freeholders, usually giving it, however, to but one landowner, possessing manorial rights. This question is a prominent one in the Agricultural Laborers' Agitation. Mr. Hughes's legal skill, as well as parliamentary efforts, have both been used in opposition to the land greed referred to. He expressed his sympathy with the Laborers' Agitation early in its progress.

But the chief work of Mr. Hughes' public and personal career, is the service he has rendered, and the labor and ability he has given to the Co-operative movement. It may fairly be claimed for him, that to his wise counsel and assistance—he himself would disclaim the word leadership in such connection—is due a very large share of its national character,—it might even be said, international recognition; while his advocacy and exposition have been marked with a thoroughly comprehensive spirit. His mind has linked the savings of the poor man's pence for the poor man's own benefit, with the loftiest ideals of social regeneration, through its large recognition of the idea of spiritual brotherhood, as well as practical sagacity, which dwells in the philosophy and practice of genuine co-operation or association. Yet he has been pre-eminently practical in his connection with the whole of this remarkable effort. He, with Mr. Ludlow, has been the legal advisor of the several societies, and the one or the other has drafted nearly all the acts which have been passed to secure their funds, and encourage their formation. Until within a brief period, these societies could own no land, could not own or mine coal lands, nor could they do a banking business. For several years they were compelled to pay income tax, a manifestly unjust ruling, as their profits were not incomes in the sense that is understood by those who are blessed with such conveniences. Their assets or profits are, in fact, trust funds, to be distributed among shareholders and customers. At present these societies return the amounts paid to their several members, so as to enable the Income Tax Commissioners to ascertain whether any of them possess more than £100 per annum from this and other resources. Under the law no individual can own shares in any one of the registered co-operative societies to a larger amount than £ 200. By a parliamentary Return, obtained on motion of Mr. Cowen, the member for Newcastle, there were in England and Wales, at the close of 1874, "790 societies, and the amount insured was £1,657,781. There were 340,930 members. The share capital at the end of 1873 was £13,334,104 and the loan capital £431,808. The trade accounts show that the cash paid for goods in the year was £12,344,780; the cash received for goods, £13,651,127; and the average stock-in-trade during the period, £1,439,137. The total expenses, in the year were £541,284, while the interest on share, loan, and other capital was £152,596. With respect to liabilities and assets, it appears that in England and Wales, the liabilities were £4,681,512; the reserve fund £83,149; and the entire assets, £4,430, 334; the value of buildings, fixtures and land, £1,361, 197; capital invested with other industrial and provident societies, £337,811; and £443,724 invested with companies incorporated under the Companies' Act. The net profits in the year were as follows :— Disposable net profits realized from all sources during the year, £958,721 ; dividends declared due to members, £861,964 ; dividends allowed to non-members, £18,555 ; and the amount allowed in the year for educational purposes, £6,864." Besides the co-operative stores, there are a large number of joint-stock operative factories and workshops, cotton mills, and foundries. In Oldham alone there are about thirty cotton mills owned by the workmen themselves, with a capital of about £1,400,000, which will represent a million and a half of spindles, or nearly one-fifth as many as are in operation in the United States. Other works are being established in connection with this remarkable growth of the idea of uniting Labor and Capital in the same hands. Mr. Hughes has been not only a faithful friend, but a bold and independent critic of his favorite cause and its operations. Addressing the Fourth Annual Co-operative Congress, held at Bolton, 1872, of which he was President, he referred to the need of some one's being paid to devote his whole time to the business of the Central Board, and protested against the narrow economy displayed in refusing to employ a secretary ; and, alluding to the hearty devotion of some of the friends of the movement, used the following language:

"'Why try to hold the movement together at all ? Why not let it slide and find its own level ?' Well, gentlemen, I have often been asked that question, and I have more frequently asked it of myself. And I will own that I have sometimes had great doubts as to the answer. Some of us have spent time which would amount to many years of our lives if added up, and not inconsiderable sums of money, in preaching and fostering this Co-operative movement. Amongst your northern associations, several old friends of mine and yours have killed themselves, without any earthly reward, at this work. Now, one can understand well enough why men should do this for a faith, if in our good old English they have got any kind of Gospel or good news to tell their fellows. But we are told that the Co-operative movement is nothing whatever but a method of doing ordinary business which will, if successful, distribute the products of industry of all kinds more equally, and amongst a far larger number of people than they reach under the old competitive system—that it is only another form of buying in the cheapest and selling in the dearest markets—resting absolutely on those two old pillars of the Temple of Mammon, and the less said about morality in connection with it the better. I have sometimes been inclined to think, while watching the development of our societies, that these critics were, perhaps, right after all, and that I and others had made fools of ourselves, and should have been certainly richer, and probably wiser, men, if we had just let the whole thing alone, and been content with getting our groceries and provisions, if we cared to do so, at wholesale prices. But such cold fits have never lasted long. It is impossible for any man with eyes in his head and a heart in his breast, not to have seen, even in the darkest times, what an educational power of the highest kind lies under this Co-operative movement for the great masses of our people. It has already done more, I venture to say, than any other religious or social movement of our day. Not even the most blind of our opponents can deny that it has made hundreds of thousands of our people more prudent and temperate, has developed in them great capacities for transacting their own business, and has made them conscious in some dim way of that highest mystery of our human life, which can only be adequately described in words with which I hope all of us are familiar, that we are members one of another, so that if one member suffers, all suffer, and if one member rejoices, all rejoice." *

The scope and character of the Co-operative movement, as it has been advocated by Mr. Hughes especially,

---

* Report of the Fourth Annual Co-operative Congress, edited by G. T. Holyoake, Manchester.

can hardly be more admirably put than in the closing words of the same address :—

"The agitators for violent political changes, for republicanism, the re-distribution of property, the nationalization of land, can scarcely conceal their contempt and aversion for bodies which ignore party politics, and are peacefully acquiring their fair share of property and land by the exercise of the silent virtues of temperance, forethought, just dealing, and fellowship in work. Well, we must be content to suffer their contempt, for with their methods and aims we have nothing in common. Extreme free-traders say that we are bringing back the evils of protection, and call us 'Socialists.' If they mean that we accuse unlimited competition of having been the cause of much of the fraud, adulteration, and rascality, which has so deeply tainted trade and commerce, we admit the fact. That is our belief; but we ask no protection against these evils from any quarter, and have already proved that we can protect ourselves. In the same way we cannot repudiate the name of 'Socialist,' in so far that it implies a belief that human society is intended to be organized, and will not be in its true condition until it is organized from the top to the bottom; but we have never looked to the state to do this for us, we have only asked the state to stand aside and give us breathing room and elbow room to do it for ourselves. And the work is going on under our eyes, in many directions, and by many agencies outside our own movement. For all these we should be thankful, and prompt to recognize and help them forward whenever we have the chance. Meantime, and especially at these Congresses, our own work must claim our special attention. But, while I trust that we shall never lose sight of the severely practical method by which we have reached our present position, I must always remind you that 'he who aims the sky shoots higher far than they who mean a tree.' And so, while in the next three days we shall be rightly engaged in the consolidation of our organization in detail, in perfecting the rules and the business arrangements of existing societies, I hope we may find time for some forecast of greater things which are behind. Our foremost thinkers have made us already familiar with the ideas of a co-operative banking system. Co-operative farms, co-operative manufacturing villages, all of which must be thought out and worked out before we have made our England (as we mean to make her) the best place for working men to live in that the sun ever shone on.

"Again, with respect to international projects, we cannot and do not wish to deny that we do entertain them. We look forward to the time when *solidarity* between the people of different nations and countries will become a fact, and when wars will be as obsolete between nations as duelling has become between men in our own country. But we are not going to preach universal brotherhood with a rifle in one hand and a torch in the other, and do not believe it will be brought any nearer by violent changes in forms of government."

Of the same general character is the position assumed by Thomas Hughes with regard to the remarkable developement of the Trades' Union movement. In 1860 he acted as Secretary of a committee charged with the preparation of a report on that subject for the British Social Science Association, a report which was presented at the Glasgow Congress. The result of the committee's labors was printed in a large and valuable volume. In the debate on its reception at Glasgow, Mr. Hughes said in commenting on the different views expressed by the employing and employed classes, that as to the latter:—

"The foundation of that difference was, that they treated the labor of their men, which was in fact the lives of their men, on the same principles as those on which they treated a dead commodity. They most rigorously applied to it the same law of supply and demand as they applied to any other commodity, thereby putting the living man and inanimate things on the same footing. Well, that might be a capital rule of thumb. They might lay down a law and act up to it; but the rule would not work. What had brought on all the discussion as to the antagonism of classes? Simply the attempt to carry that rule rigorously out. He believed that had raised those disputes, and would continue to the end of time to raise them. They must look from a different point of view. They must treat the living man according to different rules from those which they applied to the dead material.

"Here was a committee of thirty gentlemen, amongst whom were several influential employers. Two-thirds of these gentlemen started in the belief that as a rule trades' unions were in the hands of mere demagogues, not working men. But, he believed, they were now unanimous in the conclusion that this was not so. As was stated in the Report, they believed that the leaders of trade societies were generally men who represented the feeling of their class, and also able and proficient workmen, who really lived by their trade, and who had little to do with agitations. They (the committee) were at first almost unanimous in their belief that trades' unions fostered bad blood and ill-feeling between masters and men; but from the histories of all the strikes he had gone into, he was of opinion that trades' unions tended to stop strikes, and not to foster them."

He urged arbitrative tribunals as one of the better modes of settlement. In reviewing the debate, Mr. Hughes again urged that, so far as "supply and demand" were concerned, other and higher laws had to be considered. He had been defied "to distinguish between labor and other articles. He need not distinguish them, they would distinguish themselves; he said the living labor would distinguish itself by either helping or hindering its employer, and cotton goods could not help and could not hinder him. The importance of friendly feelings between masters and men had been dwelt on. Could there be friendly feeling between a master and a bale of goods? The attempt to apply the law of supply and demand to human labor, as rigorously as to cotton, coal and mere commodities, had brought on in France the French revolution; in this country Luddite riots, Chartists and rick burning; and slavery in America."

And it must be said for Mr. Hughes' view, that it is now,

scarce fifteen years later, coming to be generally accepted in Great Britain. Strangely enough, it would seem, the old fast and rigid rule is being pressed more and more in republican America, where it would appear that Co-operative politics should more readily educate the interested classes into the principles of Co-operative social economy.

Mr. Hughes however thinks there is hope even for us. In a recent article on the "Working Class of Europe," * he quotes from the poem of "John o' the Smithy" these two stanzas "—

> "But a clear keen voice comes over the sea;
> It is piercing the gloom of the waning night;
> Time was, time is, and time shall be
> When John o' the Smithy shall come by his right.
>
> "And they who have forged the pitiless round
> Which has pressed him hard in body and soul;
> Shall perish from earth when the grist is ground
> And the mighty miller shall claim his toll!"

"The author we believe," adds Mr. Hughes, "was an American, though the scene is supposed to be laid in the old world. But if so, and if he intended the 'clear keen voice' which was to declare deliverance and a bright day to the working people was to come from the west; if he meant by 'over the sea' over the Atlantic—he blundered as a seer. The principle of association, which is proving to be the Ithuriel's spear for the poor of Europe, has been of home growth. In several of its developments that principle is not likely for many generations, if ever, to find so congenial a soil in America. Trades' Unionism can never be formidable in a country where the boundary

---

* *International Review*, March, 1874.

lines of classes are so indistinct, and which has an inexhaustible supply of rich land for the discontented to fall back upon, though we quite admit, in view of the farmers' granges in Illinois and Wisconsin, and miners' combinations in Pennsylvania and elsewhere, that the design to fix the price at which one's own labor shall be sold is just as common in the Great West as in Europe."

Mr. Hughes reviews, in the article referred to, four movements: the report of the British Co-operative congress, that of the German Advance Credit Societies, the Artizan Laborers and General Dwellings Company, and the Report of the Working Men's Clubs and Institute Union. These he regards as part of one movement;—1. Unions of consumers or workers to carry on production and distribution; 2. Union of workers to obtain capital and utilize credit to their own advantage; 3. Social Union to obtain for the artizan the social advantage which club life offers the wealthier class; 4. Union to obtain healthier and improved dwellings and become their own landlords.

In concluding his review of these efforts and their effects, Mr. Hughes declares that they are ostracising the "evil spirits of irreligion and communism" and that in England "the jealousy of capital, which still exists, has no dangerous side to it," and in concluding he asserts that the Co-operative movement is the most beneficial ordering of industrial efforts for the universal good which it is at present possible to devise."

Thomas Hughes is a man of well knit frame, tall in stature, fond of athletic sports, and a good example of the 'Muscular Christian." He is Anglo-Saxon to the core. His complexion is fair, hair deep auburn, eyes blue, his head is large, high and well balanced. As a speaker he is ready and more fluent than is common with English orators, though he has a little of the hesitancy of manner peculiar to them. There is a vein of ready wit in his efforts and he is an admirable presiding officer, though there is but little magnetism in his manner.

In fact, while he never offends by patronizing ways—that the essential manliness of his character forbids,—he does not attract, except intellectually, those with whom so much of his lifework has been performed. He is a college man, and in this country would gravitate naturally to Cambridge and its social and mental influences. There is none of the comradeship of the workshop—the fraternity of common things and people,—about him. But he is a man of high purposes, manliness and vigor: a thinker, writer and worker of rare qualities, the sum of whose life when added up will prove to have been the product of sincere and wholesome effort to leave the world better than he found it. Mr. Hughes' home life is stated by his friends to be charming, and he has much personal popularity in his own social circle.

VIII.

ANTHONY JOHN MUNDELLA.

A STRANGER standing in the handsome lobby or vestibule of the House of Commons, to watch the coming and going of the ever-changing crowd, will be very likely to notice a gentleman of dark complexion, full beard, and strongly marked features, above the middle height, slightly bent at the shoulders, and with an un-English aspect in his face and appearance, who moves briskly through the throng, with a business air, and is often accosted by persons whom your chaperon, if he is well informed on the *habitués* of the place, will name to you as the prominent labor agitators, secretaries of various political associations, parliamentary agents in a large or small way, but generally identified with some reform or educational movement and effort. The gentleman referred to has the look of a keen, observant, self-possessed man who does not under-estimate his own position or capacity. He is, in the better sense, a self made man, conscious of his title to respect, giving his best to the public service for what the age has rendered unto him. If he be, as is satirically suggested by some of the press critics, something of an egotist, he at least redeems the fault by honest and wise efforts for his country and people. One can readily see that Anthony J. Mundella, junior member for Sheffield, is a man of affairs, strong in the general esteem as well as in his own, and with fair prospects of continued recognition before him.

The un-English look of his face is accounted for by the fact that he is, on his father's side, of Italian origin. Antonio Mundella was a native of Como, Italy, of good family and fair culture, who became a political refugee in 1820, in connection with a revolutionary conspiracy against the Austrians. He had been educated for the Roman priesthood, but his political bias led him away from that position. He settled in Leicester, where he undertook to teach pupils, and soon after married Rebecca, daughter of T. Allsop, Esq., of that city. Anthony, their son, was born March 28th, 1825, and is therefore in his fifty-first year. His mother, a woman of great strength of character, intelligence and ability, possessed a small property and exhibited a remarkable degree of skill and taste in embroidering lace. She was her son's teacher for several years, but when he was about ten years of age she became nearly blind from disease brought on by over application at fine lace work. The father's earnings are spoken of as small and precarious.

Anthony Mundella was first sent to a small private school, and with his mother's aid, made great progress. At ten years of age, however, he was obliged to aid in maintaining himself, and worked for nearly two years in a printing office. He was fortunate enough, on becoming apprenticed to the hosiery business, to secure a generous employer. At eighteen years he was master of his time, which had been well employed, both in business and at the Mechanics' Institute of his native town. Before he had attained his twentieth year, he married Mary, daughter of W. Smith, Esq., a manufacturer at Nottingham.

Mr. Mundella's politics are the outgrowth of temperament and experience, their naturally radical character being tempered by the wider observation and larger stakes of later life. The "stockingers" of the Midland counties were, in his youthful days, a class without much hope, and endured much of the misery that comes from poverty. The apprentice boy was an adept at writing political ballads. At fifteen he heard his own compositions sung on the streets or at public meetings. It was in the preliminary days of the chartist agitation, and on one occasion the earnest youth, then with slightly improved personal fortunes, and surrounded by influences somewhat remote from such radical opinions, identified himself in a ringing speech, with that movement. The charter, as it was called, demanded the following reforms:

"Our Union seeks the enactment of UNIVERSAL SUFFRAGE—the admission to the franchise of every man of twenty-one years of age, of sound mind and unconvicted of crime; EQUAL REPRESENTATION, —the division of the United Kingdom into equal electoral districts; THE ABOLITION OF THE PROPERTY QUALIFICATION now required of Members of Parliament, and of all qualifications except the choice of the electors; VOTE BY BALLOT—to prevent Bribery and intimidation; ANNUAL PARLIAMENTS—to insure the responsibility of the members to their constituents; AND THE PAYMENT OF MEMBERS—

rendered necessary by the abolition of the present property qualifications."*

Thomas Cooper, author of the " Purgatory of Suicides," written while he was confined for sedition in Leicester jail, writes of young Mundella's *début* as a political speaker, that he " had been appealing strongly one evening to the patriotic feelings of young Englishmen, mentioning the names of Hampden, Sydney, and Marvell, and eulogizing the grand spirit of disinterestedness and self-sacrifice which characterized so many of our brave forerunners, when a handsome young man sprang upon our little platform and declared himself on the people's side, and desired to be enrolled as a Chartist. He did not belong to the poorest ranks, and it was the consciousness that he was acting in the spirit of self-sacrifice, as well as his fervid eloquence, that caused a thrilling cheer from the ranks of the working men. He could not have been more than fifteen at that time; he passed away from us too soon, and I have never seen him but once all these years. But the men of Sheffield have signalized their confidence in his patriotism by returning him to the House of Commons; and all England knows if there be a man of energy as well as uprightness in that house, it is Anthony John Mundella."†

Mr. Mundella, at the expiration of his apprenticeship, was engaged to assist in the management of a factory, and at twenty-three he removed to Nottingham,—then as now, the centre of the English hosiery manufacture,—where he

---

* From an address of the Charter Union, issued April 17, 1848.
† *Autobiography* of Thomas Cooper, London, 1872.

became junior partner in a large firm. This was in 1848, in the midst of great political excitement. He soon became favorably known in local affairs as well as business circles, and was chosen Sheriff of Nottingham, in 1854, being only twenty-nine years of age. Since then, and before entering Parliament, he was elected to the Town Council, Presiding Alderman, Justice of the Peace, and President of the Chamber of Commerce. He took an early and active part in the Volunteer Rifle movement, becoming captain of a company.

But that part of his active life by which he has become most widely and favorably known—that of organizing the first English Council of Arbitration and Conciliation—began in 1859; when, wearied with the chronic troubles and losses growing out of "strikes" and "lockouts," and deeply impressed by his own early experiences, that neither blame or obstinacy were to be found all on one side—that of the working mass,—Mr. Mundella determined to bring about a better condition of affairs. After laboring for eleven weeks with his associate manufacturers, and in the Chamber of Commerce, he commenced his important experiment. The result thereof he has himself given in public speeches, lectures, and in evidence before Royal Commissioners appointed to inquire into its workings, and the workings of labor organizations generally.

The service rendered by Mr. Mundella in this movement can hardly be appreciated by those,—and they constitute a very large majority of American readers,—who have never investigated the conditions under which labor disputes arise. Heretofore our elbow-room has been so abundant that we have been insensible to the changed social conditions which have gradually concentrated wealth and business enterprises into fewer and fewer hands. Mr. Mundella, when visiting the United States in 1870-71, expressed to the writer his surprise at the general indifference, not to say ignorance, as to these changes, and the reasonable methods adopted elsewhere to bring them to peaceful settlement. During the past ten years, there have been four great strikes and lock-outs among the Pennsylvania coal miners, each of which involved from ten to thirty thousand working men with their families. In the town of Fall River, Mass., alone, there have been three such disasters within six years, involving from five to fifteen thousand operatives, with those dependent on them.

In Great Britain, within the six years preceding Mr. Mundella's organization of the first Board of Conciliation, there had been a number of great strikes—one at Preston, involving 18,000 cotton-mill operatives. During the year in which the Nottingham Council was inaugurated, the London building trades were on strike to the number of 10 to 12,000. Several times during the years immediately preceeding 1859, strikes and lock-outs occurred in the hosiery manufacture, taking out several thousand operatives each time. The loss of money in these struggles has not been, in the opinion of competent observers, so much to be deplored, as the increasing alienation of classes, and the fomenting of hostilities and antagonisms after each contest. In a country like England, small in area and thickly populated, with old institutions more or less hostile to the masses, this is a source of more dread than here; but the experiences England offers are a warning not to be lightly regarded by other nations.

Mr. George Potter, editor of the London *Beehive,* writing of "Conciliation and Arbitration," says—

"No man is better entitled to respectful, trustful, and even grateful attention on these matters than is Mr. Mundella, Member for Sheffield, Manufacturer at Nottingham, and in his origin a working man. He, as all even cursorily informed on the subject are aware, is founder of the Nottingham Board of Arbitration for the hosiery trade. After an experience of seven years (1861-8) from the date of its institution, it could be said of this Board that disputes between masters and men had been thereby prevented. No remedy, he contends, is complete and perfect that does not provide for prospective action. With respect to conciliation, there is no room for misunderstanding that. What, he asks, is meant by arbitration? It is an arrangement for open and friendly bargaining. Arbitration, however, seems to be something more positive and absolute than this. It, first of all, implies an arbiter, one who goes to a place in the character of a seer, a hearer, a witness. The arbiter arbitrates when, between two parties, he pronounces sentence according to equity and the best of his judgment. But he must be authorized to treat the matter in dispute according to his own will. The declaration of that will is an arbitration, and is final. Hence the meaning of authority beyond appeal attached to the epithet arbitrary.

"Mr. Mundella is one of those who have no faith in arbitration by persons who know nothing of, and have no interest in, the particular trade with which the question submitted may be connected. 'Arbitration,' he contends, 'to be effective in preventing disputes, must be the result of a system of open and friendly bargaining, in which masters and men meet together and talk over their common affairs openly and freely. Engineers cannot legislate for tailors, nor tailors for engineers ; each industry must legislate for itself.'" In this respect Mr. Mundella's view differs from that of others who contend for general boards. Mr. Potter then continues to paraphrase and quote Mr. Mundella's testimony, before a Royal Commission of Inquiry, as follows: "From 1820 to 1860," he observes, 'offences against person and property diminished ; but combinations were better organized, and strikes increased.' But let this sentence be connected with that in which he bears witness that 'the leaders of trades' unions have been among the most energetic advocates of Courts of Arbitration and Conciliation.' * * *

"In 1860, some at least of the Nottingham masters became weary of contention, and were persuaded that lockouts were not a remedy for strikes. After a century of feud, they desired an era of conciliation. First communicating with their brother masters, they brought them into the same mind. A resolution was passed, and a handbill issued. In fact the masters invited the men to meet them with a view to some arrangement. The invitation was accepted, and, at the end of three days' discussion, the existing strike came to a close by mutual concession. But this was not all. It was further agreed that, to prevent strikes for the future, 'strikes so disastrous to employers and employed,' a Board of Arbitration should be at once formed. It was to consist of six masters and six workmen. To it all questions relating to wages were to be referred, and its decisions were to be final and binding upon all parties. No sooner said than done; only, by mutual agreement, nine from each side were substituted for six. The nine workmen were chosen by the universal suffrage of their own trades' unions; the nine masters, at a general meeting of their own body.

"The Board met on the 3d of December, 1860. They had neither rules or precedents. The scheme was not universally approved by either masters or men. Some distrusted it even to suspicion; others assailed it with ridicule and sneers; a third portion (of the masters) doubted the practicability, if they did not disdain the thought, of masters meeting men on terms of perfect equality. However, the experimenters had with them a majority of the masters, and perhaps the bulk of the intelligent men. The result shall be stated as nearly as may be in the founders own words. 'Whenever men meet together with the honest desire to aim at the truth, and to do justice to each other, a good understanding is almost sure to follow.' The working-men delegates proposed a master as president; the masters, a workman as vice president—precedents which have been invariably followed. The rules originally made have never been altered. Brief and simple, they provide for arbitration on any questions relating to wages, and for conciliation in any dispute that may arise; and they intrust to a committee of four members (two, it is assumed, on each side) inquiry into cases referred to it, with instructions to settle the disputes, or, if unable, to remit them to the whole Board. This, therefore, is, after all, an example of 'settling their disputes among themselves.' Not only is no stranger called in, but no umpire, no chairman even, is appointed beyond the members of the Board, who, as has been seen, choose their own president and vice-president from among themselves. Experience, however, has convinced Mr. Mundella and the Board, that it impairs the influence of the individual and of the Board when, as has happened to himself, the president gives a casting vote. 'I consider it undesirable,' he observes, 'that one side should even appear to have the least preponderance over the other; and the employers intend, at the annual meeting, to propose the abolition of that privilege, and to substitute for it, after the example of Leicester, the vote of some gentleman acquainted, but not connected with the trade, in whose honor and justice both parties shall have full confidence.'

"Mr. Mundella does not pretend that there have been no difficulties, no mistakes; but he distinctly states that every question submitted for seven years has been successfully adjusted. 'We have had instances,' he admits, 'where employers have acted contrary to the decisions of the Board, and two where workmen have refused to accept those decisions; but the steady adherence of the majority of both parties to our decrees has always, sooner or later, brought the recalcitrants (the kickers, in fact) back to our side.' The Nottingham Board now governs the hosiery trade of Nottingham, Derbyshire, and North Leicestershire; and the number of persons employed cannot be less than sixty thousand. It is very rarely that the price originally proposed by either masters or workmen is the price ultimately agreed to. Some alterations or concessions are generally made on both sides; and the price once fixed, is considered mutually binding. But a month's notice must be given before any change of prices can be discussed. Most questions are settled in committee. The two seceders from the Board were re-admitted at their own request. For three years and a-half (the latter portion of the seven) the Board have arrived at all their decisions without voting. The Board is open to receive delegations from out-of-doors, a practice which has had a very wholesome effect; the general result being, that, by coming into friendly contact with each other, mutual confidence takes place of former mistrust, and the full force of facts and arguments on one side comes to be acknowledged on the other.

'In fact,' says Mr. Mundella, 'the less the workman is kept in the dark, the better it is both for himself and his master. On the other hand, the insight which the master obtains into the circumstances and views of the workman, tends greatly to develop his sympathies and to improve the workman's condition. And we feel that labor demands more consideration at our hands than iron, or coal, or cotton or any dead commodity.'

"Who, then, are the workmen that have seats at a Board which are producing all these beneficial effects? 'In almost all cases,' answers Mr. Mundella, 'they are prominent leaders of trades' unions;' and, he adds, 'I have found among them as much wisdom, tact, moderation, and self-denial as the best of us who are employers can show.' We now learn what, according to Nottingham experience, has been the effect of conciliation and arbitration in relation both to unionism and conflicts between capital and labor.

"Since the 27th of September, 1860," says Mr. Mundella, "there has not been a bill of any kind issued. Strikes are at an end also. Levies to sustain them are unknown; and one shilling a year from each member suffices to pay all expenses. This, not a farthing of which comes out of the pockets of their masters, is equivalent to a large advance of wages. I have inspected the balance-sheet of a trades' union of ten thousand three hundred men, and I found the expenditure for thirteen months to amount to less than a hundred pounds "*

But the member for Sheffield has not contented himself with the special work of organizing Conciliation in the business with which he is connected. He has for ten years past been active in promulgating the ideas which animate that movement, and in the advocacy of co-operation and industrial partnerships, as remedies for the present dependence of labor on wages alone, a dependence which he clearly sees to be the principal cause of the aggressive uneasiness that exists everywhere where organized industries are in operation. Mr. Mundella expresses clearly the opinion that the wages system is an inequitable method of distributing results or profits to labor. Nor has he hesitated to boldly sustain the right of organization and to defend trades' unions, in or out of Parliament, when he deemed them unjustly assailed. It was in consequence of these views, that he received the nomination and election for the Borough of Sheffield in 1868. At that time England was greatly agitated over the the shocking developments made in regard to "rattening," and other outrages, practiced by the cutlery and grinding trades, whose business is practically centered in Sheffield. Charles Reade's Novel of "Put Yourself in His Place," has presented these disclosures with pre-raphaelite fidelity, but whether designed or not, the effect of a perusal by those unfamiliar with the facts, is to make it appear that the English trades' unions,

---

* "Conciliation and Arbitration." *Contemporary Review*, November, 1870, page 551-3.

as such, were not only responsible for the Sheffield outrages, but that similar ones were the common practice among them. It was demonstrated conclusively that the offending trades were small bodies making their own policy, and refusing to act with the larger ones and federated movements that have marked later years. Mr. Mundella with other prominent friends of labor, denounced the view alluded to, and which Mr. Reade has presented with great art in his novel. A Royal Commission was in session in 1868, by request of the leading Trades' Agitators. Mr. Roebuck, who had for many years represented Sheffield, was a member of it. He gave great offence by his treatment of the Union leaders, some of whom were generally present at the sessions of the Commission. Among these was a witty Irishman named Connelly, a stone-mason by trade. This man speaking at a public meeting, called by himself and others to denounce the Sheffield atrocities, wittily and pungently asked "but what can ye expect of a Borough that sends Mr. Roebuck to Parliament?" "The Times" and other papers commented annoyingly on "Dog Tear 'em," as Mr. Roebuck has been long nicknamed from his satirical temper and speech, and that gentleman, when Mr. Connelly next appeared in the Commission-room, asked that he should not be allowed to attend the session. He carried his point and as a result lost his seat in the House of Commons. "Tom" Connelly and his friends canvassed Sheffield thoroughly, and Mr. Mundella went to the head of the poll. Mr. Roebuck, however, was returned at the next election, with Mr. Mundella as a colleague, Mr. Joseph Chamberlain of Birmingham, who was brought forward, having been returned lowest, though his vote was a large one. The author of "Men and Manners in Parliament" under the head of "The Independent Member," describes one of the most notable men in English politics in the following happy manner:

"Sitting in the corner seat of the front bench below the gangway on the opposition side is a man so old and feeble looking that the stranger wonders what he does here. His white hair falls about a beardless face which is comparatively fresh looking, though the eyes lack lustre and the mouth is drawn in. When he rises to speak he bends his short stature over a supporting stick, and as he walks down to the table to hand in the perpetual notice of motion or of question, he drags across the floor leaden feet in a painful way that sometimes suggests to well-meaning members the proffer of an arm, or of a service to accomplish the errand—advances which are curtly repelled, for this is Mr. Roebuck: the 'Dog Tear'em' of old, toothless now, and dim of sight, but still high in spirit, and ready to fight with, or to snarl and snap at, the unwary passer-by. * * * * * * *
Mr. Roebuck is a good lover and a good hater, chiefly the latter. A Parliamentary Ishmael, his hand has been against every one and every one's hand against him. Lord Palmerston, Mr. Disraeli, Mr. Bright, Mr. Cobden — in brief, every man of any prominence in the House of Commons during the past quarter of a century, has at one time or another felt the fangs of 'Tear'em' * * * In argument his style is clear and incisive, and he is a master of good, simple English, which he marshals in short, crisp sentences. His voice, now so low that it scarcely reaches the Speaker's chair, was once full and clear. As in his

best days he never attempted to raise to anything approaching florid eloquence, so he rarely varied in gesture from a regularly recurring darting of the index finger at the hon. member whom he chanced to be attacking—an angry, dictatorial gesture, which Mr. Disraeli, after smarting under it for an hour, once said reminded him of 'the tyrant of a twopenny theatre.' Now when Mr. Roebuck speaks his hands are quietly folded before him, and only at rare intervals does the right hand go forth with pointed finger to trace on the memories of the old men of the House recollections of fierce fights in which some partook who now live only as names in history."

His repeated re-elections for Sheffield are an evidence of the fact that a popular constituency may be led by a bitter tongue and a caustic wit quite as readily as they may be by energetic service and fidelity to principles and policies.

The witty writer from whom the foregoing is quoted, pays his respects to the other member for Sheffield, in commenting upon the latter as a parliamentary speaker :

"Mr. Mundella fortunately has not been discomposed by finding himself *vis-a-vis* a strong Minister. He is ready as ever to proffer advice in critical moments, and to bestow upon the House of Commons the value of the experience gained by him during his memorable fortnight's visit to Germany and Switzerland. No one can say—probably because no one dare venture to sit down before the problem—how we managed to get on at all before Mr. Mundella went that journey. But if since his return matters have not mended, it is not for lack of counsel on the part of the hon. member for Sheffield. Mr. Mundella never makes a short speech, and neither his manner nor his matter, renders a long one endurable. It is a curious contradiction of nature that a professed humanitarian who has made such great efforts in the direction of shortening the hours of labor in factories should himself unrelentingly talk to the hapless House of Commons for two hours and a half at a stretch. It does not seem fitting that, in this respect, there should continue to be one law for the factory owner and another for the hon. member for Sheffield."

"Regarded," says this writer, "from any point of view, the House of Commons has not its equal anywhere as a legislative assembly. Its composition is the most harmoniously diverse, its sense of honor is the highest, its perception of humor is the keenest, its business capacity is the largest, its collective wisdom approaches the nearest to perfection, its purity is the most stainless, its appreciation of native talent is the quickest and most generous, and its instinct is the truest of any of its compeers throughout the kingdoms of the earth. It is the one British Institution which no Briton need fear to vaunt, because foreigners are foremost in their praise of it and are united in their attempts at imitation. Next to being the Lord Mayor himself, to be a member of Parliament is, as Mr. Mundella can testify, the surest passport to distinction for mediocrity travelling on the Continent, and the simple letters "M.P." on the bearer's card, even though the bearer be Mr. Mitchell Henry, are an open sesame to all the choicest treasure-houses that lie between the Ural Mountains and the Bay of Biscay." *

---

* "Men and Manner in Parliament,' pp. 269, 270.

But this solemn "chaff," which is so characteristic a feature of English wit, must not blind us to the earnestness and comprehensiveness of Mr. Mundella's work,—especially marked in the direction of securing national education, as well as in removing all special legislation from the statute book which deals with labor offences in a spirit different from that with which other acts or offences are treated by English law. Mr. Mundella's firm employs several thousand Saxon operatives, and he is in the habit of making frequent visits to the continent. The reference made by the critic is to a special journey, taken,—as was the one in company with Mr. T. Hughes to the United States,—principally for the purpose of examining educational systems. His time was utilized to the greatest advantage, as those who met him in the United States can understand. At Washington he made a rapid survey of the Departments, and was especially interested in the Bureau of Education and its work. At the request of the Commissioner, Hon. John Eaton, he made some interesting statements, giving his views as to the value of educated labor over uneducated,—the Bureau being at that time engaged in making investigations relating thereto.[*]

His speech at the Cooper Institute, to a large meeting of workingmen, was heartily received. On these questions Mr. Mundella may be regarded as an authority and the lectures he has delivered on the subject of technical and general education are considered as valuable contributions to the discussion. He has taken an active part in the several debates on the Education Bills of 1870 and

---

[*] Circular of Information by the Bureau of Education, April, 1872.

1872, and the propositions since made for the repeal of the objectionable twenty-fifth, or rate-paying section. Mr. Mundella is an active member of the "National Education League," and serves on its Executive Committee. Favoring compulsory education, he was a member of a deputation from the League, which waited in 1870, on Mr. Gladstone. In urging their policy, he said that "without compulsion, nothing like a good education is secured. However much you may cover the land with schools; however ample the provision may be that you make for those schools, as in America, as in France indeed, and as in Holland, the results will be altogether inadequate to your efforts unless you make it the absolute duty of the parent that the child shall be in attendance, regularly and consecutively, for a certain number of years. My attention was first drawn to this by reason of the fact that I am an employer of labor abroad, that I have seen the working of this system in Switzerland and in Germany; and I have seen its contrast, too, in Holland and in France. I am conscious also," he adds, "of what is going on in America, and I am bound to say that although America has made the most ample provision of any country in the world for schools, yet American education, instead of progressing, is on the decline." He urged that the English ideal must be a high one; that there must be a comparison made with Germany and Switzerland, nations which have had a compulsory system for over thirty years, and in which he declared that he could not find an ignorant child, go where he might. He adds that—"It is not only that they are not ignorant, or that, like our own children, they have attained to the reading of a signboard, or the scrawling of a name,—that is not the education which they have enjoyed; but it is an education that is useful to them in its culture and in its assistance in acquiring knowledge in every relation of life."*

A biographical sketch says that—" Mr. Mundella's work in Parliament has been prominently in labor, education, and social questions. On entering Parliament he seconded the address. His speech on the second reading of the Education Bill was pronounced by Mr. Gladstone as pre-eminently the best in the debate.

"His knowledge of the education question has been acquired under favorable circumstances. Fifteen years ago a Nottingham house established a branch manufacturing business in Saxony. This soon after came to the hands of Mr. Mundella's firm, and he has in consequence mastered the German, Swiss, and American systems of education. In 1869 he, jointly with Mr. T. Hughes, introduced a Trades' Union Bill, which, if passed, would have put an end to the legislative strife on the question. He succeeded in obtaining temporary protection for trades' union funds till the following year. He combatted the objectionable clauses in the Criminal Law Amendment Act, and has worked earnestly for its repeal. He moved for and obtained the appointment of a Truck Commission. In 1871 he brought in the Brickyards' Bill, which he succeeded in incorporating with a Government Bill, enforcing the Workshops Act. In 1872 he carried the Arbitration (Master's and Workman's) Bill, obtained the appointment of a Factories Com-

---

* Pamphlet Report, by National Education League, Manchester, March 9th, 1870.

missioner in 1872, and introduced the Factories Nine Hours' Bill, in 1871.

"Mr. Mundella has a great capacity for work, and can and does perform the labors of two or three ordinary M.P's. His services on behalf of education before he entered Parliament deserve special mention; and the method of arbitration which the working classes of England have already assented to, and to-day are willing to substitute for the expedient of strikes and lock-outs, owes its origin and success to him. His career in Parliament has been most successful. Being returned for Sheffield in 1868, he at once came to the front in the cause of labor and won for himself a position amongst workingmen which will not soon be forgotten. The Session of 1874 saw Mr. Mundella's efforts in Parliament on behalf of the "Factory Nine Hours' Bill" crowned with success. On May 6, in a full House, he moved the second reading of his Bill; after which the Home Secretary announced the intention of the Government to deal with the matter, and pass a Bill embodying Mr. Mundella's wishes; to this he consented, and ultimately a Bill was passed, which will come into operation on the 1st of January, 1875, limiting the hours of work in factories to fifty-six a week, and preventing any child's being employed under ten years of age." *

This is the measure opposed so energetically by Prof. Fawcett. The member for Sheffield, in reply to the charge that the reduction was not desired by those whom it would affect, declared that 74 per cent. of all the mill

---

* *Beehive* " Portrait Gallery," No. 11, London, 1874.

operatives were women and children, and not ten per cent, were even negative in their support of the bill.

Mr. Mundella has heartily supported Mr. Plimsoll, in his efforts for legislation to secure protection to seamen; sustained Mr. Trevelyan's bill to extend the country franchise to the farm laborers; and voted with Sir Charles Dilke in favor of redistribution of seats. On the vote to pay the Prince of Wales's India expenses, he was with the majority, and rather strongly protested against Mr. Macdonald's assuming to be a special representative of the working class. His defence of the grant is very characteristic of the feeling with which the expenses of the crown are generally regarded by English Liberals. The member for Sheffield said. "As long as we had a Monarchy he should be ashamed to have a cotton velvet or tinfoil sort of Monarchy; he did not believe in a cheap, shabby, Brummagem Monarchy; and he always would give his vote loyally, and in consistency with those opinions which he believed to be the opinions of his constituents."

IX.

ALEXANDER MACDONALD.

THE "Working-man's Member" is no longer a myth or a terror in English politics. As Mr. Fawcett most admirably stated, in alluding to a sneer from the conservative benches over Dr. Kenealy's election to the House of Commons, the quickest way to make a demagogue innocuous or to prove that a class fear is without foundation, is to bring either into Parliament. The appearance in "the House" of the representative "working man" has made no excitement, but has practically added to the legislative capacity of that body. The next election will, without doubt, see several other labor leaders chosen, and in the mean while the two gentlemen who have secured seats, Alexander Macdonald and Thomas Burt, both men who have creditably followed the occupation of mining coal, are not only winning recognition for those who are to come on the same basis, but respect and place for themselves in that legislative assembly which is regarded as one of the most difficult places in which to secure either.

Alexander Macdonald was born at Dalmacoulter, in the parish of New Monkland, near the town of Airdrie, ten miles east of Glasgow. He is now about fifty years of age, the eldest of seven brothers, four of whom are citizens of the United States. One of them acquired some distinction as an officer of Union volunteers during the war of the Rebellion. Mr. Macdonald's family is a branch from that powerful clan of that name, which was all but exterminated at Culloden Moor, fighting in behalf of the Jacobite cause. His grandfather, then a lad, fled to the lowlands, where for a time he was quite fortunate. The elder Macdonald was bound apprentice to the sea, and took an active part in the French war, being engaged at the capturing of several of the West India Islands; and later, was taken prisoner during the war of 1812, by an American privateer. After his release and return to Scotland, he married and pursued the occupation of a miner. His eldest son, now Member of Parliament for Stafford, began his working life in the same laborious occupation at the age of eight years. The condition of the mining population in Scotland at the time has been most vigorously portrayed by Mr. Macdonald himself, in various writings and speeches. One of the latter was delivered at the last Agricultural Laborers Congress, held at Birmingham during the summer of 1875, and the miners' representative thus described his early life, its associations, disabilities, and the struggle to remove them from the class with which he is identified.

"The occupation to which I belong and from which I sprang—for I entered the mine when I was only eight years of age—was perhaps one of the lowest in condition at the time. It was at the close of the 18th century that the miner in Scotland obtained his freedom, for you will observe that previous to that time he was bought and sold with the soil. It is stated in the old chronicles of our country that blood-hounds were kept to trace miners who had run away, and to bring them back again. It was ruled by statute law that miners were obliged to work nearly all days in a year, and if they did not work, or if they committed any offence, they were to be whipped on their bodies for the glory of God—that I cannot understand—and for the good of their masters. In 1775 a law was passed to try and remove that state of things, but the law was ineffectual, for the strong grasp of the land-owner and the mine-owner (but chiefly then the land-owners, because they held the minerals) was too powerful, and it was only in 1799 that an effective law was passed to give the working miner of Scotland freedom." * * * When he began to labor, Mr. Macdonald said, "children worked in the mines, male and female, father and mothers, all together. Before the year 1825, our men had to resort to secret combinations. * * * * How were these carried on? No man was entrusted with a knowledge of their documents, and, as my information goes, they were burned secretly. The men then were working unlimited hours, and a child might have been introduced to the mine at the age of one, if the employer thought he could be of use, and the recklessness of the parent would permit. * * * How were the children expelled from the mines? How was it that a law was passed saying that no child must enter the mine before it was 12 years of age? Was it through the operation of the law of supply and demand?

* * * * Was it the mine-owners? Was it the manufacturers? No, the men determined themselves that the degrading position of their daughters, their wives, and the future mothers, should not continue. They went time after time to the legislature. I may say that the wages were not paid for three months together. * * * Why? The employers fed them, they housed them, they had a paternal regard for them, which was so very strong that they supplied them with food in order that they might spend no money save in the truck-shops or 'tommy-shops.' I ask you who released these men from that position? * * * It was the men themselves that did it. They went to Parliament. * * * The men agitated. First the law of truck was struck at, and next we attacked the badly ventilated mines. Year after year we went to Parliament, and we worked, step by step, until now. I venture to say that our position, as a class, so far as our boys are concerned, is the first of any body of laborers in the civilized world."

The early years of the member for Stafford were filled with severe toil, and arduous efforts to obtain an education. His mother watched and worked for every opportunity to send him to school. He attended in the evenings for several years, during which the working day was fifteen hours long. The effect of these exertions decided the work of his life. He was a leader of his class before he was of age, taking in 1842, an active part in a great strike, and having some time before been prominent in the agitation by which Parliament, chiefly through the efforts of the Earl of Shaftesbury (then Lord Ashley) was induced to pass an act forbidding the employment of women in the mines. The same act forbade the working of boys under thirteen, and abolished the compulsory apprenticeship of pauper children to this employment. Mr. Macdonald was also prominent, at this time, in the first formidable agitation for eight hours as a legal day's work. At the close of 1842, he determined to fit himself for the University and then to enter and pursue one of the learned professions. Six years after, in 1848, he enrolled himself a student at the University of Glasgow, and pursued his studies during the session of that and the following year, working at mining during the summer, and thereby maintaining himself and helping his mother and brothers. He continued active in support of his fellow-miners' movements. In 1850, and for several years thereafter, Mr. Macdonald taught school, and so continued until a wide-spread agitation for the abolition of the truck system, and a batch of kindred abuses and oppressions, recalled him to class leadership, and ended, for the time being, in the passage of a better mining act. Two other acts, chiefly relating to the protection of life in the mines, were passed in 1860 and 1862, mainly through the persistent agitation of Mr. Macdonald. Before this, he had come to be regarded, not only as the foremost leader of the miners, but as a trustworthy authority on all matters relating to the working, ventilation, etc., of the mines and the protection of those who were employed in them.

To the exertions and forecast of "the miners' member," as Mr. Macdonald is termed, is largely due the organization, not only of the Miners' Union in Scotland, but of their National Union, of which he has been the President since its formation. A conference looking to that end was held at Ashton-under-Lyme, in 1857. In 1863 another conference was convened, and the National Union formed. At the present time this body is a federation of twenty-three distinct societies and represents a membership of 137,956 miners. Its funds were reported in 1874 to be £157,861. The objects are stated to be the following:—

Better legislation for the management of mines; to protect the miners' lives, promote their health and improve their condition generally; to obtain compensation where employers are liable for accidents; to assist branches and members when either is unjustly dealt with; to aid them against all lock outs; to encourage the raising of local funds for the aid of permanently disabled miners, and to give a weekly allowance to disabled or aged members unfit to work.

Conferences are held every six months, or twelve months. The Northumberland Society, of which Thomas Burt, member for Morpeth, is secretary, belong to the federation and numbers 18,000 members, with a fund of £22,500. That of Durham has 40,000. The West Yorkshire district has 12,000 members, and the others from 6000 down to 600. Not over one half the Miner's Unions are represented in the National Organization, but the probabilities of a complete federation are growing. One consequence of this formidable propaganda, is the creation of "Joint Committees" in the more important mine districts. These bodies are given certain legislative functions in regard to the local arrangement of mines, etc., and consist of six miners and six mining engineers. The voting power is equal, but it is seldom that their deliberations fail of satisfactory result."

Another feature of the movements of which Mr. Macdonald is a leader, is the quite general acceptance of the plan of arbitration. In the North of England coal districts there are regular boards, now fully established and working effectively, through which agency labor disputes are in general amicably arranged. The board or court usually consists of an equal number of workmen and employers, with some person selected by both to preside. So far has this plan been carried, that in common with the more important iron mining and working districts, power is given these boards by both parties to fix, at stated periods, the rates of wages, and to make other necessary regulations. Through these causes there may be found in the mining, iron-working, and manufacturing districts, among the working operatives, men whose knowledge of the markets, their ruling rates, etc., is in every way accurate and extensive. Men like Mr. Macdonald, Mr. Burt, Mr. Halliday, and others who are recognized as labor leaders, have been trained in a thoroughly practical school, and have become experts and specialists of a high order of merit.

The President of the National Miners' Union has always been a strenuous advocate of arbitration, as well as other means of education and conciliation which will help in bringing to an end the quarrels between Labor and Capital. In a speech made during 1875, he argued that—

"Employers and employed are engaged in a joint enterprise: that joint enterprise results in sending a certain commodity to market which the public buy, and they receive in return — both employers and workmen — a certain amount of money. That amount is to be divided between the owners of the collieries and the workmen; and I contend that when the division has to be readjusted, the workmen have a perfect right to know how the readjustment is to take place, and the employers have not a right to make this reduction in an arbitrary manner. If the workmen resent the reduction, then," said Mr. Macdonald, "the employers in the public interest are bound to submit the matter to arbitration. I don't want to destroy anything," he said; "I want to bring about that which will give peace and security; I want to effect that which will give working men and employers contentment in the future, enabling them to settle peacefully and fairly whatever disputes may arise, instead of by the old brutal method of strikes and lock-outs."

The following resolution was reported by the speaker and passed with others of a similar character :—

"This Conference strongly recommends the establishment of Boards of Arbitration and Conciliation, supported by sound organization, together with co-operative collieries, as the best means of arriving at the true interest of capital and labor, invested in the mines of the nation, as this Conference is of opinion that until this be accomplished, strikes and lock-outs will occur, and the rights of the workmen be entirely ignored by a large number of employers."

Mr. Macdonald, while closely attending to the public and parliamentary interests of his laboring clients, finds time to take active interest in the political reforms in progress. He early advocated the participation of the Trades' Unions, as such, in political demonstrations. Some of his strongest speeches have been made at their meetings. He was a candidate for the House in 1868, canvassing the Scotch borough of Kilmarnock. It is claimed that in order to prevent his election, employers quite generally began to discharge such of their workmen as supported him. In order to prevent the personal suffering consequent on this, Mr. Macdonald withdrew from the canvass. Since then he has twice visited the United States, travelling extensively therein.

At the Nottingham Trades' Union Congress in 1872, and at subsequent annual meetings of that body, he was elected chairman of its parliamentary committee. At the last general election he was elected to the House of Commons from the Borough of Stafford, standing at the head of the poll. In Parliament he at once found a prominent place, representing, as he practically does, so much larger a constituency than the one that elected him. At the last Trades' Congress, held in Liverpool, January 16, 1874, he was among the most prominent members.*

---

*It may be well to state the representative character of the British Trades' Union Congress. At the Liverpool sessions there were present 280 delegates, representing over 100 Unions, and representing a membership of nearly 700,000, several Unions and Trades' Councils, numbering from 20,000 to 140,000. Among those in attendance, besides Mr. Macdonald, M.P., were Mr. Burt and Mr. Plimsoll, M.P.'s. Mr. Henry Crompton, a well-known Positivist, Lloyd Jones, Joseph Arch, George Ogden, and others. The objects for discussion therein and agitation during the ensuing year, were stated to be,—The repeal of the several enactments which removed Trades' combinations and the matter of contract between a wages-laborer and an employer, out of the general law, and provided specially for the class affected. This has since been accomplished. Also, consideration by Parliament of what

As a member of the House of Commons, Mr. Macdonald, like his fellow-member, Mr. Burt, the member from Morpeth, formerly a working miner, has declared that he does not consider himself bound to represent working-class interests only. He has taken quite an active part in debates on education, taxation, church, and other matters, serving on the Trades' Inquiry Commission, besides being a hard worker on the Coal Trade and other Committees, and in attendance with frequent delegations on Ministers. The witty writer, who under the name of "The member for the Chiltern Hundreds," has described the House of Commons, does not appear to like the member for Stafford, and thus gently satirizes him over the compliment he pays to Mr. Burt: "Mr. Burt has, he himself proclaims, worked as a miner in Choppington Colliery. He looks like what he is, and speaks with the most remarkable accent ever heard within the walls of the House of Commons. But he bears himself modestly, shows a perfect command of the subject he discusses, and is short

---

limit should be placed upon the summary jurisdiction of magistrates, which deprives citizens of the right of trial by jury, and an inquiry by a royal commission as to the whole subject of the unpaid magistracy and their powers. Reduction of the qualification of jurymen, to admit workmen to discharge the civic duties of jurymen, and payment for the duties so discharged; alteration of the law so that workmen or their families may be able to sue employers in the event of injury or death from accidents due to negligence; a workshops regulation bill for women and children, and the extension of the Factory Act to bleaching and dyeing works; an act to prevent truck, by making compulsory weekly payments to workmen in the current coin of the realm; and last, an act for the better protection of seamen's lives by preventing the sending of ill-found and unseaworthy vessels to sea.

and pithy in his treatment of it. * * * No one can complain that Mr. Macdonald, the second professional 'workingman's candidate,' is tiresome in his reminders of his earlier status. He is secretary of the Miners' Association for Scotland and president of the Miners' National Association, if you please ; but not a working man. * *. * Mr. Burt is lost in the obscurity of the seats usually filled by the rank and file of Irish members. But no position less prominent than the front seat below the gangway, and no companionship less distinguished than that of Mr. Fawcett, Sir Charles Dilke, Lord Edmund Fitzmaurice, and Mr. Roebuck will suit Mr. Macdonald ; and as he stands fully a pace forward on the floor of the House, with right hand on hip, buff-coloured waistcoat fully displayed, and a respectable-looking slip of paper lightly held in his left hand, one might, without incurring just rebuke for the error, take him for a prosperous pastrycook or even a luxurious linendraper. His discourse, too, would foster the illusion, having in it no more of the pith and marrow of Mr. Burt's simple speech than his voice has of the Northumbrian miner's deep burr, or his manner of that winningness which is born not so much from the sort of feeling that animated the rhetorical yeoman,

'Too proud to care from whence he came,'

as from the unconsciously expressed conviction that after all the thing is not what the father was or what the youth may have been, but what the man is." *

Mr. Macdonald is a man just above the medium

---
* "Men and Manner in Parliament," pp. 197-9.

height, broad shouldered, full chested and compactly built. He has strongly marked features, with high cheek bones, prominent nose, and somewhat heavy lower jaw, manifesting both strength of will and combativeness. He dresses with scrupulous neatness, usually wearing his broad-cloth coat buttoned over the breast. Mr. Burt on the other hand is a younger man, of rather slender but sinewy figure, while his features are refined and delicate in mould, and he impresses a stranger as one whose constitution, naturally none too robust, has been impaired by the hard labor he has endured. The impression given is decidedly favorable. One who saw both gentlemen at the Liverpool Trades' Congress says in an unpublished letter, that "Mr. Macdonald affected somewhat in dress and attitude the member of Parliament, while Mr. Burt moved about with a simplicity and ease that was noticeable. When speaking he appears to be completely absorbed in his subject, so that his entire forgetfulness of self and indifference to rhetorical effect suffices in a short time to make the hearer forget the Northumbrian dialect, which is very pronounced. His powers of expression are very superior, his language simple, concise and well chosen, and his style not at all declamatory. His sense of the ludicrous is marked and what he says is often enlivened by quiet humor." Of the member for Stafford, Mr. Macdonald, it is said by the same writer that "in his speeches in the body in question he identified himself thoroughly, and apparently with the utmost sincerity, with the cause he champions, while he manifested a decidedly independent spirit in the expression of his own opinions on questions upon which the Congress was divided in sentiment. He impresses one as a man who would make a bold stand in the face of an adverse majority, though his combative vehemence and earnestness would doubtless turn the scale in his favor in many cases and enable him to carry the majority of a popular audience with him. He speaks with fluency and vigor, but is a little too prone to declamation, and his language sometimes lacks the accuracy and polish incident to thorough scholarship and rhetorical training. Despite a faint trace of self-consciousness, or at least, the appearance of it, he produces on the whole the impression of a strong and earnest character, and seems well calculated to wield a large and commanding influence over the minds of the class with which his life has been so closely identified."

Mr. Macdonald does not seem to have the faculty of winning the approval of his opponents—a circumstance which does not detract from the esteem of his supporters and may doubtless be regarded as a proof of the sincerity and courage with which his views are presented. The London *World*, a free lance in critical journalism, describes him with a decided touch of acerbity in writing of the part he took in the debates relative to the Labor legislation of the last session and in that on the 16th of July, 1875, relating to the expenses of the Prince of Wales on his Indian trip. Mr. Macdonald had declared that every such grant did more to make the English workingmen disloyal than all the efforts of Republican agitators, and spoke of himself as representing that class. The writer in the *World*, whose articles read like those of the witty author of " Men and Manner in Parliament," first compliments Mr. Burt, the member for Morpeth, as " a real and substantial addition to the representative power and character of the House of Commons," and says that "his sterling merit receives the acknowledgment of respectful and interested attention whenever he wishes to speak, in the most fastidious, aristocratic, and uncompromisingly critical assembly in the world." He then dissects the member for Stafford in a strain which if racy, cannot be considered as complimentary:

"Mr. Macdonald, the other titular working man's representative, is much better known and far less liked. I do not know whether he ever worked with his hands in the sense that Mr. Burt, if he boasted at all, might claim to have done, but I should say not. He has communicated to the undoubting 'Dod' the interesting fact that he was 'educated at Glasgow University,' from which I gather that neither grammar nor good manners forms a portion of the training received at that renowned institution. Mr. Macdonald would probably feel insulted if he were regarded as a working man, but it is impossible to consider him as a gentleman. There is about him a vulgarity which has a touch of originality in it, even as the position he assumes is without precedent. Mr. David Davies, the member for Cardigan, though not professionally a working man's candidate, is, as he has often told the House, a man who once lived by the labour of his hands. He was, I have heard, a sawyer, and I'll wager our time against that of Greenwich that he was a top-sawyer. Mr. Davies has not much of a drawing-room air about him, and he speaks the English of Llanfairfechan. But no man feels uncomfortable in his company, for the simple reason that he is at ease with himself, being strong in the sense of his own honest intention, and careless about what other people are thinking of him. Mr. Macdonald is as uneasy as a barn-door fowl that has borrowed for use a peacock's tail, and goes in mortal fear lest it should fall off. He is in a constant state of unrest, torn by the conflicting emotions of desire that every one should see the tail, and dread lest some one should observe the stitches by which it is fastened on. See him now, whilst Lord Elcho is speaking on Mr. Cross's Employers and Workmen Bill! He might have found an opportunity of delivering his own empty and ill-made phrases half an hour ago; but observing Lord Elcho with a bundle of notes in hand, he crossed over, and sitting down in the gangway simmering with satisfaction at thus holding easy converse with a live lord who will some day—thank Heaven—be a peer, he said he would follow him, and so secured the advantage of filling up the interstices in his talk by familiar references to 'the noble lord opposite.' In the meanwhile he is sitting on the front corner seat below the gangway, the most prominent and commanding position in the House of Commons, and is leaning forward anxiously waiting Lord Elcho's sitting down, the signal for his own uprising. When the time comes he jumps up with ill-disguised anxiety, lest the Speaker should name some one else, and so deprive him of the satisfaction of speaking in a debate in succession to a noble lord. This anxiety set at rest by the Speaker's complaisance, he begins with—'Mr. Speaker,—Sir,' and proceeds in an irritatingly impressive way to say nothing, interspersed with sickening iteration of the unctuous phrases, 'the right hon. gentleman at the 'ead of her Majesty's Government,' 'the right hon. gentleman the 'Ome Secretary,' 'the noble lord opposite,' and 'the R'y'l Commission of which I believe I had the honour to be a member.' Of counsel, of information, or of suggestion, Mr. Macdonald's speeches in the House of Commons are absolutely void. That tail, being a foreign substance, is always tickling him and recalling his attention to himself. If you listen to his speeches you will observe that he sometimes says 'we,' but his favorite construction of sentence involves the constant use of the pronoun in its singular number. It was a strikingly characteristic of him that when the Royal Commission on the Labour Laws came to draw up their report he should have dissented from the conclusions. If you examine the expression of dissent you will find that there is very little in it, and nothing at all that could by any construction offend the noble lord and other distinguished persons with whom he had the lifelong pleasure of being temporarily associated. But it was necessary that the tail should be brought out and spread in this highly advantageous position. To be one of the 'we' who declare the judgment of a Royal Commission was satisfactory; but to be the 'I,' with a whole paragraph to yourself, indicating less that you are wiser than your fellows, and a truer friend of the working classes—for Mr. Macdonald's vanity does not take even that comparatively robust form—than that you were there, a person duly and specially authorized by her Majesty to make an inquiry in her august name, and that you sat at the same table on a footing of ceremonious equality with a 'noble lord,' this was something worth living for, and as a last lingering grip of the fleeting honour—the ultimate drop in the cup of your wonted luxury—we had this paragraph all to itself, lifting Alexander Macdonald out of the ranks and placing him on a pedestal where the tail might be soothingly spread out in the winking sunshine that pretended not to see the stitches."

The London *Beehive*, under date of July 24th, comes to the defence of Mr. Macdonald, in a manner not less vigorous than the critic's assault. Being the official organ of the English Trades' Societies, its views are significant as to the esteem in which Mr. Macdonald is held by a common constituency. It describes the *World* as "not absolutely a scandalous production," but as one that seeking "out commercial and other cognate immoralities" revels in their exposure "with a piquancy of phrase" which is sensational. It protests against the "smart exaggeration" by which it seeks to injure the "usefulness" of the "labor representatives" and adds:

"We think it may be said that the constituencies that returned Mr. Macdonald and Mr. Burt to the House of Commons were not particular—in fact, cared nothing—as to the intonation of their words, nor did they trouble themselves as to provincial phraseology or accent; they did not scan too closely the agreement of nouns and verbs, or other peculiarities by no means confined to the working men members of the House of Commons, and of which Messrs. Macdonald and Burt are far from being the extremest examples in the House. The working men want realities rather than semblances, men who will speak out plainly in the manner natural to them, the thoughts, the wishes, and the wants of their class, not mincing dealers out of pretty and correct sentences."

The praise given to Mr. Burt is spoken of as being " as unnecessary as it is tardy and insincere. Its censure of Mr. Macdonald may be replied to in the same way. The working men of Stafford did not know nor did they care what such men as those who write in the *World* might think about the appearance, the manner, or the language of Mr. Macdonald."

As to Mr. Macdonald's pursuits and education, the *Beehive* writer says that the working men know that he has labored with his hands, and that he "has never in any way tried to conceal the fact; but upon all necessary and fitting occasions has made it known. Nor does Mr. Macdonald claim to have a full University education. He simply makes known the fact that out of his earnings as a miner, he struggled to give himself something of the advantages desirable from the University of his native district. The attempt was creditable, and the success not to be questioned, when the detracting and cramping toil of the mine is taken into account, as well as the other depressing circumstances attending the daily trials of a workingman's life. But upon what he acquired as education in Glasgow University, Mr. Macdonald has never rested any claim to the support of the working classes. His claims are far better founded. They rest on tasks voluntarily entered on, perseveringly pursued, and successfully accomplished, for the amelioration of the class of workers amidst which his lot was cast. He labored to rescue women and young children from the—to them—demoralizing, degrading, and crushing toil of the mine; to shorten the hours of labour for men, improve generally the conditions under which they worked, and to increase the payment received for their labour, and as a consequence to augment the comfort of their homes."

X.

THOMAS BRASSEY.

THE member for Hastings is an example of a man not dwarfed by having had a very capable and even distinguished father. The positivist phrase " Captain of Industry " is often used in a meaningless way, but personally applied to men like the Brasseys, father and son, it possesses an admirable appropriateness. The father was notable for having been one of the earliest and largest of railroad contractors and employers. But he is more noticeable also for having been among the largest, but as is generally agreed, one of the fairest employers of labor to be found in his day and generation. The son has followed his father's example in spirit, if not in fact, by devoting a great deal of practical knowledge, wide experience and finely cultured capacity, to the introduction of a better mode of dealing with labor, in law and society, in business and government alike.

Of late, the character and work of the Brasseys, father and son, have been made quite widely known. The first

has been introduced to the public by Sir Arthur Helps' attractive biography; and the last by his own writings, besides legislative, and other public efforts, bearing on the relations of labor to capital and to society in general.*
John Ruskin seems almost to have had the senior Brassey in his mind when he wrote of "mastership" to his artisan friend, Thomas Dixon, cork-cutter of Sunderland, the second of the remarkable letters, since published in a collected form.† Ruskin says; "there are just and unjust masterships;" and adds, that though co-operation is better than the latter, "there is very great room for doubt whether it be better than a just and benignant mastership." He thinks that the wages system might be made so just that it should be "sufficient and regular" to each "according to his rank;" that by it "due provision shall be made out of the profits of the business for sick and superannuated workers; and by which the master, *being held responsible as a minor king or governor for the conduct as well as comfort of all those under his rule*, shall on that condition be permitted to retain to his own use the surplus profits of the business which the fact of his being master may be assumed to prove that he has organized by superior intellect and energy."

The elder Thomas Brassey was among the first persons in England to enter regularly into the business of railway construction, which he did in 1834, at the suggestion of the elder Stephenson. At that time, this sort of work had

---

* "Brassey's Life and Labors." Arthur Helps, Roberts, Boston.— "On Work and Wages." Thomas Brassey, Bell & Daldy, London.— "Articles on Co-operation." *Contemporary Review, London.*

† "Time and Tide." John Wiley, New York, pp. 6, 7.

not "begun to run in grooves, * * * but required new modes of operation, and the creation of skilled labor of a new kind; also the management of larger bodies of men than hitherto had been brought together for public works, and a more rapid movement of these *armies* of laboring men, from place to place, than had ever been requisite."* Mr. Brassey continued actively engaged in this business until 1870,—a period of twenty-eight years, during which time he contracted for, and constructed 6,498¾ miles of railroad, more than two-thirds of which was in other countries than his own. He constructed roads in France, Germany, Italy, Switzerland, European Turkey, Sweden, Denmark, Spain, Austria, Russia, the East Indies, the Australian Colonies, South America and Canada. The variety and extent of these operations have given the greatest value to his experience in the management of labor and to the testimony borne by himself and by his sons. Mr. Brassey handled enormous sums during his business life, amounting, his biographer states, to "seventy-eight millions" (pounds) "of other people's money, and upon that outlay retained about two millions, and a half. The rest of his fortune consisted of accumulations."† His profit never exceeded three per cent. It is recorded of him that he never had but one lawsuit, was never knowingly wronged by an agent or employee in any money transaction, was always enlarging the compensation of those who worked under him, when they made extra exertions, or when it was evident that their industry, skill and enterprise had largely carried

---

* Helps' "Life of Brassey," p. 27.
† "Life of Brassey," p. 158.

through a successful contract; that he declined all honors or public position, and always bore his testimony to the good conduct of workmen when properly treated. In truth a perusal of Arthur Helps' work will illustrate what Auguste Comte must have had in view when he urged that the "Captains of Industry" were to be the future leaders of the civilized world, and that moral force itself would be the best law to keep them in the highways of just dealing and fair stewardship. It would be difficult to imagine young men becoming sordid and mean, or mere drones, who had the good fortune to be reared in such an atmosphere as that of the Brassey household.

The eldest son, Thomas Brassey, now member for Hastings, was born at Stafford in 1837, and is therefore in his thirty-eighth year. His father was born in 1805, at Buerton, in the parish of Aldford, in Cheshire. He was the son of John and Elizabeth Brassey of the same parish. The family is an ancient one, having owned and occupied for nearly six centuries an estate of three or four hundred acres, at Bulkeley, Malpas, Cheshire. The Brasseys are of the most direct Anglo-Norman stock, the founder of the family having been a soldier in the army of William the Conqueror. The Bulkeley manor is still a favorite family residence. In addition thereto, the grandfather owned land at Buerton, and also rented a large farm from the Marquis of Westminster. Mr. Brassey, senior, was articled at sixteen to a land surveyor. He early became connected with the management of the property on which Birkenhead, the flourishing town on the Cheshire side of the Mersey, near Liverpool, was built. It was the accident of supplying stone to George Stephenson for the construction of the Sankey Viaduct, on the Manchester and Liverpool Railroad, that led to Mr. Brassey's becoming a contractor. He had, two years before, married Maria Harrison, daughter of a forwarding agent doing a large business in Liverpool. Mrs. Brassey has survived her husband. His biographer says: "It is always a difficult matter to speak in praise of those who are living, and who may not like to read commendation of themselves. But, notwithstanding this necessary reserve, it is but right to mention the fact that Mr. Brassey's first connection with railways was partly due to the advice which he received from his wife." The domestic sacrifices that were imposed on her by the engagements of her husband can readily be seen in the frequent change of residence required by them.

The eldest son was partly educated in France, owing to the fact that his father was engaged there. The family changed their residence eleven times during the first thirteen years of Mr. Brassey's new business career. These changes and his subsequent necessary absences from home, threw the entire charge of the education of her sons into Mrs. Brassey's hands, until they were old enough to go to the public schools and the university. The eldest son was sent to Rugby and then to University College, Oxford. After graduating he studied law, and was called to the bar at Lincoln's Inn in 1864. As he was certain to inherit a large fortune, his professional studies must have been prompted chiefly by a desire to prepare himself thoroughly for the public life on which he soon after entered.

One of the most interesting chapters in the biography of his father is one in which extracts are made from letters written to Sir Arthur Helps by the present Mr. Thomas

Brassey. They contain interesting facts, delicately stated, in relation to the character, tastes, etc., of his father. They show also the influences under which his own mind has been formed. He speaks of the powers of observation his father possessed, of the interest he took in all engineering projects and plans, of his love for oratory, sculpture and fine architecture, and his careful observation of the commercial and agricultural resources of the country through which he was passing. His son says: "Whenever he travelled abroad he was a busy sight-seer. He used to visit the churches, the public buildings, the picture galleries, with the keenest interest. He would seldom leave a great city, though the primary object would probably have been some matter of business, without giving almost as much attention to its works of art and its architectural monuments as the ordinary traveller, whose only object is the love of art or change of scene.

"I remember, during my Rugby days, an agreeable journey with him to the South of France: his object being to inspect the works on the Lyons and Avignon Railway, at that time under construction. After he had completed his examination of the line, he determined to devote a couple of days to an excursion from Avignon to Nismes. On our way from the station at Nismes to the hotel, we passed the Maison Carrée, so justly celebrated for the exquisite character of its architectural proportions. I do not think he had heard much about this building, perhaps he might never have heard of it before, but he immediately appreciated its great beauty, and remained at least half an hour on the spot that he might examine that admirable monument of ancient art from every point of view." Mr. Brassey speaks in discriminating terms of his father's love of sculpture and admiration for porcelain; his recognition of finely proportioned ships — yachts especially — and his delight in fine reading and good oratory. In politics the elder Brassey was a Conservative, but never endeavored in any way to influence his son's political opinions. In business matters he was always his own amanuensis, never employing a short-hand writer, until late in life and after a stroke of paralysis. No letters were unanswered. Of his father's kindliness of character, Mr. Brassey says, that "he evinced at all times the most anxious desire to assist young men to enter upon a career in life." He always urged "those who sought his advice, to begin by giving to their sons a practical knowledge of a trade." He possessed great patience, a remarkable power of business statement; was kindly in judging of others, even to a fault; sought to avoid all offence to those about him; accepted gracefully, but not servilely, social distinctions, and, his son continues: "in all he said or did, he ever showed himself to be inspired by that chivalry of heart and mind which most truly ennobles him who possesses it, and without which one cannot be a perfect gentleman." The father, thus affectionately described, died December 8, 1870, and was buried at Catsfield, Sussex. He left a widow and three sons; Thomas, then, as now, member for Hastings; Henry Arthur, the member for Sandwich, and Albert.

Mr. Thomas Brassey entered the political arena soon after leaving the university, as an avowed liberal, independent and moderate. He unsuccessfully contested, in 1861, the borough of Birkenhead, with whose early prosperity his own family was identified. He was returned for

Davenport in 1865; but a general election followed immediately, in which he lost his seat. He was, however, elected at Hastings in 1868, and again in 1874.

During his parliamentary career, Mr. Brassey has generally acted with the liberal party, but he has in several instances shown his independence by defending and voting for propositions not accepted by Mr. Gladstone's ministry. He has acted usually with the advanced liberals on matters of education, franchise, and the labor laws. It is his position in regard to the relations of labor and capital, and his extensive knowledge of practical matters that enter into them, that make his career one of marked prominence and gives him an influence not usual in men so young in years and public life. The writer of the biographical sketches embodied in the *Beehive* "Portrait Gallery," who represents very closely the judgments and opinions of intelligent labor in England, says of Mr. Brassey's position, that "he is nearly always found on the side of the workingmen, and, it is needless to say, that what he utters on such occasions is received with more than ordinary attention by the House, and tends powerfully to forward the just claims of the working people. To this it may be added that on all questions connected with labor, Mr. Brassey is accessible to those who act on behalf of the workingmen, and in him they always find a safe and friendly adviser.

"But the most notable service rendered by Mr. Thomas Brassey to the labor movement in Great Britain was the publication of his instructive and important book, entitled 'Work and Wages.' This is not in any sense a controversial work, and it deals scarcely at all with the opinions of employers of workingmen as such. It simply gathers together the recorded experience of his father's life, not only as a great employer of labor, but as an employer who had carried on his operations in nearly all parts of the world; and it adds to this recorded experience the results of his own careful study in the chief fields of our great industries, and proves his case from this in a very clear and masterly manner. What the importance of that case is to the British workingman will be easily enough understood when we state the matter in dispute between capital and labor to which it refers. Putting the building trades on one side, all the great industries of England are carried on with reference to foreign markets, and therefore have to be regulated in regard to the cost of production by a real or presumed foreign competition. All attempts made by workingmen to better their condition by advanced wages or shortened hours of labor in these trades have been met by the cry that if such demands were granted we should lose our trade through foreign competition. This was the 'wolf' always at hand to alarm the timid, and in this cry all men's throats had become musical who had any pretence to be friends of capital or students in the science of political economy. The friends of workingmen who had studied the question knew how hollow and unreal all this pretended fear was. They knew that Continental labor was nominally cheaper, and that Continental hours were longer; but they inferred very correctly, from the actual and daily increasing predominance of English manufactures in foreign markets, that English labor was practically more valuable. To them it was clear that their skill, energy, and perseverance, in connection with their superior machinery and other advantages, gave better results than Continental manufactures had obtained; and they knew also that workers on the Continent were not satisfied with their condition, and that in regard to work and wages they were struggling to attain to the British artisan's standard.

"Over and over again these things were urged by the advocates of labor in England, but the Press was closed against them, and their facts and argument, therefore, never reached the ear of the general public. In such circumstances Mr. Brassey's book was just what was wanted. It was peculiar in its character, as it drew its facts from a special source. Its logic was the logic of life. His father had employed hundreds of thousands of Englishmen, and he had also employed men in large numbers belonging not only to every country in Europe, but to every land, north, south, east, and west, where any great works requiring skill or labor had to be constructed. He had not only to employ the native worker on the spot, but had to calculate the value of the men of different classes and nations, as commodities to be imported or exported for the economic performance of the work on hand. He had, in fact, to look at the question every way, in the most honest, practical, and unprejudiced manner, and his deliberate verdict was that, *all things considered*, the labor of the Englishman was the cheapest labor in the world. It is true he got more wages and was more his own master, being less amenable to arbitrary dictation that any other worker; and yet he was decidedly the cheapest, when the value that he gave in return for his wages was properly taken into account.

"We cannot here state the variety of tests by which Mr.

Brassey proved this in his very valuable book. We state simply, but most emphatically, that he did prove it in such a manner as to leave no doubt on the mind even of the most prejudiced, and by doing so he has put to flight a phantom which can now only be called up again by the utterly ignorant, or those whose purpose it is to keep alive a profitable superstition. This is but one out of the many valuable points in Mr. Brassey's book, but it is the one of most practical value to workingmen in reference to wages and hours of work. The labors of Mr. Brassey, generally in relation to questions of capital and labor, are characterized by much fairness, and he does not confine his views to one set of questions. At the last annual Congress held at Halifax,* Mr. Brassey presided, and delivered an inaugural address, characterized by great thoughtfulness, and overflowing with sound practical advice of the very best kind. The services rendered by Mr. Brassey * * * are willingly but unostentatiously given. He is a capitalist, and a friend of capital; but he is, beyond this, a friend of justice and fair dealing. * * * Mr. Brassey comes to the side of workingmen in this way, and what he has already done, without a touch of partisanship, gives a cheering promise of what he may do in the future to help forward England's workers on the grand path of self-improvement and self-elevation, along which they are at present moving.

"We have not noticed in this brief sketch the study which Mr. Brassey has given to nautical questions; but he is well known by the attention which he has given to them, and the useful practical works he has performed in relation

---

* Co-operative congress of 1873-4.

thereto. He served as a member of the Select Committee on Compulsory Pilotage. He is now a member of the Royal Commission on Unseaworthy Ships. He has also published pamphlets on 'Organization of our Naval Reserve,' and on 'Recent Admiralty Administrations.' Mr. Brassey has made several voyages, including several visits to the Mediterranean, cruises in the Baltic, and on the Norwegian coasts; and has also ascended all the navigable rivers on the east coast of the United States, to the highest point which can be reached by sea-going vessels. He is the author of 'Notes on Algeria,' letters describing a journey in Syria and Palestine, as well as journeys in Norway and the United States. He has also published important pamphlets on Trades' Unions, Co-operative Production, Wages, the Duty of the Church in relation to the Labor Question, and on Education in America."

He has been among the contributors who, in the *Fortnightly* and *Contemporary Reviews*, have written papers bearing on such topics as are named in the *Beehive* sketch.

The valuable book "On Work and Wages," which is referred to in the foregoing quotations, is worthy of careful examination. It is written in a liberal and comprehensive spirit, and deals with its chosen themes in a manner altogether different from the usual tone of the all-wise editorial writers who seek to instruct the public every time a dispute culminates in a strike, or grows to the dignity of an agitation. Mr. Brassey's little volume gives a historical sketch of Trades' Unions and strikes, and adds chapters on demand and supply, maintaining that the "Cost of Labor cannot be determined by the Rate of Wages;" comparing the "Industrial capabilities of different Nations," showing that "Dear Labor stimulates Invention;" discussing the "Hours of Labor" and the "Rise of Wages," in other countries than England. Then follow a "Comparison of the Commercial Progress of Nations;" and a discussion of the question whether labor is becoming dearer. The "Influence of American wages on the English labor market," is a valuable chapter. Mr. Brassey thus sums up: "The influence of the price of labor in the United States has been felt in this country (Great Britain), and no economist can doubt that it will soon be felt in those branches of industry in Germany in which the wages are so much below the English rates of pay."* Mr. Brassey's concluding chapters discuss the "Alleged Physical Deterioration of the Laborer,"—giving a negative answer to the theory,—the "Fluctuations of Wages;" "Co-operation," "Piece-work," and "Courts of Conciliation."

Mr Brassey read a very interesting address before the Social Science Congress at Norwich in 1873, being a genreal review of the labor market at that period. Speaking of shortening the hours of labor and of the effects of this policy on English production, Mr. Brassey refuses to regard a limitation of the hours of labor as an evil in itself. He says of the theory he combats—"I cannot share in this view. Because some may make an unwise use of their newly-acquired advantages, that is no reason for returning to a former state of things; when in the general depression of trade an undue pressure was brought to bear upon the working-

---

* "On Work and Wages," p. 207.

man. No doubt, says Sir Arthur Helps, hard work is a great police agent. If everybody were worked from morning until night and then carefully locked up, the register of crime might be greatly diminished. But what would become of human nature, where would be the room for growth in such a system of things? The use of leisure requires education, and that education has not been fully given to the mechanics, miners and puddlers of former generations." *

A more recent article shows a considerable advance in literary skill on the part of Mr. Brassey, as well as of capacity to handle his chosen themes. In the article alluded to he reviews the subject of "Co-operative Production," giving a very clear and comprehensive account of the movements in that direction, not only in Great Britain but in other countries also. After summing up the facts relating to co-operative stores, Mr. Brassey proceeds to those of production. He reviews at length the difficulties in the way of managing such enterprises, shows the want of administration, knowledge and skill, and the disinclination to place the needed power in the hands of managers. Mr. Brassey says :

"When co-operative production has been introduced into all branches of industry successfully and on a sufficiently extensive scale, we shall then have the universal gauge or measure of the workman's rightful claims. From the day when the workman will take his part in the deliberations which accord to capital its fair rate of interest, and to the wage-earner his due, from the day when the workman may count with certainty on a just and equal participation in the profits of every enterprise in which he is engaged, in proportion to his merits, strikes, it is to be hoped, will cease, and workmen will be devoted to the successful prosecution of the industry in which they find their

---

* "Wages in 1873." London, Longmans, Green & Co.

employment. If it should appear an exaggeration of the powers of human nature to adopt the principles on which Fourier insisted, and to regard all labor as a pleasure, it is possible to conceive conditions, in which labor would appear neither irksome nor distasteful. The laborer might have more satisfaction in working under the direction of persons selected by himself, than he now experiences under the authority of an employer upon whom he is entirely dependent as the distributor of wages "*

He points out that capitalists and employers of labor are not, as a class, regardless of the rights of others, and declares " that the disposition to be liberal towards workmen is developed, as a general rule, in proportion to the extent of the business and the capital of the employer." Struggling ones are more apt to be selfish and grinding. He takes exception to the theory that the intermediate class, persons of moderate but independent incomes, is becoming smaller; and points out the fact that the average size of farms in the United States is stated at 154 acres, and that in seventeen representative counties the farms of England are but 152 acres each. He urges the advantage of individual over corporate business control, and quotes Erastus Bigelow of Massachusetts, against the system of corporations. The article embraces an account of all the known productive co-operative efforts, and gives very interesting details of the sub-contract and piece-work plans adopted by his father and other great railway contractors, claiming for them the character of co-operative effort. Another statement of value is one relating to "piece-work," in iron ship building. He also discusses the "partnership of labor" plan as introduced in coal mining by Messrs. Briggs & Sons, and by Messrs. Fox, Head & Co., in manufac-

---

* "Co-operative Production.—*Contemporary Review*, London, *July*, 1874.

ture. The latter scheme gives every one a pecuniary interest in success and profit, proportioned to service rendered. Wages and Salaries are paid at ordinary rates. Capital receives a specified interest rate. A fund for repairs and plant is to be maintained, also one against loss by bad debts. After these sums are paid the profits are divided between capital and labor. This scheme, Mr. Brassey says, has worked well for eight years, and he adds:

> "In that interval, amid the many fluctuations to which their trade is always subjected, they have paid between £6,000 and £7,000 to their workmen by way of bonus; and the result has been eminently satisfactory to the employers. They think they have a superior class of workmen, and that they stay longer at the works. They obtain the best prices for their manufactures. They have no disputes, and pay no contributions to standing committees or courts of conciliation. Thus, the employers are well content with the arrangements they have made; and the conduct of the workmen shows that a feeling of mutual satisfaction prevails."

The closing paragraphs of this article are so thoughtful and worth considering, as illustrating what a wise representative of the capitalist class thinks of the probable tendencies of the Labor Agitation, that they will bear reproducing. Mr. Brassey alludes to the fact that travel is no longer confined to the wealthy or well-to-do classes, but that working-men circulate more freely from country to country. Their class interest will, he thinks, bring them closely together, and so make "them regard with stronger aversion those national struggles in which, from motives of personal ambition, their rulers in past ages have been too ready to engage. Already we see in Germany a party being formed whose sympathies are for France. The originators of the movement are the artizans in the two countries; and, as their numbers will probably increase, they may exercise a valuable influence in promoting the blessed work of reconciliation."*

So, too, he regards "the solidarity of the two peoples" as surer guarantee for "a close and permanant alliance," between Great Britain and the United States," than the most elaborate contrivances of diplomacy." Appealing for a better feeling in his own land, Mr. Brassey writes in closing:

"As union is most earnestly to be desired between the same classes in different countries, so it is not less desirable between different classes in the same country. If it is hard for the privileged few to appreciate the difficulties of the masses around them, who are struggling forward in the battle of life, it is still harder, we may rest assured, for the poor to appreciate the peculiar trials of the rich. We may plead for princes their isolation, and for the nobly-born the absence of many powerful motives which fire the ambition of men of modest station and lead them forward to a career of usefulness and distinction. We may urge on behalf of the rich that they are a tempting prey to designing men, and can seldom earn the gratitude reserved for those who are believed to practice the virtue of self-denial; but we may rest assured that the mass below them, contending for bare existence, have little sympathy to spare from the constant troubles of their own lives, for trials that to them must appear artificial and self-imposed.

"Whatever the poor may feel towards the rich, the duty of the rich towards the poor is too plain to admit of misconception. Whether moved by considerations of policy, or by the nobler impulses of humanity, it must be the object of our universal solicitude that no class in society should be exposed to the fatal influences of despair.

"Multitudes there must be in every city contending amid waves that threaten destruction; and when, with anxious glances they seek a refuge from the storm, can they descry the happy isles in which they may repose? The land, if seen, is far away, their bark is sinking,

---

* *Contemporary Review*, July, 1874, p. 232.

and their only hope the aid of those who have already gained the shore.

"An idea prevails in certain quarters abroad that there is no sympathy between the affluent classes in England and the masses of their less fortunate fellow-countrymen. Much more truly may it be affirmed that in no other country is the same deep interest felt in the welfare of the poor. It is because this sympathy exists, that in England we have as yet been spared the miseries of social disunion; and from this the most dire calamity which can befall a nation Heaven grant we may remain for ever free!"*

Mr. Brassey is a fine type—physically and mentally—of the English gentleman, descended from an estimable family, of a class which represents the very best stock in a land where so much store is set on ancestral qualities. Coming, too, from an immediate parentage so honorably identified with the broadest activities of modern civilization, possessed of all the advantages the best education and wealth can afford, he unites therewith a positive character, and a kindly breadth of judgment and experience which are sure to make him hereafter a man of more marked influence in English politics. He is a man of comely appearance; of middle stature, well knit, athletic frame, kindly but thoughtful face, large, brown eyes, hair, and light side-whiskers. His head is large and well balanced, and the forehead is broad and open, a fair index of the mind. His manners are grave but courteous, and, like his father, Mr. Brassey is always accessible. He has been an efficient co-worker in the Plimsoll agitation, so far as Parliamentary action is concerned; in other matters he has commonly given an active support to measures like those of Mr. Trevelyan and Sir Charles Dilke for

---

* *Contemporary Review*, p. 232–3.

extending the franchise and redistributing seats. So well grounded is the popular faith in Mr. Brassey's purity of purpose and just intent, that even when he takes adverse ground on a labor or political question or dispute, as he has recently done in the great lock-out of miners in South Wales, no one has questioned his sincerity of motive. Mr. Brassey is married, and children are growing up by his hearth-stone. The advent of men of his stamp in the public life of any country is an event always to be welcomed; but their activity (for Mr. Brassey is not alone) in British politics is a matter of congratulation to the people of England, and of service to all others, for the light they will be able to shed on different sides of the world's great social and economic problem—the Labor Question.

XI.

SAMUEL MORLEY.

THE late Richard Cobden, speaking in favor of Electoral Reform in Great Britain, argued that the wisest policy to pursue was for those in power from time to time to garrison present institutions with new forces and fresh recruits. This is a favorite idea with the member from Bristol, Mr. Samuel Morley, and presents a fair statement of the philosophy which guides his political life. It is not a difficult thing to indicate the party affiliations of an English gentleman, who is at all active in public affairs, when you have named the family and other class associations from which he sprung, or in which he moves. So too, if he is in the House of Commons, his position may be generally apprehended by naming the borough he represents, if there is even a slight knowledge of English political history. For many years past, no one but an "advanced" politician in the field of finance or electoral reform, has sat for the borough of Finsbury. It would not be possible for any one other than a leader in the economic school known by the name of that great manufacturing burgh, to sit for Manchester: and Bristol, for which Mr. Morley has sat since 1868, has not sent to Parliament for many years any one but an independent Radical. For a century it has been marked for opinions of this cast; and at various periods of popular agitation, its people have grown impatient at delays and hastened the progress of needed reforms by significant disorder and turbulence. The passage of the reform bill of 1832 was accelerated by the riots at Bristol, quite as much as the later one was by the fall of the Hyde Park railings under the orders of the Reform League. Mr. Morley, by his birth and early associations, as well as his mature convictions, fitly represents the ancient borough for which he sits.

Samuel Morley is an elderly gentleman of striking appearance, bearing in his open and benignant face, the evidence of a benevolent character as well as of a firm and thoughtful mind. He possesses wealth, public spirit, a courteous and kindly disposition, and a courage which leads him readily to champion a right cause or vigorously expose wrong doing. He belongs to the wealthy middle class—the manufacturing and commercial interests—which have given to modern England so many of its best citizens. He is the youngest son of John Morley, of London and Nottingham. His father was the head of one of the largest hosiery manufacturing firms in England, and his sons have succeeded to the business. Samuel Morley was born in 1809, and is in his sixty-sixth year. He is one of the finest looking men in the Commons and one of those most sure to be noticed by a stranger. In 1841, at the age of thirty two, Mr. Morley was married to the daughter of Samuel Hope, a well known banker of Liverpool.

Mr. John Morley was a prominent laymen in one of the leading evangelical sects, and his sons from their childhood were the friends of the foremost nonconforming divines of England. This association began to influence Mr. Samuel Morley at a period when all liberal thoughts ran largely to political action. Among those with whom the Morleys were on familiar terms, was Dr. John Pye Smith, a famous Biblical scholar, whose activity was marked in many other fields. Dr. Smith was an ardent supporter of Joseph Hume, the sturdiest financial reformer England has seen for a century past; and later in life, he was an ardent supporter of Cobden and Bright in their anti-corn-law struggle. His influence largely affected Mr. Samuel Morley's life and principles, and on the latter's entering public life, he was recognized both by the public and his co-religionists, who form an important element of the Liberal party, as the rightful heir to political convictions like those of his learned friend.

As a large employer of labor at Nottingham, Mr. Samuel Morley is known as the friend and supporter of Mr. Mundella in all his earlier efforts to introduce, as a remedy for labor troubles, the Boards of Arbitration and Conciliation which have since proved so fruitful of good results. In his public career, Mr. Morley is recognized as an authority on all legislation on questions relating to capital and labor. His opinion on some of these matters is expressed very clearly in a letter addressed to a Mr. Kelley of Bristol, who was actively engaged in the organization of the Agricultural Laborers' Unions, and at the same time in promoting the establishment of arbitration boards. Mr. Morley writes :—

"I very heartily sympathize with you in the efforts which you are making. * * * These boards are, I am convinced, the very best remedy for the evils and misery which come from lock-outs and strikes. They serve to make masters and men think about the justice of their respective claims, and prevent the enormous loss of labor, and consequently of capital (which is only accumulated labor's results), which presses most heavily in time of strike on the workman and his family. I sincerely hope your efforts will be crowned with success. It is most opportune to have everywhere the boards formed and ready to act before the differences arise, and to have them consist of the most strictly upright and honorable persons, capitalists and laborers in the various localities."

It was not until 1865 that Mr. Morley entered Parliament. Having been, after sharply contesting Nottingham, unseated at the close of his first session on account of informalities, which in no wise affected his own character or political purity, Mr. Morley did not again offer himself as a candidate until 1868. He then stood for Bristol, and was elected in November of that year, and again in 1874. He identified himself with the Liberal Ministry, generally supporting their measures. Among his earliest votes was that cast for the disestablishment of the Irish Church, a measure which he was convinced, he said, would strengthen, not weaken Protestantism. Mr. Morley represents that portion of the nonconforming sects which do not fully accept the political leadership of Mr. Miall or the policy of the Liberation society. He is disposed to compromise on the "Erastian" principle—that of concurrent endowment. But like Mr. Miall he is a strenuous opponent of all compulsory supports of a state Church, or other religious body. Mr. Morley very early entered with great activity into the agitation for public education, and when the act of 1870, establishing School Boards, was made law, he became a candidate for the Board of London. So much are his presence and influence valued in this field, that when business cares and public duties compelled his absence from its deliberations for several months and he tendered his resignation, he was unanimously asked by his colleague to withdraw the request. No better idea can be given of the great work that is being done in this important field than to present the following brief statement of the result in London, made by Mr. George Potter, editor of the *Beehive*, who, with a Mr. Lucraft, was elected to represent the working class in this body. It will be remembered that many of the foremost men in England have stood for and been elected as members of School Boards.

Mr. Potter says, that in 1871, the London Board decided to build accommodation for 112,000 children. In these new structures eighty-five schools have already been opened, twenty-two more are being constructed, and work on seventeen others will soon be commenced, making a total of 127 new buildings, which will accommodate 105,000 children. In 1871 there were enrolled in the "efficient" schools of London (before the labors of the Board begun); 208,250 children. At the close of 1874 the number was 343,100. The average daily attendance was at the first date 171,767; at the last it was 256,394, being 84,624 more. The cost of these schools is about $49 for each child, which is about 48 cents on each dollar of assessed valuation. The amount, spent or to be provided for, up to March, 1875 was £1,031,392, 7s.5d., or nearly $5,157,000.

As a business man of large experience, Mr. Morley has already shown himself efficient in the preparation and carrying of necessary legislation. Several measures have been proposed and carried through by him for the improvement of commercial law and especially of Bankruptcy proceedings. He has urged with great earnestness the passage of an act to enable the Public Works Loan Commissioners to make advances to the limited owners of entailed estates for the building and improvement of the laborers cottage—being one of a series of propositions to which Mr. Morley has closely devoted himself, all looking to the improvement and elevation of labor, and the correction of abuses which have grown up in the shadow of inherited privilege and wealth. Mr. Morley votes in nearly every instance with Sir Charles Dilke for redistribution of seats, with Prof. Fawcett in measures for the suffrage and education of laborers; with Messrs. Mundella, Macdonald, Burt and others for the abolition of special legislation as applied to workmen; with Mr. P. A. Taylor in opposition to the game laws and against the unpaid magistracy, though he is in commission for Middlesex county where he resides; with Plimsoll on the shipping bills, and with Sir Wilfrid Lawson on the Permissive Liquor act. He does not usually follow the "irreconcilables"—now recruited from four in the last House to eighteen in the present one—into the lobby, when they divide the House upon a royal grant or modification of the civil list. In financial matters, Mr. Morley is consistent in his efforts to reduce taxation. He was among the earliest friends of the Reform League, giving freely of his means to that and other similar movements. He was one of the first public men in England to recognize the importance as well as the justice of the Agricultural Laborers' movement; and presided at the Exeter Hall meeting, when Joseph Arch made his first speech to a London audience, supported by such widely varying champions as Cardinal (then Archbishop) Manning and Charles Bradlaugh. The speech of the latter consisted of a single ringing resolution in which it was declared that the only remedy for the laborers distress and wrongs was in an equitable settlement of the Land Tenure question. The London Times editorially referred to it as the important event of the meeting.

Mr. Morley was also the Chairman of the second meeting on the same question, when in 1874, the farmers of the eastern counties inaugurated an extensive lock-out. Mr. Morley's speech was a strong one, though free from all bitterness.

He had, he said, "not the slightest doubt as to the propriety of his being there that evening to express deep and earnest sympathy with the agricultural laborers. The life which the poor fellows lived was a disgrace to Christians of this country."

"Deeply anxious to see an end put to the present state of things, he had tried very hard," he added, "during the last fortnight, to procure the intervention of men of position, influence, and independence." It was a duty to cheer on every man, mechanic or peasant, "in the determination to do something towards raising his own social position."

Speaking of his sympathies with the laborers, he declared, that these were no new opinions or feelings: he had "always felt and thought that working men have a right to meet together and decide the price at which their labor shall be sold." As to locking out those who unite for this purpose until they dissolve their Union, he regarded it "as a positive act of tyranny, an interference with the rights of Englishmen;" and he, for one, had made up his mind to "help them in every practicable and possible way to maintain their position."

It is said eulogistically but apparently with truth, that Mr. Morley's "moral instincts are noble and unselfish, and his natural disposition is generous and liberal. Knowing that his great wealth comes to him through the industry of those whom he employs, he never forgets their claims in the indulgence of any caprices of his own. His chief pleasure consists in promoting works of usefulness and aiding purposes of philanthropy. Unpretendingly plain and rigidly abstemious in his own habits and mode of life, he knows no luxury but that of doing good. His love of truth amounts to a worship. His sense of justice is quick, strong, and steadfast. His hatred of oppression is a passion. These are the sentiments that form and fire his oratory, which by virtue of a simple and straightforward strenuousness, often transcends the highest flights of eloquence, at once more catching in its influence and more abiding in its results."*

---

* *Beehive* "Portrait Gallery," London, 1874.

PART III.

PARLIAMENTARY AGITATORS.

XII.

SAMUEL PLIMSOLL.

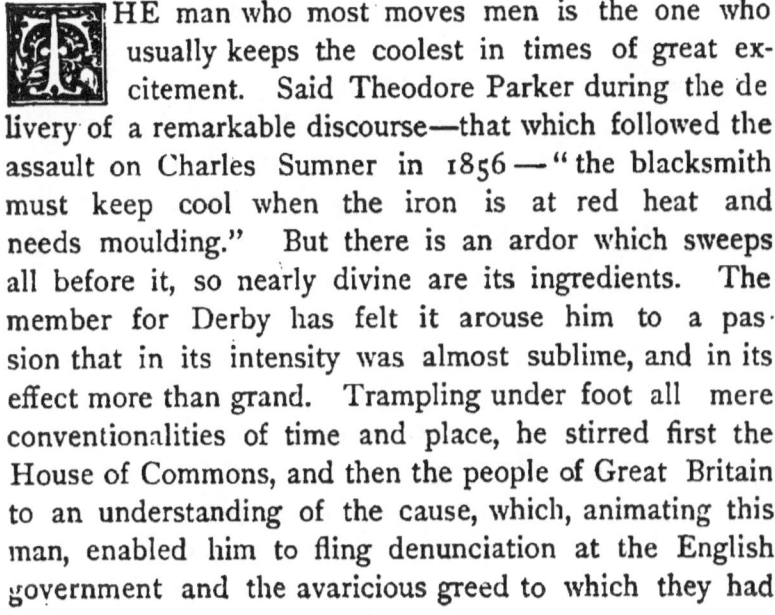

THE man who most moves men is the one who usually keeps the coolest in times of great excitement. Said Theodore Parker during the delivery of a remarkable discourse—that which followed the assault on Charles Sumner in 1856—"the blacksmith must keep cool when the iron is at red heat and needs moulding." But there is an ardor which sweeps all before it, so nearly divine are its ingredients. The member for Derby has felt it arouse him to a passion that in its intensity was almost sublime, and in its effect more than grand. Trampling under foot all mere conventionalities of time and place, he stirred first the House of Commons, and then the people of Great Britain to an understanding of the cause, which, animating this man, enabled him to fling denunciation at the English government and the avaricious greed to which they had cringed! Parliamentary history records no incident more striking than when Mr. Plimsoll woke the echoes in St. Stephens, on the 23d of July, 1875, and shamed a nation into action. The words he uttered, so smiting in their directness, sounding in their terrible invective like the denunciations of an Hebrew prophet, recall that marvellous arraignment of Warren Hastings which alone would have made Edmund Burke renowned as an orator. Samuel Plimsoll is no Edmund Burke—he is not a man of genius in the sense usually understood by the term, but he is possessed of that deep sympathy for human suffering which is so rare and so much more ennobling than the merely intellectual, however massive, can ever be.

The member for Derby is now in his fifty-first year. He was born at Bristol in 1824, being the fourth son of the late Thomas Plimsoll, Esq. His mother was Priscilla, daughter of the late Jonas Willing, Esq. He was privately educated by Dr. S. Eadon, M.A., M.D., and married in 1857 Eliza Ann, daughter of the late Hugh Railton, Esq. Mr. Plimsoll's own business being that of a coal merchant, his attention was called to the condition of the English marine service, and the horrible recklessness exhibited towards the sailors, as to their treatment and their lives. In the coal trade Mr. Plimsoll has amassed a large fortune, which he has for some years past been spending freely in furtherance of the great work he has undertaken. His wife sympathizes with him fully, and this true gentleman and lady, with their children, live in the plainest style suitable to their social position, economizing closely in order to have the means wherewith to meet the possible judgments that may attend the libel suits that have beset the agitation inaugurated by him. Moncure D. Conway writes from London * that

"Mr. Plimsoll's madness was not that of the intellect; it was a sort of divine passion, breaking out with thunder and lightning. This man has dwelt on the scene of poor wretches struggling amid the waves to an extent hardly appreciable by the gentlemen of England who live at home at ease. He is a nervous gentleman, too; thin, pale-faced, with an affection of the eyes which makes it necessary for him to wear colored spectacles. He has often reminded me of the portraits of Washington. * * * He and his wife have for many years devoted themselves with absorbing enthusiasm to the work of saving seamen. * * * Mr. Plimsoll was induced to seek a place in Parliament, not by any personal ambition, but purely for the sake of his cause. By his persistent inquiries and agitation he succeeded, against many powerful influences to the contrary, in making out a case for investigation, and the facts brought to light were such that no Government could dare to withhold support from his reform. A week ago he was one of the happiest men in England. At a dinner, where I had the pleasure of meeting him, he said that he had been privately informed by a member of the Government that they had substantially adopted his bill, and meant to put it through. The crowning success of his cause appeared just at hand."

It was upon that exultant moment that Mr Disraeli's cruel nihilism broke like thunder in a clear sky. Mr. Plimsoll however seems to have been prepared. He heard during the day what was coming, and went to the Commons armed for whatever might happen. Early last spring, speaking to a distinguished American who had a wide naval experience and personally knew the great need of Mr. Plimsoll's exertions, that gentleman said that he expected to go to the Tower before his work was accomplished, as there would be no remedy made successful, until the lightning of public indignation had struck

---

* *Cincinnati Commercial*, August 6th, 1875.

those who were fattening on wholesale murder. If Mr. Plimsoll was mad there was evidently method in it.

It has been apparent from the first that the agitation, begun by the member for Derby as a work of pure humanity, had drifted into an issue of political importance, and the last incident bids fair to aid the overthrow of the Disraeli ministry. Mr. Plimsoll's practical defeat of the Conservative Premier is a political blow more severe than the personal insult which Daniel O'Connell aimed at him, when he imagined him to be a lineal descendant of the unrepentant thief on the cross. Mr. Plimsoll, when he published his remarkable volume "Our Seamen" dedicated both the large and cheap editions to "The Lady, Gracious and Kind, who seeing a Laborer working in the rain, sent him her rug to wrap about his shoulders"—thereby recording his admiration of an incident narrated to the honor of the Queen herself. His politics are however of the advanced radical order, and in Parliament and before the people, he votes for and advocates the measures, which are tending so rapidly to making England shoot that Niagara, to which Thomas Carlyle has so vividly referred. Dod's Parliamentary Manual classifies Mr. Plimsoll as an "advanced Liberal." He voted for the disestablishment of the Irish Church in 1869, and with Mr. Miall in 1871; supports Sir Charles Dilke's proposition for a re-distribution of seats, Mr. Trevelyan's bill for the extension of the franchise to Agricultural laborers, demands the abolition of all rate-paying clauses, supports the labor legislation and is an active advocate of arbitration, co-operation, temperance, and national compulsory education. Mr. Plimsoll was a candidate in 1865, but unsuccessful. He was elected in 1868, and was re-elected in 1872. Before entering on this portion of his life, Mr. Plimsoll was known as a successful merchant, the author of important pamphlets on the Export and Indian Trades, published in 1862, and as one of the most efficient of the honorary secretaries to the London Universal Exposition of 1851. He himself says he was induced to seek a seat in Parliament in order that he might thereby advance his agitation, and in the strangely interesting book he has written, "Our Seamen"—all the more attractive because wholly and purposely void of any literary pretensions,—he appeals to the people in this wise: "I do not wish to represent Parliament as indifferent to the interests of workingmen. * * * Parliament will act readily enough if people out of doors make it a prominent question; and, so thoroughly satisfied am I on this point that I begin to doubt whether I was right in trying to get into Parliament with the object of getting this done. It seems to me at least doubtful whether I should not have done better to have endeavored to rouse people out of doors to the urgency of the matter." He then declares that if he fails to obtain a Royal Commission of Inquiry, he shall resign his seat, and do that. "I will then, as God may help me, and with such fellow-workers as I may find, go from town to town, and tell the story of the sailors' wrongs. For, if the workingmen of Sheffield, Leeds, Birmingham, and Manchester only demand justice for these poor men, the thing is done. The workingmen of Derby have done their part; for when, moved by the sailors' wrongs, I asked them to send me to Parliament to seek for justice, they sent me by over 2000 majority." *

---

* "Our Seamen." Popular Edition, Virtue & Co., London, p. 120.

Mr. Plimsoll's sympathies and exertions are, as he states, the result of personal knowledge both of the life of workingmen as a class, and of the particular dangers to which British sailors are exposed. On the latter point, his special experience as a coal merchant and shipper has been supplemented by frequent coasting and other voyages, undertaken for health and amusement. Both Mr. and Mrs. Plimsoll are fond of the sea. On one occasion, they went from London to Hull, on the Yorkshire coast, a voyage which skirts the most dangerous portions of the British shores. The steamer in which they took passage appears to have been greatly overloaded, and a very severe storm was encountered; the vessel, crew, and passengers were in great peril, and in their gratitude for their escape Mr. and Mrs. Plimsoll promised themselves to undertake their present agitation. How well and thoroughly it has been performed, the later incidents which have made Mr. Plimsoll's name a "household word," prove beyond question. The larger part of the expenses have been borne by himself, and all the earlier portion came from his own purse. After the member for Leicester had thoroughly informed himself, as he then believed and has since proved, he prepared a volume, octavo in form, containing photographs of the original documents, drawings, measurements, insurance policies, etc., which he had obtained, beside the remarkable narrative accompanying them. This was published at his own cost, and by him widely distributed. Among the pathetic appeals which abound in this singularly tender and sympathetic exposure of a horrible system, Mr. Plimsoll says: "Now, you who read these pages—somebody shall read them, if I have to give away the whole edition—will you help me to put these things right?* He adds his address and says no one need fear to burden him too heavily with correspondence.

In the pages immediately following, Mr. Plimsoll gives some autobiographical facts, the narration of which heightens the general impression made by a review of his labors—of his genuine simplicity, sincerity, and intensity of character—not lacking by any means in an apt and notable amount of sagacity and adaptation of means to ends. Mention has been made of the social position of his parents. It will appear that Mr. Plimsoll himself, soon after his own active life commenced, was greatly reduced in circumstances, and through that fact came to have the experiences which he thus utilizes to arouse interest in the class for which he pleads:

"I don't wish to disparage the rich, but I think it may be reasonably doubted whether these qualities "—he has alluded in a preceding paragraph to honesty, industry, generous comradeship, and courage—" are so fully developed in them; for, notwithstanding that not a few of them are not unacquainted with the claims, reasonable and unreasonable, of poor relations, these qualities are not in such constant exercise, and riches seem in so many cases to smother the manliness of their possessors, and their sympathies become not so much narrowed as, so to speak, satisfied—they are reserved for the sufferings of their own class, and also the woes of those above them. They seldom tend downward much, and are far more likely to admire an act of high courage, like that of the engine-driver

---

* "Our Seamen." Cheap Edition, Virtue & Co., London, p. 107.

who saved his passengers lately from an awful collision by cool courage, than to admire the constantly exercised fortitude and the tenderness which are the daily characteristics of a British workman's life.

"You may doubt this. I should have once done so myself, but I have shared their lot; I have lived with them. For months and months I lived in one of the model lodging houses, established mainly by the efforts of Lord Shaftesbury. * * * I went there simply because I could not afford a better lodging. * * * Don't suppose I went there from choice—I went from stern necessity—and this was promotion too,—and I went with strong shrinking, with a sense of suffering great humiliation, regarding my being there as a thing to be carefully kept secret from all my old friends. In a word, I considered it only less degrading than spunging upon friends, or borrowing what I saw no chance to pay.

"Now what did I see there? I found the workmen considerate for each other. I found they would go out (those who were out of employment) day after day, and patiently trudge miles and miles seeking employment, returning night after night unsuccessful and dispirited; only, however, to sally out the following morning with renewed determination. * * And I have seen such a man sit down wearily by the fire (we had a common room for sitting and cooking everything), with a hungry, despondent look—he had not tasted food all day—and accosted by another, scarcely less poor than himself, with "Here, mate, get this into thee," handing him at the same time a piece of bread and some cold meat, and afterwards some coffee, and adding: 'Better luck to-morrow; keep up your pecker.' And all this without any idea that they were practising the most splendid patience, fortitude, courage and generosity I had ever seen. You would hear them talk of absent wife and children, sometimes these in a distant workhouse (trade was very bad then), with expressions of affection, and the hope of seeing them again soon; although the one was irreverently alluded to as 'my old woman,' and the latter as 'the kids.'"*

Mr. Plimsoll says he "soon got rid of miserable self pity there." He urges that workingmen are not to be estimated merely from the small per cent. who are idle or of drinking habits. He proceeds to say that "emulous of the genuine manhood all around him, he "set to work again," and by preparing himself more thoroughly for his business "than had previously been considered necessary," he was "soon strong enough to live more in accordance with his previous life." He adds, "but I did not leave all at once. I wanted to learn the lesson well; and though I went reluctantly, I remained voluntarily, because the kindly feelings I took with me had changed into hearty respect and admiration." †

He recites many incidents of mutual and generous help, and gives a number of pathetic incidents of bereaved families encountered by him in the course of the investigations he has made of late years. Mr. Plimsoll deprecates all literary character and merit for his book, and declares that he would not have written it had he not addressed it as a personal appeal to a correspondent. But its effect is in some respects that of almost the highest

---

* "Our Seamen," pp. 108-9. † Ibid. p. 110.

literary art. The explanations relating to the ships are lucid and clear, and at the close the reader has a good idea of the processes of the "homicidal system" which he has fairly denounced as murderous in character. Remembering that the House of Commons which listened awe-struck to Plimsoll's outburst on the 23d of July, which cheered during its progress and only interrupted when he became apparently indecorous, is practically the same assembly that a few years ago greeted Gladstone with ironical cheers and laughter, when he declared the unenfranchised masses of England were "the same flesh and blood" as themselves, and that the London press which derided Disraeli and sustained Plimsoll, is the same that nicknamed the Liberal Statesman "Flesh and Blood" Gladstone, in scorn of his so-called sentimentalism, it cannot but be perceived that the constant infusion of the Democratic spirit, is teaching the supercilious that there is "nothing common or unclean" that the Divine spirit has created and blessed. A London letter in the N. Y. *Herald* cleverly illustrates by the Plimsoll incident how Mr. Disraeli mistakes the present English temper, and finds excuse for indifferentism in the weariness of reformatory politics which there as elsewere, has made for itself a temporary period of recuperation before it goes forward to more serious ends. The correspondent says under date of July 24,[*] that—

"The reign of mutual compliments and good will, of the interchange of bland civility and deferential courtesy which Mr. Disraeli has striven not unsuccessfully to introduce at Westminster, was very

---

[*] N. Y. *Herald*, August 8th, 1775.

suddenly interrupted * * in the House of Commons. The Plimsoll incident I regard as the natural Nemesis upon the principles on which the Prime Minister has undertaken to manage Parliament. Of course, we do not want any more drastic legislation at present. We want to be as we are, at rest, and we are thankful accordingly. But Mr. Disraeli, whose theoretical acquaintance with the English character is as profound as his contempt for its idiosyncratic traits is sincere, chooses to convert what should be merely a season of politic inaction into a period of bland badinage. It was said by Chamfort of the ancient monarchy of France that it was a monarchy tempered by songs; it may be said with equal truth of the government of Mr. Disraeli that it is a despotism tempered by jokes. Perhaps this is the natural reaction after the political asceticism and gloom of the Gladstonian era, just as the excesses of the Stuart Restoration followed upon the artificial severity of Puritanism. But I think Mr. Disraeli has already begun to go too far. His fooling is certainly exquisite, but it is excessive, and the British Senate is beginning to rebel against it."

Mr. Disraeli is himself a compromise, and it is not possible for a man who is intellectually "shifty," to understand the spirit which makes men like Mr. Plimsoll a power. "Flesh and Blood" more than "facts and figures," except as they deal with them, are coming to the front. "A clever mountebank" is the severe judgment some have passed on the English conservative leader. It certainly seems as if the limits of his power were found, but that he is, as yet, unconscious of the fact. His airy reference to the scene in the House of Commons as the "Plimsoll incident," at a subsequent civic dinner, points to this, and his misapprehension of the spirit in which his purpose to throw over a bill for the saving of human life in order that he might avoid the unpopularity of retaining his followers beyond the period at which their annual field sports usually begin, has been received by the people of whom he is now the chief commoner, illustrates his inability to regard a thing so real as any less a compromise than other ordinary political measures.

The *Herald* writer, who is probably Edmund Yates, judged by the internal evidence of the style, says that—

"Mr. Plimsoll may at least boast that he has studied the subject. By profession a coal merchant, he has had large practical insight into the details of our system of marine transit, and it is experience that causes him to feel so profoundly the magnitude of the evil he is bent on remedying. Where, it may be asked, did the opposition to Mr. Plimsoll's movement originate? Where else should it than with the representatives of the shipping interest? The gentry who metaphorically go down to the deep, and whose business is thereon, have no motive in particular for caring for the welfare of their craft or for that of the sailors whom they employ. The former, * * * are heavily insured. The latter are but men who, if they are lost on the high seas, can be replaced easily. Now, the shipping interest—that is, the interest of the ship-owners—is represented with unusual strength in the House of Commons, and it is from the representatives of this class that the resistance to Mr. Plimsoll's agitation proceeds. Rightly or wrongly, Mr. Plimsoll regards Mr. Edward Bates, the member for Plymouth, as the gentleman immediately interested in the perpetuation of these many abuses, and it was the presence of this gentleman which raised the member for Derby to such an intensity of wrath. * * Mr. Bates is a conservative of the new type—a wealthy, one-ideaed merchant, who feels that he has a stake in the country, and that he must protect his interests. The House of Commons is just now swamped with such as these, and Mr. Plimsoll's suspicions are at least plausible. But Mr. Disraeli can afford to offend Mr. Plimsoll, and cannot afford to irritate the plutocrats, shippers, merchants and others who are the backbone of the conservative party."

Mr. Plimsoll's allegations in brief are that under the present English system, or want of one, ships are constantly being sent to sea utterly unfit to encounter the weather; that they are regularly overloaded; that they are in many cases over-insured; and that this fact is a premium on the practice of sending to sea and overloading the most rotten hulls as well as those otherwise unseaworthy, and that sailors, under present legislation are arbitrarily compelled to sail in a vessel, for service in which they have signed articles, though they may afterwards become conscious of her utter unseaworthiness. British seamen can be arrested without warrant, on complaint of owner or captain, and taken aboard their vessel, or if they still refuse to sail, they can, at the option of the authorities, be imprisoned for several months for each offence. An English vessel may, unlike an American built ship, change its name at the owner's will. Here it cannot be done without the consent of Congress, after being once registered. English seamen may be discharged at will in a foreign port; an American shipped crew cannot be so dealt with, unless there be three months' extra wages paid over to the consul for the men's use, and to prevent them becoming a public charge. The bill which Mr. Disraeli roused Mr. Plimsoll's righteous indignation by attempting to postpone, only attempted to extend to the British Board of Trade more power to do what was in principle already conceded to it; namely, to prevent unseaworthy ships from sailing, and to see to it that ships were not overloaded. These two are the practical points towards which Mr. Plimsoll's agitation and demands have lately tended. They do not cover all that he deems necessary. The bill which he himself introduced provides in addition for the compulsory survey of all merchant ships,—a measure which is now optional with the owner. Of the measure brought forward by the Government in place of this one, Mr. G. W. Smalley writes to the New York *Tribune* that the bill "is pregnant with no principle, or none that is new. The object is only to enable the executive to do more rapidly what they can do already: stop unseaworthy vessels about to leave British ports. That power was given by the acts of 1871 and 1873 to the Board of Trade. Under these acts they have during the last two years stopped 558 ships for survey and 58 because overloaded; and all the latter and nearly all the former proved unseaworthy. The process of detention, however, is not summary, and there are not officers enough. The present bill enables the Government to appoint forthwith a sufficient number of officers, with— as far as can be made out from Sir Charles Adderley's rather confused account—powers to stop vessels on their own discretion. The bill does nothing more than this, except to free sailors (when one-fourth of the crew complain that their ship is unseaworthy) from responsibility for costs if she proves not so, and does not oblige them to desert in order to complain. Against inward bound ships, which drown more sailors than outward bound, no power is given."

He adds an account of the opposition indignation to the insufficient measure and writes—

"The *Times* declares that the new bill does not bear out the promise given, and will not do even as a makeshift for the coming winter. The *Standard* itself admits the House did not relish Sir C. Adderley's proposals, and while it does not believe Mr. Plimsoll's bill can be passed, pronounces its principles sound, and advises the Government to adopt it in part. If they refuse, there will still be time for other meetings to repeat the demands of those already held—possibly even to convince the Government that for once it is wiser to legislate in accordance with a public opinion so overwhelming as to be practically unanimous."*

Mr. Plimsoll explains in "Our Seamen" how it is possible to make over-insurance so general. "Lloyd's Underwriters" are not as in the United States, chartered insurance corporations, but private persons and firms, whose general designation is derived from their having first met in "Lloyd's" coffee-room, near the London Exchange. The business is conducted through shipbrokers, who, acting for the owners, proceed to the underwriters' room, and offer the different risks that may have been given them. There are perhaps fifty persons present engaged in marine underwriting, and the several risks may each be divided among one-half or the whole. So if a vessel is lost, the total to each individual or firm is usually too small for them to contest payment, however much they may be convinced of the scandalous nature of the transaction. The ship owners are the power in these cases; not the underwriters, as is usually the case on this side of the Atlantic. It was stated by the secretary of *Lloyd's Register*, an institution unconnected with the underwriters, that no British vessel had been broken up for thirty years past. They are sent to sea until they founder and fall apart from utter rottenness. *Lloyd's Register* or classification is a mercantile convenience which grew up in consequence of the extension of marine underwriting. It is a merely voluntary marine survey, and to honest ship-owners, as Mr. Plimsoll has repeatedly asserted the majority are, a great convenience and advantage, making their ships more saleable, if they

---

* N. Y. *Tribune*, August 9th, 1875.

desire to dispose of them. To follow the details of ship-owning practices, as described by Mr. Plimsoll, would fill a goodly volume. Extracts from speeches made at the Liverpool Trades Congress in April, 1875, by Mr. Plimsoll and some of the delegates—practical shipwrights and workmen—will best illustrate these practices. Mr. Knight, a leading mechanic employed in iron shipbuilding, said: * * "To-day the vessels that were built were composed of the worst materials that could possibly be got. He had seen piles of iron plates punched and almost every two out of three were broken before they were put on the sides of vessels. He had seen the iron so bad that when the plates were open after they had been fastened to the side they could not be caulked with the proper material because the iron would not stand it. Another thing to be complained of was inferior workmanship; and this arose to a great extent from the abolishing of the apprentice system. Scarcely one lad out of thirty employed in the yards was ever bound to the trade of iron shipbuilder. Men went into the yards at the ages of 24 to 27, having worked before in attending masons. Other evils were the cutting down of prices by employers, and piece work. * * * The piece-work system only made even good men scamp their work, because the prices were so low they could not make a living at their work. There should also be an inspection of ships by practical men." Mr. Morgan, a ship-carpenter, described wooden ships so rotten that a stick could almost be driven through their sides, and said he had worked himself on a ship where in order to drive and fasten a staple an iron plate had to be placed on the other side.

Mr. Mathew Callahan, Treasurer of the "Liverpool Seamen's Protective Society," offered a resolution to support a measure embodying the following principles:—

1. "That there shall be a compulsory periodical survey of all merchant ships, under the authority of the Board of Trade, such survey to include the hull, spars, sails, rigging, machinery, and gear, to prevent ships being sent to sea in an unseaworthy condition; 2, that an officer of the Board of Trade shall inspect the forecastle for the accommodation of the seamen, and the quality and quantity of the stores and provisions for the sailors; 3, that there shall be a load-line or conspicuous mark on each vessel, showing the depth of loading and of surplus buoyancy, and that some rule of freeboard be enforced to prevent vessels being overladen; 4, that each ship, according to her tonnage, shall be efficiently manned by able seamen; that examinations in practical seamanship be established, and certificates of competency be granted to able seamen, the use of false certificates to be punished as a misdemeanor; 5, that apprenticeships be restored under proper regulations and conditions, and that the number of foreigners in British ships be limited to at least one-third of the crew; 6, that advance notes be abolished, and in lieu thereof that allotment notes be granted of two-thirds the monthly pay to those who require it for the use of their families; 7, that wages due to seamen be paid immediately on the termination of the voyage, or if not paid within two days, that they be compensated with extra pay for being kept waiting; 8, that punishment for breach of contract, or of articles of agreement by owners, or masters and crew, be placed on a footing of perfect equality; 9, that local admiralty courts be established in all ports for the settlement of disputes."

Mr. Plimsoll is a popular as well as an excitable speaker. His words do not halt by the way, but usually muster and march with speed, swift to the purpose before him. He has no hesitation in using good, simple Anglo-Saxon terms, and is as direct in public meetings as he was before the House of Commons, when he described the "burglarious intention" with which his bill was "burked;" or of speaking of the "maritime murderers inside and outside the House," who aim to "secure a continuance of the murderous system." The expressive epithet of "Ship-knackers" applied to a class of men who never own a sound ship, and seldom any, but charter old and worthless crafts, and send them to destruction and their crews to death, is a term which in England will be enjoyed for its racy directness. There is a regular occupation, in London and other large cities, of men known as the "Knackers." It consists in buying old and worn-out horses, as well as buying and removing dead ones. If there is any work left in the former it is utilized till the last. Then the animal is killed. The flesh is generally converted into food for dogs and cats, in the sale of which there is a large trade and a considerable number of persons employed. To say that a horse is only fit for the "Knackers' yard" is to say that it ought to be dead. The applicability of the term to the purchaser of rotten ships can readily be made. At Liverpool Mr. Plimsoll said:—

"There were people who bought old ships, and only old ships—who never had a good ship, and never meant to have a good ship—and sent them to sea; and the public curiosity was excited to know what the government meant to do to stop that sort of thing, and who the people were who could sleep in their beds when their bread was, so to speak, made out of dead men's bones." *

---

* From a return issued July, 1875, by the Board of Trade, it appears that of the total number of vessels detained by the Board of Trade under the Act of 1873, for "alleged unseaworthiness," there were found seaworthy, 15; found unseaworthy, 464; survey pending, 18—total stopped, 497. Forty-eight more were stopped for "alleged overloading," and the Return states that "in no instance in which the Act has been put in force has the allegation of overloading or improper loading been found groundless."

Again, in describing the manner in which ships' hulls were weakened by lengthening amidships and other ways, he said in the same speech that—

"* * He had since given information of two ships which were single riveted where they ought to be double riveted, which were cut in two and lengthened with the same scantling, and in which big beams had been cut away to make room for tanks, steam engines, and thrashing machines, without proper means having been taken to strengthen them. He thought people who were content to make money like that—well! they used to hang people; and they had hanged a great many people who were better than some ship-owners."

In retorting on a ship-owner who was present, spoke to the Congress and had described his speech as "sensational," Mr. Plimsoll said:—

"He had no doubt it was, because he felt strongly on the subject; but it was a very sensational thing to be drowned, and he wanted to stop that."

It is this intense sincerity which has made Mr. Plimsoll a power, which will keep him a popular public man in other movements, and which prevented his anger in the House of Commons from becoming merely sensational, and lent to the solemn denunciation with which he closed his very remarkable protest, somewhat of the same spirit that must have dictated the words which he quotes with such terrible force:

"In the name of the God of all justice and of all mercy I protest against any further delay. I demand that the Merchant Shipping bill be proceeded with from this hour *de die in diem* until through committee, and failing this, I lay upon the head of the Prime Minister and his fellows the blood of all the men who shall perish next winter from preventible causes, and I denounce against him and against them the wrath of that God who hath said, 'Ye shall not afflict any widow or fatherless child. If thou afflict them in any wise, and they cry at all unto me, I will surely hear their cry, and my wrath shall wax hot, and I will kill you with the sword, and your wives shall be widows, and your children fatherless.' How much hotter must be his indignation and wrath against those who reduce unhappy women and children to that deplorable condition, and who leave their own fellow-creatures, guilty of no crime, to a violent and sudden death!"

Mr. Plimsoll's personal and public vindication was rendered complete by his subsequent withdrawal of the unparliamentary language used in the House, without retraction of any alleged facts as stated by him in his memorable outbreak. To this was added the subsequent passage of a Shipping Bill, which provides provisionally for two of Mr. Plimsoll's important demands:—1. The appointment of competent surveyors to examine ships as to their seaworthiness; 2. Allowing one-fourth of a crew to lay complaint, or if their number exceeds twenty, any five of them, and requiring the examination of a vessel as to overloading or seaworthiness, without being required to give surety for cost of detention, as now required. Mr. Plimsoll gave notice before the session of Parliament closed, that he should move at the next session for a Commission of inquiry into marine insurance, its nature, risks, business, etc., and should press a more elaborate measure for the protection of life and property at sea.

XIII.

SIR WILFRED LAWSON.

THE habits of the English people are so fixed,—especially in the maintenance of their personal customs, as not to be lightly dealt with. No one obtaining entrance into public life and selfishly seeking public favor would deliberately select, if choosing an issue or hobby to champion, such a one as the subject of this sketch has taken under guardianship. The last place in the kingdom, wherein to advocate the Prohibitory Liquor Law, would seem to be the House of Commons. There are men of single ideas and purposes who have won large places for themselves, in a legislative body, which though flattered as the "best club in Europe," often appears to a looker-on to be a nearer approach to a bear garden, and is moreover an assembly whose prejudices are more easily roused and more difficult to overcome than is the case with any other similar body in the world. And of all questions on which to obtain a hearing, or through which to become recognized and esteemed, that of liquor legislation would appear to be the most dubious.

Sir Wilfred Lawson, Bart., President of the United Kingdom Temperance Alliance, and author of the "Permissive Liquor Bill," has however accomplished that remarkable feat. A recent letter published in the Boston *Post* says of the member for Carlisle,—the city formerly so long represented by Lord John Manners,—that:

"Sir Wilfred's special hobby is prohibition. He as regularly introduces a "Permissive Bill" into the House of Commons every year as the late Mr. Berkeley, of Bristol, did a "Ballot Bill," thinking perhaps that by a similar persistency he will meet with a similar final success. He is the chief of the famous United Kingdom Temperance Alliance, a large and powerful body, with £150,000 at its disposal, and having the object of promoting temperance by political enactment. But Sir Wilfred is far from being a stiff and sour fanatic. Strange to say, this great temperance advocate, who absolutely refuses to let the House live in peace, never bores it, and is always welcome when he rises to speak. He is in fact one of the most genial and popular of all Her Majesty's knights and burgesses. Not only a prohibitionist, but also a radical of radicals, he is yet socially hand in glove with the most obstinate of Tory squires in the House. He puts his case in so witty and genial a way that even the twenty-five brewers who sit as members of Parliament cannot find it in their hearts to stay away from the treat of hearing him. Moreover, he has wit—I doubt if there is a wittier speaker in England; certainly, since the defeat of Bernal Osborne, he has not a rival for wit in the House of Commons. He does not pretend to be a teetotaller, nor does he profess to desire to enact teetotalism as a statute. He essays to provide a mild check upon the intemperance of the country. Indeed, for a rider of a hobby, Sir Wilfred is exceedingly reasonable and moderate." On the last occasion of introducing the permissive bill, which is regularly done at every session, "there were nearly five hundred members—a remarkable House—present to listen to him.".

This Parliamentary leader of the temperance issue, is the eldest son of the late Sir Wilfred Lawson, Baronet, of Brayton, Cumberland, and is now himself the wearer of the title and possessor of the family estate. A remarkable individuality of character and ability evidently runs through the family. The Baronet's brother, William, now a resident of Massachusetts, is very well known to many persons in the United States, having travelled extensively therein, and having been a careful student of our institutions, and also from his connection with a remarkable agricultural co-operative experiment at Blennerhassett Farm, near Brayton, the results of which he has told in a very interesting volume.* In the first chapter Mr. Lawson describes the method followed by his father in educating his sons. He says :—

"I had the advantage of being the son of parents who were more anxious that their children should be happy and good than that they should be learned or great. My father had my education conducted—in a religious manner—at home, where I acquired a little Latin and Greek, and a few other things; and where, as is the case with many other youths, anything in the shape of lessons were not attractive to me, and I learned as little as possible. I had,

---

* "Ten Years of Gentleman Farming."

before I was eighteen, travelled several times on the Continent of Europe, and had visited Egypt and Palestine; but circumstances never brought me in contact with rich or great people, and I had not much of what is called "*knowledge of the world;*" nor, as I always had the prospect of enough wealth to enable me to live without working, did I form what are called "business habits." Trained as a shooter of animals, a hunter of Cumberland beasts with hounds, and a trapper of vermin, I found myself in the spring of 1861, in my 25th year, without an occupation; without many acquaintances,—except among the poor, whom I had not learned to despise because they spoke bad grammar, and took their coats off to work;—and without the reputation of having been successful in any undertaking except that of the mastership and huntsmanship of my brother's fox-hounds."

The younger brother takes life seriously—like Mr. Gladstone "on the Treasury benches," he is always in earnest,—and being without the genial humor and clear wit of his brother, the Baronet, could not and does not make a fair public appearance. But the allusions made to their paternal home show the character of the influences that surrounded them both, illustrating how in their own way each has struggled for the amelioration and advancement of their country and its people.

The temperance agitation in Great Britain, though often marked with features somewhat akin to the fever and excitement of the Moody and Sankey "revivals,"—as witness Father Mathew's crusade and progress,—has not, as in the United States, had the support of any considerable body belonging to the "ruling" and respectable classes.

Not until late years has it exercised a perceptible influence on public opinion, in any wide spread or national sense.

"The United Kingdom Temperance Alliance," which had before confined itself to "moral suasion" entirely, took a "new departure" in October, 1857, and commenced an agitation in behalf of the Permissive Liquor bill. The purpose of the measure is shown by the following statement: The bill provides that on application of any District (meaning the civil divisions called parishes, or the boroughs and any sub-division of them ;) the votes of the rate-payers shall be taken as to the propriety of adopting the provisions of this act ; but that a two-third vote shall be necessary for any affirmative. When adopted it prohibits all liquor traffic in the District for common purposes. In other words the Lawson bill is in intent similar to the measures offered in several of our State Legislatures under the name of "local option" laws. The first division had in the House of Commons was in 1863, and polled forty members in the affirmative. In 1869, the bill received ninety-four votes.

The out-of-door agitation has been persistent; growing year by year in activity and interest. The *Times* has treated Sir Wilfred Lawson and the Alliance with more than ordinary respect ; the most significant tribute which has as yet been paid to the movement's growth and importance. The "Licensed Victuallers Association," as the Guild or Trades society of inn-holders and keepers of public houses is termed, is a wealthy and powerful body, exercising a great influence and welded together by the strongest ties of self-interest. It represents an important "vested interest,"—one of those which a British legislator ordinarily regards as specially committed to his cares. "Interests," not men and women, except as their well being affects, "interests" and property, are regarded as the chief object of solicitude for which that remarkable mixture of fiction and fact, precedents and principles, known as the "British Constitution," was believed to have been framed and recognised. An examination of Hansard will show that the "Malt Tax," and excise regulations in relation to this traffic, have occupied a very large share of legislative attention during the last half century. From the drinking habits of the people, the Government derives a considerable portion of its revenue. The consumption of articles paying duty or excise, as intoxicating liquors, was per capita, at the dates named, as follows:

	1853	1863	1873
Wine, gallons,	0.25	0.35	0.56
Malt, bushels,	1.49	1.67	1.98
Spirits, home and foreign, gall.	1.10	0.85	1.23

As compared with imported or exciseable articles of food, such, for instance, as bacon, butter, cheese, eggs, sugar, tea, etc., the proportion is quite large, though probably not so much so as it appears in the common arguments of the Alliance advocates. In the foregoing figures it will be perceived that the increase in twenty years of the consumption of wines and of spirits, is much greater than that of malt liquors. Still the intelligence of the British masses is so great a fact in the sum-total of their improvidence, pauperism and vice, that it is really strange that the Alliance had not at an earlier day the support of the many notable persons who are now found on its platforms, or contributing to its at present large fund. As now constituted, it does not follow that all who sustain its efforts are themselves abstainers from all intoxicating liquors. Sir Wilfred Lawson himself does not make strenuous demands for this, or do more than urge, as he did in a notable speech at Sunderland, that Parliament "go to the people" with the question he presents. He said:

"I won't touch the licensing power with my tongue. For generations the House of Commons has protected over it; and the cleverest men have tried their hands at it, and I am not going to make a fool of myself by trying to bring in any licensing bill."

This was doubtless said in reference to the advice repeatedly urged by the Hon. John Bright and others with whom Sir Wilfred Lawson has acted in all other political matters, that he should draft and present some stringent license measure, for which they could all vote.

"That," continued the Baronet, "is not the object of my bill. We leave the licenses with the magistrates, if licenses are to be granted at all; but we move the previous question; we say, go to the people and ask whether they want licenses at all; we go in the old-fashioned way. I say, keep the power of electing the best men in the best houses; bad as they are at the best, go on doing the best. In those places where the people, by a large majority, say we will have no licenses, there the magistrates shall stop their evil work, and the people shall be free."

The strength of this agitation, or rather of its effects, may be seen in the fact that the passage, in 1872, of a law shortening the hours to which public houses could be kept open at night, giving more power to magistrates assembled in the Quarter Sessions, to grant or withdraw licenses, and requiring a register of all offences committed in public houses and under the influence of liquor, aided very materially in the defeat of Mr. Gladstone's ministry when, soon after, Parliament was dissolved, and an appeal was made to the country. The "Licensed Victuallers" with the brewers and distillers, exerted themselves to the utmost against the Ministry and its supporters. It speaks well for Sir Wilfred Lawson's personal popularity that he was returned for Carlisle, as before, at the head of the poll.

In the House of Commons Sir Wilfred Lawson is among those whom the author of "Men and Manner in Parliament" notes as independent members. After a witty reference to the length of Mr. Mundella's speeches, this author writes: "It is a pleasant change when, from the seat below, Sir Wilfred Lawson rises to discourse on the evils of the liquor traffic or the evils of war. 'The honorable and amusing baronet,' as Mr. Knatchbull-Hugessen, himself never guilty of being amusing, peevishly called him, has done what few men have accomplished. He has thrown an air of gentility over teetotalism, and has made 'a man with a mission' a welcome interloper in debate in the House of Commons. As a rule Parliament votes men with missions impracticable bores, and will not listen to them. But it is always ready to hear Sir Wilfred Lawson, and is rarely disappointed in its expectation of being interested and amused."

He has a way of seizing a commonplace idea, dressing it up in some incongruous fashion, and suddenly producing it for the consideration of the House of Commons. The simple glory of war was illustrated by Sir Wilfred Lawson "when, a few nights after both Houses of Parliament had voted their thanks to Sir Garnet Wolseley and his troops, he incidentally summed up the practical results of the expedition as being comprised in Great

Britain's having gained possession of "a treaty and an old umbrella." *

In further illustration of Sir Wilfred Lawson's power of graphic illustration and humorous wit, T. H. S. Escott, a keen and observing writer, speaks of the Baronet as redeeming the session of 1874 from the "absolute dulness of monotony." He thus describes the House on one of the Permissive Bill divisions:—

"Let the reader suppose that it is a Wednesday in June. The speaker took the chair at 12 o'clock. The motions and notices of motion are speedily dispatched, and it is understood that Sir Wilfred Lawson will be allowed, for the ventilation of his hobby, the period that must elapse before the hour hand of the clock, just under the Peer's gallery, points to the fatal ten minutes to six. On hearing the order of the day, Sir Wilfred merely moves that the Bill be read a second time, reserving himself for its fuller advocacy till later in the afternoon. It is but a languishing and wearisome talk up to three o'clock. The Speaker, bored presumably to exhaustion, adjourns for a chop, returning in ten minutes. Sir Wilfred Lawson rises; * * and in a very short time the house is full. It is Sir Wilfred Lawson's special vocation to show that compulsory teetotalism and solemn dulness need not go together, that

---

* "No Treaty!" shouted out an honorable member anxious for truth, "well, never mind!" said Sir Wilfred; it doesn't much matter, for I don't suppose the treaty would be worth any more than the umbrella?' The honorable baronet's style of speaking is well suited to his humor, and greatly adds to its effect. He does not * * make a speech to the House. He just has a chat with it, and being a man of sense and humor he is a thoroughly enjoyable companion.—"Men and Manner in Parliament," pp. 152–4.

cold water and witticisms are not necessarily inconsistent, and that the praises of Rechabitism afford just as good an opportunity for the exhibition of sportive fancy and a lively humor as lyrical panegyrics on the most exquisite vintage of France or the Rhine. * * Sir Wilfred Lawson is always ready to relieve the monotony of business, and, even though the theme of total abstinence is not under discussion to lend him its glowing inspiration, he will find his inspiration in any casual topic that may crop up. When the honorable baronet is fairly launched upon his theme, every alternate sentence that drops from his lips is the signal for an outburst of 'loud laughter.' He welcomes those ebullitions of merriment, as he informs his audience, with grateful satisfaction, for the cause which at first provokes smiles is, he remarks, generally in the end crowned with triumph." *

But amused as is the House of Commons at the speeches of the champion of this legislation, it is not to be set down that Sir Wilfred Lawson is no more than the " Professor of the art of buffoonery," which Mr. Escott says, in speaking of him, that the House of Commons requires to make up its usual characteristic. He is, on the contrary, a very cool, clear-headed, logical and persistent worker in a yet unpopular field, who uses the intellectual weapons at his disposal with an effect which is yearly becoming more apparent in the gains the movement he leads is making in Parliament and before the country. In general politics, Sir Wilfred Lawson is counted among the more moderate Radicals;

---

* "The House of Commons: its 'Personnel' and its Oratory." *Fraser's*, October, 1874.

interested mainly in ameliorative policies and measures, such as National Education—Arbitration as a substitute for War, and for strikes and lock-outs in labor disputes,—the reduction of taxes and extension of the franchise. He votes with Mr. Plimsoll for legislation to procure the protection of seamen, with Mundella, Macdonald, Morley, Burt, Cowen, and others in matters of labor legislation, with Prof. Fawcett on matters of education, pauperism, woman's suffrage and measures of a social, economical character, while on general politics he follows the lead of Mr. Gladstone. Though he is one of a class, small but increasing, who "sit below the gangway" of the House, and are counted as "Independents," a cordial and sincere support was given by Sir Wilfred Lawson to Mr. Gladstone when in power, and to the party when in opposition. In the country, before the masses, the temperance baronet steadily gains in general influence and personal popularity.

Sir Wilfred Lawson's last conspicuous appearance in Parliament was during the debate on the proposed visit of the Prince of Wales to India, and his speech was thus described by the vivacious Lander, correspondent of the Louisville (Ky.) *Courier-Journal,* for August 9, 1875:

"Later, Sir Wilfred Lawson, celebrated as the originator and staunch supporter of the permissive liquor bill made the telling speech of the evening. He took exception to Mr. Macdonald's statement—Mr. Macdonald being ostensibly a workingman's representative—that the workingmen took a great deal of interest in this question: 'Why the House of Commons has reduced itself to such a position that very few people take any interest in their proceedings.' At this sally the House roared. Sir Wilfred would have been glad to hear that the Prince was going to make a private visit to India. He was one who commiserated and sympathized with princes. They really deserved sympathy; for they were barred from public life, and if they went into the army, it was said their promotion was the result of favoritism. Altogether they had hard lines, for all they were permitted to do was to provide vapid amusements for stupid people. They could not go out of doors without being stared at by mobs, while next day the penny-a-liners devoted columns to their movements. He did not wonder at the Prince getting very tired of all that sort of thing—tired of laying foundation stones, opening institutions, uncovering statues, and eating charity dinners. If the Prime Minister had proposed it on the ground that the Prince wanted pastime, Sir Wilfred would have had great difficulty in opposing him; but he said that the travelling was to educate the Prince, and a friend of his on the Opposition Bench connected with India told Sir Wilfred that it was desirable that the future ruler of India should become acquainted with the subjects he would have to govern. This Sir Wilfred disputed altogether, for the whole constitutional doctrine of England is that the king reigns, but does not govern. If this was to be an educational mission to teach some one to govern India, why not send the Prime Minister? The Prime Minister has stated that the Prince of Wales ought to be placed on his travels in a position that would impress India with the dignity and station he occupied, but the sum of £140,000 would enable them to do nothing of the sort. Why, all the great Mogul people would beat him quite hollow. He could not compete with them in magnificence and pomp, and, if they outdid him, more harm than good would be done. England got possession of India by an admixture of force and fraud, and now holds it by force. She can only continue to hold it by fair and honest dealing, and not by indulging in costly shams. 'Hear! hear!' and unlimited 'oh's and laughter greeted Sir Wilfred Lawson's effective, witty speech, of which I have given a meagre skeleton. When he clapped the climax by saying that if there was the shadow of a shade of dissatisfaction with monarchy, it was provoked by such votes as this, there were cries of 'Divide,' which, however, passed unheeded."

XIV.

EDWARD MIALL.

THE power of agitation has received, in the life of the ex-member for Bradford—the Editor of the *Nonconformist* and the animating spirit and organizer of the "Liberation Society"—one of its most conspicuous examples. Studying the history of the Established Church of Great Britain, and observing how closely it is interlinked with every governing interest; how it is interwoven with the crown and its dignity; with the landed and hereditary aristocracy and its supremacy; with the history and splendors and policy of every phase of English life since the Eighth Henry made it a political body and dependent on the State, it is difficult now to realize how near that great establishment is to its downfall. When this is once comprehended, it is easy also to see that like that of the blind Sampson in the temple, its destruction will be followed by that of other long cherished institutions. But what is not so easy of comprehension is to recognize how much of this swiftly approaching result is due to the energetic spirit of one man—Edward Miall—who has literally spent himself in the work of preparation. For several years he sat in the House of Commons as member for Bradford, Yorkshire, the principal centre of English woollen manufactures. Ill health prevented Mr. Miall from becoming a candidate at the last general election, and it is not probable that he will ever again endeavor to secure a seat. Yet, he remains a distinct and positive force, to be counted upon in the sum of English Radical efforts. The author of "Men and Manner in Parliament," speaking of those who have "Fallen from the Ranks," writes that " Mr. Miall is missed, though not for the sake of his charms of oratory. To tell the truth, there were few speakers in the House more painful to listen to. 'His style was of the worst order of Dissenting preaching, and there was a specially painful vigor in the way he was wont to wrestle with himself for words—pumping them out one by one as if they came from a well in which the gearing had got out of order—that could not be excelled by any young student fresh to the conventicle from college, and desirous of impressing critical deacons with the amount of wisdom which must underlie utterances so weightily deliberate. It is, however, probable that this mannerism, which had of late years grown upon him, was the outcome of that failing health and strength which finally resulted in his retirement from public life; and it speaks eloquently for Mr. Miall's force of character that in spite of such personal disadvantages, and though known as the uncompromising advocate of principles peculiarly obnoxious to the majority of his fellow-members, he always compelled the respectful attention of the House of Commons, and carried into his retirement the assurance that his absence would be regretted and his place not easily filled."*

While this critic has overdrawn the disadvantages of Mr. Miall's method and manner as a speaker, there is no doubt that he is not gifted in that direction. The matter is more imposing than the manner, and his speeches are capital "campaign" documents, bristling as they do with facts, well presented, and clothed in that nervous and vigorous English of which Mr. Miall is a master. As a controversial writer the editor of the *Nonconformist* is among the most influential and trenchant. A fair specimen of his nervous style may be found in the following extracts from a critical paragraph in relation to the Hon. W. E. Forster, written at the time of Mr. Gladstone's retirement from the leadership of the Liberal party. The article has significance in that it outlines Mr. Miall's views, and enters an objection to Mr. Forster's leadership, growing out of the famous debate on the Education Act of 1872, herein alluded to.

"Mr. Forster's qualifications for leading the Liberal party in ordinary times are pre-eminent. He is a rugged speaker; but he can generally speak, and forcibly too, to the point. His industry is indomitable. His political knowledge is extensive, and, within certain limits, varied. His political sympathies incline more steadily towards democratic views than towards those which terminate in oligarchical rule. He is a favorite in the House, but more so among those who sit opposite to him than among those who sit behind him. He is candid, flexible, and courteous to his foes—less so, even in his Parliamentary speeches, to his friends. What he may be in the lobbies to the former, we do not know. What he is to the latter, we cannot profess to admire; he is not conciliatory, he is not attractive; he has no healing or binding influence. * * * He would probably fitly and fully ex-

---

* "Men and Manner in Parliament," p. 33.

press the wishes of the party in relation to topics within a purely secular range. His views (unless we have mistaken them) are characterized by breadth, generosity, faith, and courage. But opinion—and, we may add, Parliamentary opinion—is approaching another and a much higher class of questions. Not even Mr. Forster can long postpone a consideration of ecclesiastical policy. How is he disposed to deal with that huge and richly endowed monopoly which, while its very existence overrides every sentiment of justice, is rapidly tending in practice to give enormous development to sacerdotal assumptions? We do not ask his opinion of disestablishment. * * * But in what direction will Mr. Forster be likely to lead the House? * * * We believe he has very little spiritual sentiment—for he has avowed as much—and that his ecclesiastical outlook, if he has ever distinctly shaped it to his own mind, is predominantly Erastian, and would ultimately rest upon 'concurrent endowment.' Now, men deeply interested in freeing religious institutions from State support and control, can take no active part in committing the leadership of the Liberals to a statesman so completely at variance with themselves upon what they regard as the most important political problem of the present age. They have no choice but to refuse binding themselves to an allegiance they could not conscientiously render."

Mr. Miall is the leader of those in England who accept the voluntary method, who desire the entire disseverance of the State from all religious bodies, believing that under such conditions only can the broadest religious activity and progress prevail. They hold the same view with regard to the public schools, seeking the entire separation of all denominational influence from the elementary training, which they desire shall be had at the public expense.

The struggle by which Mr. Miall and his friends are able to look from their Mount Pisgah, and into what they deem the Promised Land, is full of interest to the historical student. The statute books are not entirely free from provisions requiring and compelling the Christian

Dissenter to pay rates for the purpose of sustaining the Established Church and its priests. Not many years have elapsed since Lord Mansfield delivered a famous opinion by which he declared "that non-conformity being no longer a crime, the natural liberty of the Subject was in favor of the Dissenter." The passage of the Toleration Act, he said, "renders that which was illegal before, now legal; the Dissenters' way of worship is permitted and allowed by this Act; it is not only exempted from punishment, but rendered innocent and lawful; it is established, it is put under the protection, and is not merely under the connivance of the law." Disabilities remained. The Dissenters' inability to take the form of oath required, prevented them from holding office, or, for a time, of sitting in Parliament, and until within a few years from being educated in the State Universities. During the last fifty years or so, the more public spirited among them, especially the Quakers, maintained a passive resistance to the collections of tithes, church rates, and Easter dues, just as at the present time they oppose the payment of rates and fees for school purposes, which are, it is charged, practically made denominational in character. In the old agitation, the more determined allowed their goods to be distrained rather than voluntarily pay such taxes. It became an understood policy at the sale of such distrained goods, not to bid against the owner, and so the "church" got in general more scorn than profit. So odious became these seizures, that Parliament slowly and at long intervals, passed acts compromising the rates in some way, and in a few instances abolished them altogether.

The more recent and directly national and political

bearings of the issues relative to "Church and State," have, however, gathered around the active public life of Edward Miall. What some of these are in a more directly social and personal way, is stated by the *British Quarterly* in an article reviewing a debate in the House of Commons. It refers to Sir Roundell Palmer's defensive reply that the "Establishment no longer inflicts wrong on those who think it right to dissent;" and says: "Whatever may be the case in the great centres of population, it is certain that in the small towns, and especially in the rural districts," where it is asserted the Church is a great blessing, "petty persecution, aiming at the suppression of dissent, is as rife as when the Establishment would persecute by law. Is the dissenter a farmer? He is kept by church landlords and landladies out of a whole district, as carefully as the rinderpest itself. * * Is he a shop-keeper? He must hold his head low, and consent to sell his principles with his wares, or he loses half his custom. * * * Is he poor? So much the worse for him, when coal, blankets and soap are distributed at Christmas; when parochial charities, intended to be unsectarian, are dispensed, or when misfortune makes him a fitting object for the help and sympathy of all his neighbors." "Nay," continues the reviewer, "he may be wholly independent" of all pecuniary considerations, equal in fortune, culture, grace, refinement to the more fortunate, but he also "pays the penalty for conscientious non-conformity in the social exclusion and the haughty contempt" which makes English country life so hard to bear.*

---

* "Mr. Miall's motion for Disestablishment," *British Quarterly Review*, July, 1871, p. 183.

The editor of the *Nonconformist* is a son of Moses and Sarah Miall, of Portsmouth, and was born in 1809. He is therefore in the sixty-sixth year of his age. Belonging to a family prominently identified with the congregational body, Edward, with two of his brothers, was educated for the ministry, at Wymondley, Hertfordshire, in a theological institution founded by a Mr. Coward, and in after years consolidated with the new College, St. John's Wood, London. After his ordination he was called to Leicester, as the pastor of an Independent Chapel there. His induction into the ministry was at a time when England fermented with the Reform Law and Emancipation agitations, and there naturally grew up a searching consideration of the relations of "Church and State," with the connections between "civil and religious liberty," which latter was then the shibboleth of the Whig party. From the ranks of the non-conforming sects in England has often come the impulse and movement which has led to great reforms. Divisions in their own midst, during the earliest years of Mr. Miall's ministerial life, as to the limits of agitation, and how they should allow themselves to participate therein, led him to a careful consideration of these questions. The country Dissenters considered themselves in advance of those who lived in the metropolis and larger cities. Doubtless they were, for it is easy to understand that disabilities, legal and social, would be more perceptibly annoying in localities where the "peer," "squire," and "rector" held almost undisputed sway. In the cities, clergymen and their principal laity constituted a society sufficiently large and cultured enough to relieve themselves from personal annoyance. Under the impulse given by the Reform Bill of 1837, the provincial Dissenters felt that they must organize. Several associations were in operation at this time,—one, the "Ecclesiastical Knowledge Society," undertaking the task of publishing all matter relating to legal disabilities and church oppressions. Another was known as "the Religious Freedom Society." Neither of these efforts was other than tentative in character, and they were aimed solely or principally at the redress of "practical grievances," such as a church-rate seizure, or any personal or social wrong-doing on the part of their politico-ecclesiastical opponents.

It was this want of broad and logical basis and purpose to their movements that brought Edward Miall to the front, and created the *Nonconformist* newspaper, and the "Society for the Liberation of Religion from State patronage and control." Its original designation was that of "The British Anti-State-Church Association." This was found cumbersome and inexpressive—for it by no means embodied the principles on which the movement was founded. There were and are many advocates of "concurrent endowment" by the State of all religious worship, while Mr. Miall and his associates desire entire freedom from State aid or political control. The movement originated in the Midland and manufacturing counties, and seems to have created some surprise elsewhere. The direction of this effort centered at Leicester, and through Mr. Miall was not there pre-eminent, it owed much of its early activity to his energy and zeal. It was determined to publish an organ, under the name it now bears—the *Nonconformist*. A writer in the *Beehive*, sketching the life of its editor, says:—

"The prominence subsequently given to the name, person, and labors of Mr. Miall in the matter, was, as some would have regarded it, a thing of the merest fortuity; but others are inclined, no doubt, to take a very different view. We believe we are but stating the simple fact when we relate that he and his friend, the Rev. J. P. Mursell, came to town at the request of others to engage as the editor of the projected journal a gentleman of undoubted sympathy in their opinion and object, as well as of the highest eminence and of tried experience as a public writer. In this errand they did not succeed. As they returned, they were pacing together the railway platform at Rugby waiting for the Leicester train. Suddenly, as the circumstance is told, Mr. Mursell said to his companion, "you must do it yourself." The answer of Mr. Miall was to the effect that the idea was altogether new to him; and it was easy to conceive much of what would immediately come to the lips of a man committed to the Christian ministry, settled to his mind as pastor of a church, and with a rising family to be considered in any new movement he might be solicited to make. However, Mr. Mursell pressed his suggestion in a form sufficiently impressive to obtain from his friend a promise that he would not then put a final negative upon it, but would, before answering yes or no, give it that deep and serious consideration which such a proposal so urged demanded at his hands."

Having undertaken the work, he left his active ministerial labors, and has ever since devoted himself to the work he has since performed. How great the task, can only be fully understood by a thorough apprehension of the conditions by which it has been surrounded. The Established

Church and its patronage has been, with remarkable sagacity, interwoven into every part of the political and social conditions that have governed England since the Reformation. It is enormously wealthy, its annual income being variously estimated at from sixty to ninety million dollars. The Episcopate is, politically speaking, an important portion of the system; the two Archbishops and twenty-seven Bishops being practically appointed by the Crown. Nominally, they are elected by the diocesan clergy, but that is only a form, as the Queen sends to the Synod a letter or *congé d'élire*, naming the person selected. They are only required to ratify the nomination, and have not power to reject. There are 13,261 benefices in the Church, all of which are the subject of public or personal patronage. The congregations or communicants, as such, have no power of selection or right of choice, and the vestry is entrusted only with civil functions; care of buildings, collection of rates and tithes, etc., as also certain powers over the parish in the way of assessing and disbursing money, providing for the poor, schools, etc. These latter functions have been curtailed of late years. The "rector," or "incumbent," becomes thereby possessed of certain privileges, landed and magisterial in many instances. The Crown holds a number of livings at its bestowal; there are 4,521 in the gift of members of the House of Lords. The Bishops sit therein as "Peers Spiritual." Catholic patrons are required to transfer the gift of their livings to the Crown. A considerable number, nearly as many in fact as are in the gift of the Peers, are at the disposal of private gentlemen and ladies. The Universities and other institutions are also largely possessed of this patronage.

It was no wonder then that Warburton should declare that the Church "has been of old the cradle and the throne of the younger nobility," or that Goldwin Smith speaks of it as "a mere bulwark of the oligarchy." Mr. Gladstone himself sounded the key-note to its downfall when he declared, in 1836, speaking in the House of Commons, that—"A Church establishment is maintained for the sake of its doctrines, not of its members—they have no right whatever to an advantage over other subjects of the State." The eloquent churchman was defending the establishment, while in truth he gave the key-note for its assailants. The diversity of doctrines it shelters produces sub-divisions, almost as numerous as the articles of faith on which it is presumed to be founded. As the Dean of Canterbury acknowledges in a notable review of some "Nonconformist essays,"*—"The first step for an Anglican apologist must ever be the abandonment of logic. * * Any one of his arguments, which begin so fairly, will, if carried out, land him either in Rome or Geneva." He adds, however, that this is not to be regarded "as fatal to his position." It shares in that "the predicament with everything else. that is English. There is not an institution in our realm that is logically defensible,"—and he adds, with characteristic English pride, that every such institution is now, or is in the course of being made, "the best that can be had under the circumstances."

This, then, is the institution Edward Miall undertook to destroy. He has seen its kindred organization go down in Ireland, and now hears his Liberal associates pleading for time to prepare for a disendowment as well as dises-

---
* *The Contemporary Review*, August, 1870.

tablishment of this powerful and wealthy institution. A great many forces help just now to bring the ripening issue to a head. Ritualism within, dissent without, but more than either, the spirit of secular and scientific inquiry and activity, which instinctively rebels against sacerdotal assumptions,—these all tend to but one result. A very influential element at this time is the revolt of the agricultural laborers against the degraded poverty and condition in which they have heretofore been sunk. Out of the eleven or twelve millions claimed as communicants of the establishment, the farm laborers have always formed a large proportion. But more and more the lowlier and less prosperous sects have obtained a commanding control of this class, until now, under the leadership of such teachers as Joseph Arch, William Ball and others, usually local preachers or exhorters themselves, they are in the full tide of vigorous agitation. Men like Mr. Miall have with tongue and pen prepared the way, and are now skilfully binding up their sheaves and gathering the harvests. In the movement just alluded to, the established clergy have unwisely arrayed themselves, as a rule, against the people. This mistaken policy is political suicide, as it has aroused other classes to a logical apprehension of the intimate sympathies that naturally result between State ecclesiasticism and the English landed oligarchy.

Mr. Miall is a man of stoutish form, about the middle height, with dark hair, eyes and complexion, wears a full beard, and peers out with a keen but kindly look from behind his spectacles. He is a man very much esteemed for his social and personal qualities, as well as admired for his intellectual capacity and activity. Though he is a voluminous writer, only a few volumes of controversial matter or of observations and descriptions made on journeys taken for his health, constitute his published works outside the columns of the *Nonconformist*.

Mr. Miall was first chosen for the House of Commons in 1855, and again, ten years later, as member for Bradford. His name had meanwhile several times been presented as a candidate, but without success. In Parliament, his general course has been that of an advanced Liberal. During the American civil war, Mr. Miall and his paper were warm advocates of the Union cause. He has favored the increase of the franchise, vote by ballot, ameliorative and corrective laws for labor; sustains the demand for a redistribution of seats and the extension of the franchise to the counties, as well as the abolition of the rate paying qualifications. In the debates on public education Mr. Miall has been the leading opponent of all denominational control. The measure passed in 1872, under the management of the Hon. W. E. Forster, then Vice-President of the Privy Council, and Chairman of its Committee on Education, was bitterly opposed by Mr. Miall, who regarded certain clauses as strengthening Church or denominational control over the schools. The ministry were denounced as having led those he represented "through the Valley of Humiliation," and were warned that the effect would be felt at the polls. There is no doubt too that the dissatisfaction thus engendered aided in producing that reduction in the Liberal vote which enabled the Conservatives to regain power. Mr. Miall obtained two important Royal Commissions of Inquiry during his parliamentary career, one relating to education, and the other calling for an account of clerical incomes and endowments. In the first report he made a suggestion, the adoption of which marked a distinct step in the growth of the educational system. That suggestion was to the effect that all grants for school purposes should be given only for improvements in the secular studies laid down by the "Minutes of Council," and over which inspection was maintained.

On other or minor political matters Mr. Miall followed the leadership of Mr. Gladstone, at least up to the time of the passage of the Forster Education Act in 1872, when he practically took a position of entire independence. But it is of course on his advocacy of Disestablishment of the State Church that his reputation must rest. In 1856, he first introduced a practical proposition for the abolition of the Irish State Church. The Liberal party had for many years been hostile to this oppressive institution, but there was a wide divergence as to the means to be adopted. The question of disestablishment was first broached over forty years ago, by a motion of Mr. Faithfull, made in 1833. The subject was so unpopular that Lord Althorp declined to reply and moved the previous question. Mr. Miall's motion and speech, the latter especially, received marked attention. Fourteen years later, (in 1868) Mr. Gladstone declared that "in the settlement of the Irish Church, that Church, as a State Church, must cease to exist." Mr. Miall witnessed that triumph, and on the 9th of May, 1871 rose to move the formal Disestablishment of the English State Church itself. It is evident that he will not have to wait as long as he did in the case of its *confrère*, the Irish Episcopal Establishment. The

British Quarterly Review, the organ of the non-conformist party in politics and affairs, says of the debate and Mr. Miall's speech that preceded it, "a large house — a speech which the most competent critics in England have pronounced to be of the highest class—a seven hours debate sustained, for the most part, by members of the greatest mark—a weakness of argument and of tone on the part of the opponents of the motion which has excited general surprise—a division almost exactly tallying with the calculations of those at whose instance it was taken—leading articles and correspondence on the subject in every journal in the Kingdom, and an almost universal impression that disestablishment is nearer at hand than it was thought to be before the motion was submitted—if these do not satisfy the most ardent of "Liberationists," the patience which has hitherto distinguished them must have given way to unreasoning haste."*

Of their leader's efforts the same authority says: "If Mr. Miall has not acquired favor as a Parliamentary debater, he has made two speeches which will live in the political history of this half century." Of the latest, one of his supporters "happily said that it seemed to him as though it were the condensation of the thought of a lifetime;" "but in truth," continues the reviewer, "the speaker had to disengage his mind from many thoughts which had for years engaged the highest powers of his intellect and the warmest sympathies of his heart. He had to remember that he was standing, * * * on the floor of the House of Commons, and that he was addressing not

---

* *British Quarterly*, July, 1871, p. 98.

the eagerly responsive readers of the *Nonconformist*, but the cold and critical readers of journals of a very different type. And further, while avowing that the religious side of the question was that which most powerfully affected his own mind, and conscious that the most potent forces he could employ were those which derived their force from religious considerations, he had to leave that vantage ground, from the admitted unwillingness of the House of Commons to deal with the subject in its spiritual aspects, and to take the lower ground involved in objections of an exclusively political and social character. It required no small degree of self-restraint, and of practical skill, for a speaker of such antecedents as those of Mr. Miall to keep strictly within the lines which he had laid down for himself, and the unstinted admiration expressed by all the subsequent speakers, and especially by public journals, which * * * were little likely to be biassed in his favor, have shown conclusively the completeness of his success." *

These encomiums are sustained by the later praise of a non-partisan writer already quoted. They are echoed by others. The writer before quoted from the *Beehive's* "Portrait Gallery" closes a sketch of Mr. Miall by a reference to adverse criticism that was made in his own denomination, upon his leaving the pulpit for the editorial chair, and by declaring that time and his life work has amply justified the decision, adding that Mr. Miall has lived "to see others besides himself doing the same thing, and to hear them applauded for it. In fact it was a quondam preacher in the pulpit who coined and gave currency to the phrase

---

* *British Quarterly*, p. 99.

of 'priesthood of the press.' All such objections have now passed away; and nearly every observer can perceive that the man who did and has done what it fell to Edward Miall's lot to do, required the ardent devotion of a Prophet, to say nothing of priesthood of any kind, to help him along and to carry him through. * * * Whether it will fall to Mr. Miall's share to reap the harvest for which he has so wisely sown and so well toiled, no man knows, as none, perhaps, less cares than he. Let some men, they may not be many, be clear that they have done what they could, and they are content to leave the matter of reward in the unerring hands of Him who only knows how to apportion it, 'but to him that soweth righteousness, shall be a sure reward.'"*

---

* *The Beehive*, London, Jan. 2, 1875.

XV.

HENRY RICHARD.

THAT portion of the Island of Great Britain which gives a title to the Heir Apparent to the British Crown, has not for a good many years been remarkable for devotion to the class system whereby the English Empire has been governed. The Welsh are, in the main, a working people; small farmers, delvers in the mines, workers at the forge and furnace; and they are a race with very marked characteristics, preserving their old traditions and literature with a zeal which has in itself proved to be an education. These traits have lent to their politics a good deal of intensity. The earlier chartist agitation found formidable materials among them for stormy demands. One movement, known as the Daughters of Rebecca, originating in an organized opposition to turnpike tolls, which had become a grievous monopoly in the principality, became in the southern portion a serious political insurrection, at one time presenting a formidable aspect, and requiring a considerable force for its suppression. Ordinarily, however, the Welsh are a quiet and very orderly people. The gentleman whose name heads this sketch is a representative man—a genuine leader of the best Welsh elements,—and is beside, a man worthy of large recognition because of his worthy aims and character. He may be said to be not merely a member for the coal-mining and iron-forging constituency who have sent him to the House of Commons, but to be in fact a member for all Wales.

Henry Richard was born in 1812, at Tregaran in Cardiganshire, and is the son of Rev. Ebenezer Richard, a minister of the Calvinistic Methodist persuasion. His mother was Mary Williams, and both parents were of unmixed Welsh descent. The father, indeed, represented one of the oldest landed parishes in the region, and the son was carefully educated and became especially versed in all that related to the Principality itself. He had occasion to mingle much with the working people, and thereby acquired a wide knowledge of the great trades' union movements, their aims, hopes, and spirit. This experience, joined with hearty sympathy have secured for him the confidence of the constituency he represents, and have given him considerable influence in the House of Commons on the Labor questions which have formed so important a part of English Legislation.

Mr. Richard married in 1866 Augusta Matilda Farley. He was for some years an "Independent" minister at Marlborough Chapel, Southwark, London. But his first public reputation was won as an advocate of popular education, and in defending his own people—the Welsh—

from what he regarded as false reports made by a government commission which was sent in 1846, to enquire into the state of education among them. Mr. Richard prepared and delivered an elaborate lecture, afterwards published in book form, as were also a series of letters printed later in the London *Morning Star*, — in both of which he replied and refuted the adverse criticisms. The effect of these publications were so marked that Gladstone took occasion to pay a tribute to Mr. Richard and the ability he displayed, when he addressed, in 1873, the National Eisteddfod, as the annual Welsh meetings are termed, which of late years have done so much to revive an interest in the ancient Welsh lore—the source of the Arthurian legends. Mr. Gladstone said in his opening speech :—

"I will frankly own to you that I have shared, at a former time, and before I had acquainted myself with the subject, the prejudices which prevail, to some extent, with respect to Wales, and I come here to tell you how and why I have changed my opinion. It is only fair that I should say that a countryman of yours, a most excellent Welshman, Mr. Richard, M. P., did a great deal to open my eyes to the true state of the facts by a series of letters which, some years ago, he addressed to a morning journal, and which he subsequently published in a small volume, which I recommend to all persons who may be interested in the subject."

The title of this volume was "Social and Political Condition of the Principality of Wales." Mr. Richard has also published a life of Joseph Sturge, and an essay on "The Present and Future of India." The work to which Mr. Richard has more especially devoted his life has been the advocacy of peace, and the establishment of international arbitration as a substitute for war. In pursuance of this work, he has travelled extensively, and his face is one well known in all the chief continental cities. The earlier efforts made by him were taken in conjunction with Elihu Burritt, as early as 1846, and resulted in the convening of a memorable series of Peace Congresses held from 1848 to 1852, at Brussels, Paris, Frankfort, London, Manchester and Edinburgh. The London Congress in 1850 will be remembered in the United States from the fact that it was attended by a number of the most prominent of our anti-slavery advocates—Garrison, Phillips, Tappan, Lucretia Mott and others—and in England by the interest that was aroused by the presence and eloquence of the now venerable quaker lady. These gatherings gave to the peace movement its first world-wide recognition. They attracted public attention, and secured the pacific advocacy of Cobden, Bright, Lamartine, Arago, Humboldt, Liebig, Visschers, Suringar, Chevalier, Coquerel, Sir David Brewster, Varrautrap, Cormenin, Victor Hugo, Emile de Girardin, Beckwith, Garnier, and many others.

The Diplomatic Congress of Paris, in 1856, at which the representatives of Great Britain, Russia, France, Sardinia and Turkey assembled to frame and ratify the treaty concluding the Crimean war, was marked by notable steps forward in the movement of which Mr. Richard is a foremost champion. At that time that gentleman, accompanied by Joseph Sturge and Mr. Hindley, M. P., proceeded to Paris and obtained interviews with the Plenipotentiaries there assembled. "The views of Mr. Richard and his friends were on that occasion so heartily entered into by Lord Clarendon and his colleagues at the Conference, that they, in consequence, embodied them in the celebrated Protocol recommending States to have recourse, in cases of disputes, to the good offices of friendly Powers. Mr. Gladstone has pronounced this high sanction of pacific principles to be 'in itself a great triumph.' It has subsequently been repeatedly acted upon by various countries, and especially by Great Britain and the United States, in reference to the Alabama difficulty, finally settled by arbitrators nominated by other Powers." *

It will be remembered that the Congress of the United States unanimously passed during the session of 1872-3 a resolution favoring the principle of international arbitration. This action was part of the result obtained by Mr. Richard through his long-continued agitation. In July, 1872, he carried a similar motion, after a notable speech on his part, followed by a vigorous debate, by a majority of ten on a total vote of 190, the number of members present. Since that date, besides the vote in the American Congress, similar motions have been passed by the Legislative assemblies of Italy, Sweden and Belgium. The latest adherent to the policy is Holland. The leading advocate of arbitration in the Netherlands Parliament, thus announced his success in a letter to Mr. Richard:—

THE HAGUE, Nov. 27, 1874.

DEAR SIR:—I have the satisfaction to inform you that this day, after two days of debate, we carried our motion on International Arbi-

---

* *The Beehive*, March 13, 1875.

tration (of which we gave notice on the 12th of October), by a majority of 35 against 30, in the second chamber of the States General of the Netherlands, 15 members being absent.

It appears that some of our opponents made a political question of it. But a proposition to adjourn the discussion until a later day was rejected in favor of my counter-proposition to leave our motion to its own inherent merits, without any further defence from our side and to close all further discussion and vote at once. This proposal being adopted, the Minister for Foreign Affairs, whilst approving the principle of our motion, disputed its opportuneness, and doubted the advisability of a small country like ours accepting it and so taking an initiative so important. After his speech, the debate being closed, the motion was carried, as above stated.

I hope, dear sir, that although this success may not be a brilliant one, all our English friends of kindred mind with ours will rejoice in it, and that you, dear sir, in particular, will acknowledge that M. Von Eeck and myself have redeemed the pledge we gave you during your visit to this country, that we would do our best in this direction. I remain, dear sir, yours most truly,

T. P. BREDINS,
M. P. for Dordrecht.

This movement was stimulated on the part of Mr. Richard by an extended Continental journey, undertaken shortly after his success in the British Parliament had been achieved. The biographer of the *Beehive*, already quoted, writes that Mr. Richard "visited Italy, France, Austria, Holland, and Belgium to secure interviews with influential members of their respective Legislatures, and obtained in various instances, promises of early action, of which the fulfilment in most cases has already proved the importance. During this journey Mr. Richard was welcomed by a continuous series of ovations and banquets in the chief Continental cities. Addresses of congratulation also poured in upon him from all quarters. One from Italy was signed by almost all the eminent men in that country, including General Garibaldi, the Presidents of the Senate and of the Chamber of Deputies, Signor Lanza, the ex-President of the Council of Ministers, and by a host of other leading Italians. But one of the most acceptable of these addresses was that from the working men of Venice, in which they testified their earnest gratitude to him for his pacific efforts, inasmuch as it is mainly upon the working classes in every nation that the burdens of war fall. *They* furnish the 'food for cannon'; *their* wives and widows and orphans suffer most grievously from war; whilst the titled and wealthy classes carry off the honors and spoils, but avoid most of the risks and privations. This representative address has afforded a deep and peculiar satisfaction to Mr. Richard. For, in common with his friends and associates throughout life, such as Richard Cobden, John Bright and Joseph Sturge, it has been his sincerest earthly ambition to render solid service to those classes of his countrymen who most need such help—the great and numerous ranks of the toiling millions who constitute such an important proportion of the population, that efforts for their benefit and elevation constitute the truest form of patriotism."

Mr. Richard was elected for the Welsh borough of Merthyr, in November, 1868, and again in the subsequent elections. His opponents were Lord Aberdare (formerly Mr. Bruce, Home Secretary under the Premiership of Mr. Gladstone), and a Mr. Fothergill—both of them large land-owners and employers. Mr. Richard's votes, however, were nearly double those polled by these rivals. The constituency he represents is emphatically a working one;

as the district of which Merthyr is the centre, is one of the heaviest coal and iron-mining and working portions of Great Britain. It has been within three years the seat of two great labor struggles, the first being a strike for higher wages, and the second a lock-out on the part of employers, in consequence of the refusal of the men to accept a reduction. Over one hundred thousand men and boys were thrown out of employ for several months, the employers having raised a large fund and formed a close union in order to accomplish the result they desired, which was the breaking up of the Laborers' Combination by the process of starvation. The miners yielded, but yet the employers could not be accounted wholly successful. The extent of the lock-out was brought about by the determination to prevent the men of other districts from supporting the unionists in those places where the struggle was first inaugurated. Practically the iron workers supported the miners. The iron masters as well as the colliery-owners were induced to strike hands and close all the works, the *employés* of which, though in every way innocent except as to sympathy with the men originally involved, were thus compelled to suffer for many months. Not less than half a million persons were involved in the matter, and the distress was very general. The *Beehive*, which is the recognized organ of the British Trades' Unions, wrote of Mr. Richard while the lock-out was in progress, that "many anxious days and weeks have been devoted by him to endeavour to bring about a satisfactory solution of the difficulties involved; and although his circumstances, as unconnected with the iron trade, or with any other branch of commerce, have placed him in a position of much disadvantage and delicacy, when pleading with the masters on behalf of their men, he has not shrunk from repeated attempts in this direction. In January, 1875, the Associated Employers of South Wales issued a document referring to one of Mr. Richard's communications, saying:—'The Council of the Association of Colliery Owners have received and taken into their earnest consideration, a letter of the 25th of December, written by Mr. Henry Richard, M. P., to the Chairman of the association.' The masters then explained in detail their reasons for arriving nevertheless at a conclusion adverse to Mr. Richard's wishes, and concluded by stating their decision :—' No Board of Conciliation, no method of arbitration, can either remove the existing distress, or qualify the necessity for a reduction of wages.' Hence the responsibility of the painful events which have taken place was entirely assumed by the employers, whilst Mr. Richard has watched and seized every opportunity of advocating the cause of his distressed constituents."

Shortly after his entrance into the House of Commons, Mr. Richard made a speech which aroused much interest, exposing the political intimidation and other unlawful acts practised against their poorer tenants by many of the Welsh landlords. It had the effect also, of checking the abuses whereof he complained. During the debates on the disestablishment of the Irish Church, and on the question of National Education, Mr. Richard took bold and radical ground, urging the abolition of the State Church in England.

The *British Quarterly Review** in an article on Mr.

11* * July, 1871.

Miall's motion on this subject, made on the 9th of May, 1871, speaks of Mr. Richard as supporting the motion in in a speech whose "facts 'and figures * * admirably supplemented Mr. Miall's exposition of principle; while so far as the Principality is concerned, they demolished some of the boldest allegations of the advocates of the existing system." It refers to his having shown that Wales cannot be considered as part of the territory over which the establishment has shed the beneficiary influences which its defenders claimed for it during the debate under consideration."

Mr. Richard has also urged the perfecting of a complete system of National and compulsory education. He is strongly opposed to all denominational supervision or interference, and resisted, with Mr. Miall and his friends, the bill of Hon. Wm. E. Forster, passed in 1872, which, it was charged, extended and even increased that influence. Mr. Richard made for himself a considerable reputation and influence, on the liberal benches, by bearding Mr. Disraeli, at the very first session, at which the Tory leader resumed power, in an attempt to repeal the obnoxious section of the last Education Act, and also by resisting a bill relative to endowed schools, which, though it commanded the united conservative vote and a majority therefore of the House of Commons, the Prime Minister felt obliged to withdraw. In this effort, Mr. Richard gained an unusual triumph, as a party man, in rallying to his support, such ex-ministerial Liberals as Bright, Lowe, Goschen, Coleridge, and others. His recent votes have been given for re-distribution of seats, the agricultural laborers' franchise and other propositions.

"The Member for Wales," as he is sometimes called, is a handsome, and genial gentleman, well educated, and with the ease of a thorough man of the world. He has traveled much, has mingled with the leading men of other lands, is a fluent and ready speaker; well informed and conscientious writer and debater, and more than all, a man of kindly heart, quick sympathies and a strong and vigorous intellect.

PART IV.
POPULAR LEADERS.

XVI.

GEORGE JACOB HOLYOAKE.

 JUNE day in 1867 witnessed a remarkable meeting in the town of Rochdale, Lancashire. This is the home of John Bright, but it will be much longer remembered as the scene of a fruitful experiment begun twenty-three years before the day on which the town was agitated so pleasantly. The cause of this excitement was the opening and dedication of the finest business building in the borough—one of the finest in the county—for the use of the famous Co-operative Society known world-wide as "The Rochdale Equitable Pioneers." The building stands at the head of Toad Lane, the narrow hilly street in which the co-operators first opened a store. At this dedication ceremony and banquet, with a subsequent public meeting in the evening, were present gentlemen like Thomas Hughes and Walter Morrison, both members of Parliament, Vansittart Neale, William Pare, and others whose services and sympathies have made their names widely known. But in that gathering, either at banquet or meeting—the latter being presided over by

the Mayor—there was no guest more honored than the gentleman whose name is at the head of this sketch—George Jacob Holyoake.

A conspicuous figure in English affairs, social and political, for now nearly forty years, he has been the founder and organizer of one most notable movement, and the advocate and historian of another still more remarkable. Mr. Holyoake's double title to fame, as the founder of the "Gospel of Secular life" (the Rev. Mr. Molesworth in his later English history has so designated the "Secularist" movement) and the historian of "Co-operation," must give him no slight hold upon the esteem of his times and the respect of the future. He has won from the bitterest of his opponents a large measure of admiration and confidence. Into his fifty-eight years of life have been crowded the labors of a century in agitation and literary work. A man of notable appearance, above the middle height, slender of frame, he impresses one as being wiry rather than strong, nervous and spare, with a striking head and face. His features are sharp cut and marked with rather thin nostrils and mobile mouth, indicating a capacity for sarcastic speech, which is not belied by the facts. Mr. Holyoake wears a beard and mustache, which become the artistic and well poised head. The dark hair, now gray, is brushed back of his ears, revealing a long head, the larger part of which is set well forward, with a strong, though not broad forehead. The general intellectual expression is one of thoughtful acuteness. Individuality is evident in every expression, from the sharp high-keyed voice, the keen eyes looking out humorously from under heavy lids and brows, and the slight nervous but characteristic gestures which accompany his speech. He is a man of wit as well as knowledge. Radical though he has always been, and that on topics that have usually ostracized their advocates in English society, his social tact has enabled him to conquer personal prejudices, so that there is scarcely a public man more welcomed by all with whom his work brings him in contact—no matter to what class they may belong.

The men of Birmingham have been termed the Yankees of England, and there is something in the nervous temperament and expression of Mr. Holyoake, which recalls the best New England type. He was born in that town in 1817. The family from which he is descended were once well known armorers, and in days gone by, possessed a valuable freehold, but none of it descended to the branch of which Mr. Holyoake is a member. Work was his only inheritance. He is accustomed to say "he was born with steel and books in his blood." His father was a famous worker at the forge, and his mother inherited and conducted a small button-making business—the old fashioned horn button with copper shank. Both parents were persons of more than ordinary intelligence. At six years of age, the future agitator and journalist began work in his mother's shop, which was continued several years, until the introduction of machinery broke up the business. It was an occupation which gave employment then to a large number, and conducted as it was by persons with small capital, it was mostly carried on at home. George and his brother Austin (who died during the past year) were kept busy at school and shop. The elder brother was afterwards employed at a tin-plate factory. When Mr. Holyoake was twelve years of age, and from that time until he was twenty-two, he worked at the Eagle Foundry, where his father had been foreman of the whitesmiths for forty years. The son bore the reputation of being a good workman. He has often declared that he could resume with success either of the trades he learned when a youth, not having forgotten his skill therein. He gave early evidence of his ability, having invented several machines before arriving at manhood, and laboring steadily to qualify himself for the profession of civil engineer. The Mechanics' Institute and the workshop were his college, and the thoroughness of his preparation is evinced by the character of the works on educational matters he has since written. Among them are "Mathematics no Mystery," "Practical Grammar," "Logic of Facts," "Public Speaking and Debate." Of this latter, so competent an authority as Wendell Phillips has spoken in high terms. In furtherance of his intention to pursue the profession of civil engineering, Mr. Holyoake's name was placed, through the intervention of Mr. Lloyd, a magistrate of Birmingham, upon the staff of George Stephenson, then in the earlier years of his memorable career. Circumstances, however, led the young workman away from this design, and enlisted him in the discussion caused by Robert Owen's doctrines and plans.

Mrs. Holyoake, the mother of our keen-witted youth, was a woman of strong religious convictions, and her sons were steady attendants on the Baptist Sabbath Schools. The founder of the Secularists and Editor of the *Reasoner* became a teacher himself in the religious society where his mother worshipped. But other influences were at work.

The Mechanics' Institute of Birmingham was the resort of many young men who have since become known in public affairs. In 1837, Mr. Holyoake, then twenty years of age, heard Robert Owen lecture for the first time. He almost immediately identified himself with the new movement, and before he was twenty-three he was appointed one of the "Social Missionaries," as the lecturers on Mr. Owen's Social Science were termed. Before this period, however, he had tried himself in public, by teaching and lecturing in the Mechanics' Institute, of which he for a time acted as Superintendent. His activity was not confined to social studies and self-improvement, but early took the political bent it has since followed. He was a member of the famous "Birmingham Political Union," from which sprung the Chartist movement, and which has thus exercised a decided influence on English opinion. William Pare, for many years its Town Clerk and one of the most respected citizens, was, next to Mr. Owen himself, the foremost champion of the captivating social philosophy of the founder of New Lanark. Mr. Holyoake came next. Like Mr. Pare, who died within the last two years, he has never deserted his first standard. Apparently, amid all the more exciting discussions and contests in which he has been engaged or led, it is co-operation and the hopes it holds out of social regeneration, that have commanded his heartiest exertions and maintained the strongest sway over his mind.

The social condition about him—he was born and reared in the very center of English factory life, being of it and in it—was such as to attract his deepest sympathies and arouse his most earnest activity. In his very interesting history of "Co-operation in Rochdale," he gives a graphic picture of the "state of trade," and "agitation," at the time the association of "Equitable Pioneers" was formed.

The flannel weavers of Rochdale "who were," he says, "and are still, a badly paid class of laborers, took it into their heads to ask for an advance of wages." This was near the close of 1843. Mr. Holyoake describes how some employers, more liberal than the others, made an experimental advance—the wages to be reduced if others did not come up to the standard. This did not work and a "strike" was determined upon. A trades' union deputation was a dangerous business then,—for the men who were made members of it. After the excitement was over, these leaders found it impossible, as a rule, to obtain work, and were generally compelled to emigrate or seek other occupations. This was the state of affairs which the flannel weavers had to contemplate. However, a strike was determined upon. The result was, not an advance of wages, but the "Equitable Pioneers," which a few of the wiser men started as a means of helping themselves and their class in the straits to which they were reduced. Mr. Holyoake tells this preliminary skirmish so well and it has to do with so much of his own life-work, that it is not inpropriate to give a portion of the story in his own language, especially as it is a good illustration of his literary style.

"At this period the views of Mr. Robert Owen, which had often been advocated in Rochdale, recurred to the weavers. Socialist advocates, whatever faults they else might have, had at least done one service to the employers — they had taught workmen to reason upon their condition — they had shown that commerce was a system, and that masters were slaves of it as well as the men. * * * And if the men became masters to-morrow, they would be found doing pretty much as masters now do. * * The socialism of this period marked the time when industrial agitation first took to reasoning." He quotes Ebenezer Elliott's epigram to deny that such societies ever found place in England.

> "'What is a Communist? One who hath yearnings
> For equal division of unequal earnings;
> Idler or bungler, or both, he is willing
> To fork out his penny, and pocket your shilling.'

"The English working class have no weakness in the way of idleness; they never become dangerous until they have nothing to do. Their revolutionary cry is always '*more work!*' They never ask for bread half so eagerly as they ask for employment. Communists in England were never either 'idlers or bunglers.' When the Bishop of Exeter, * * troubled Parliament, in 1840, with a motion for the suppression of Socialism, and an inquiry was sent to the police authorities of the principal towns as to the character of the persons holding those opinions, (the same who built in Manchester the Hall of Science, now the Free Library, at an expense of £6000 or £7000,) the answer was that these persons consisted of the most skilled, well conducted and intelligent of the working class. Sir Charles Shaw sent to the Manchester Social Institution for some one to call upon him, that he might make inquiries relative to special proceedings. Mr. Lloyd Jones went to him, and Sir Charles Shaw said that, when he took office as the superintendent of the police of that district, he gave orders that the religious profession of every individual taken to the station-house should be noted; and he had had prisoners of all religious denominations, but never one Socialist. Sir C. Shaw said also, that he was in the habit of purchasing all the publications of the Society, and he was convinced, that if they had not influenced the public mind very materially, the outbreaks at the time, when they wanted to introduce the general 'holiday,' would have been much worse than they were, and he was quite willing to state that before the government, if he should be called upon to give an opinion.

"The followers of Mr. Owen were never the 'idlers,' but the philanthropic. They might be dreamers, but they were not knaves. They protested against competition as leading to immorality. Their objections to it were theoretically acquired. They were none of them afraid of competition, for out of the Socialists of 1840 have proceeded the most enterprising emigrants, and the most spirited men of business who have risen from the working classes. The world is dotted with them at the present hour, and the history of the Rochdale Pioneers is another proof that they were not 'bunglers.' No popular movement in England ever produced so many persons able to take care of themselves as the agitation of Social Reform. Moreover, the pages of the *New Moral World* and the *Northern Star* of this period amply testify that the Social Reformers were opposed to 'strikes,' as an untutored and often frantic method of industrial rectification; as wanting foresight, calculation, and fitness; as an irritation, a waste of money and temper. And when a strike led, as they often have done, to workmen coercing their comrades, and forcibly preventing those who were willing to work at the objectionable rate, from doing so, the strike became an injustice and a tyranny, vexatious, disreputable, and indefensible."*

It was of the class thus described by Mr. Holyoake that the Rochdale co-operation movement sprung. The same sort of men and women were assembled, 7000 strong, at the celebration mentioned in the opening of this sketch. These men were the sturdiest supporters of the union cause in England, and their co-operative funds, and those of societies that had sprung from their example, were the savings banks that kept them and their families from pauperism during the weary two years of the cotton famine.

Mr. Holyoake's own life diverged just before the time the Rochdale movement was first under way, from the general course and causes he had been advocating, into other and quite as marked channels. He had drifted early into Unitarianism; later becoming a Theist—a position to which he is perhaps nearer still than any other, religiously speaking. He was at any rate a moderate Freethinker; not specially pronounced in the ranks. He was moreover an active Chartist speaker. A writer in the *Beehive*, sketching the lives of prominent co-operators, says:—

"It was lecturing to the Chartists in their room in Cheltenham "On Home Colonization," in 1841, that led to his imprisonment in Gloucester Gaol. A question was put to

---

* "History of the Rochdale Equitable Pioneers," Part I., pp. 7, 8. Türbner & Co.

him as to his theological opinions; his rule was never to introduce them into his lectures and other subjects, and it was because he had not introduced them that the question was put to him. Usually Mr. Holyoake refused to answer such questions, as being irrelevant and impertinent, but at that time a case had occurred in the town which led the public to believe that social advocates were timorous of avowing their opinions. Resolved that this should not be said of him, Mr. Holyoake answered the question directly and explicitly, and was ultimately tried at the Gloucester Assizes for the answer he gave. Mr. Justice Erskine, who tried him, admitted it was an honest answer, and gave him six months' imprisonment as an encouragement to youthful candor. Mr. Bransby Cooper, brother of Sir Astley, the chief magistrate of the county, visited the gaol before the trial and told Mr. Holyoake that he would not be allowed to speak in his own defence in court. Mr. Holyoake said in that case he would try, and he spoke nine hours, fifteen minutes. Being satisfied towards evening that the court was hearing him, he concluded his defence at half-past nine at night. Mr. Knight Hunt, who became editor of the *Daily News* on the retirement of Mr. Charles Dickens, personally reported the trial in full." *

The question addressed to Mr. Holyoake was as to his belief in the truth of some quoted portion of the Bible, and his reply was in other words from the same volume, not usually used in such a manner. He was tried under an old law, on a charge of blasphemy—and his trial and conviction was the last one of the kind in Great Britain. Mr.

---

* London *Beehive*, June 5, 1875.

Holyoake in his subsequent organization of the society of Secularists, an account of whose aims may be found in the sketch of Charles Bradlaugh, did not mean, as he has repeatedly since avowed, to organize Atheism or Theism into a sect, but rather to find a common band of association by which those who believed in the right of free inquiry could be socially protected by the creation of an organized public sentiment strong enough to ensure respect. Its platform was so drawn that no one need be excluded. The Gospel of Common Life—the daily duty of an every-day world was announced to be its aim. The future was to be left to itself. Mr. Holyoake delivered a remarkable lecture about these days, on the "Organization of Ideas—not Arms," which dealt with the views already indicated. He included the idea that there was a secular side as well as a religious part to every moral issue, and that there should be perfect harmony among all parties in working for that side, irrespective of theological views.

During the ten or twelve years following his incarceration in Gloucester Jail, Mr. Holyoake was actively employed as a lecturer on co-operative topics, and in organizing and lecturing to Secular Societies. His labors were chiefly confined to the manufacturing districts, though in 1847, or '48 he took up his residence in London where he still lives. He was for several years editor of the *New Moral World*, the organ of co-operation as represented by Robert Owen. He then commenced the publication of the *Reasoner*, which was continued for about fifteen years, thirty volumes being published in all. It numbered among its contributors Prof. Francis A. Newman, William J. Linton, Joseph Mazzini, and other distinguished persons. He was also editor with Mr. Linton of a Chartist publication, "The Cause of the People," and assisted in the editorship of the famous *Leader*, for which he wrote regularly over the signature of "Ion." He has also edited the "*Spirit of the Age*," the "*British Leader*" and the "*Social Economist*"—the latter in conjunction with Mr. E. O. Greening. As a contributor to the press and in general literary work his labors have been immense. He was for several years, and probably still is, connected with the *Daily News*, besides being the London correspondent of The Newcastle *Chronicle*, and Birmingham *Post* among provincial papers, and a frequent correspondent of the New York *Tribune*. Mr. Greeley was greatly attached to Mr. Holyoake, and the latter dedicated his "History of Co-operation in Halifax" to the eminent editor. His connection with American affairs has been quite intimate, though he has never visited the United States. The *Beehive* writer already quoted, sketching his services to the co-operative cause, says: "Being one of those who in 1842 and 1843 visited Rochdale as a lecturer, he encouraged the recommencement of the co-operation in that town, and wrote many years later the history of the famous store which began there in 1844, a history which has been translated into German, Italian, Spanish, Russian, and circulated or reprinted both in India, America, and Australia. Mr. Holyoake never stipulated or received any advantage from the copyrights of his works, his idea simply being to advance the objects they represented. * * At many of the meetings of the Association for Promoting Social Science, Mr. Holyoake has read papers illustrative of co-operative principles and progress. He has edited several of the reports of the annual co-operative congresses, and has contributed to the *Co-operative News*, besides publishing numerous small pamphlets, as new methods of co-operative development seemed to require discussion." In the introduction to the Report of the Congress of 1872, Mr. Holyoake thus pleasantly speaks of the general condition of his favorite movement at that date. The paragraph gives a clear view of its progress and has therefore merit besides what it gains from the cheery way in which it is put. He says :—

"The Italians have a proverb, wonderful in its sagacity for that quick-witted people; it is this: 'Those who go slowly go far.' Then Co-operation may be expected to go far, for it had the courage to go very slowly and to keep on going. And it has gone both slow and far. It has issued like the tortoise from its Lancashire home in England; it has traversed France; it has overrun Germany; it has crept under the frozen steppes of Russia; the bright-minded Bengalese is applying it; the soon-seeing and far-seeing American is turning over the idea; and our own emigrant countrymen in Australia are endeavoring to naturalize it there. Clearly Co-operation has become what the *Times* used to call an 'established fact.' Like Liebig's new essence of beef, or a good chronometer, Co-operation is unaffected by change of climate. It remains fresh and wholesome and goes well; and we may say more, looking at its progress now, it goes fast as well as far."

While writing for the *Leader* in 1852 Mr. Holyoake's criticism of the Abolition movement here and the policy of Mr. Garrison excited sharp discussion, and brought from Wendell Phillips one of the most masterly orations of his Anti-slavery life. It was made in the Boston Melodeon, January 27, 1853, and is published in a volume of collected speeches, under the title of "Philosophy of the Abolition movement." The gist of Mr. Holyoake's criticism is in this paragraph, which follows a partial quotation of Garrison's famous declaration, that "I am in earnest,—I will not equivocate—I will not excuse—I will not retreat a single inch—AND I WILL BE HEARD." "Ion" wrote—"This is a defence which has been generally accepted this side of the Atlantic, and many are the abolitionists among us whom it has encouraged in honesty and impotence, and whom it converted into conscientious hindrances. We would have Mr. Garrison to say 'I will be as harsh as *progress*, as uncompromising as *success*.' If a man speak for his own gratification, he may be as harsh as he pleases; but if he speaks for the down-trodden and oppressed, he must be content to put a curb upon the tongue of holiest passion, and speak only as harshly as is compatible with the amelioration of the evil he proposes to redress."

The writer's own philosophy of agitation could not be expressed in terser or more appropriate words than are embraced in the last sentence. His life and methods are the evidences of his adherence to the view thus expressed. It brought upon him, however, not only the sweeping splendors of Mr. Phillips' reply, but bitter criticism among friends and whilom associates at home. One of them wrote in reply to "Ion" a harsh review, closing with this caustic personal attack: "We have spoken harshly; but not more harshly than seemed good, nor without truth.* * In an age whose great evil is the absence of faith, he sets himself to undermine the very ground of faith; in a time of narrow sects and exclusive individualisms, which prevent all combination for the sake of progress, he preaches atheism, which is the justification of selfishness. * * * It may be harsh to say of him that he is an ill-conditioned cross between the Atheist and the Jesuit, an obsequious seeker of success; that we doubt his sincerity and bid men beware his guidance. It is harsh as truth."*

It is the old difference of methods. No truer and braver life has ever been spent in the service of man, than that of him who penned this severe judgment. Artist, poet, defender and servant of liberty; the writer thereof had, like Garrison, no choice in his temperament or heart, for any words that did not express the whole of the truth as he saw it. Yet the same hand writes recently, that without Holyoake's efforts much of what has been achieved in England, in free thought and broader fields of work would have been impossible. There will always be those who, like George Jacob Holyoake, will counsel a wise moderation. These things are a matter of temperament as well as of conviction, and results will always be appealed to as vindicating both views.

There is no radical question or reform movement occurring in England for the long period of Mr. Holyoake's active life, in which he has failed to take a prominent part, and to do good service, often the very best, by pen and tongue. After his removal to London, he and his brother Austin, were associated together in a publishing house, which issued the *Reasoner*, and also many books and pamphlets that otherwise might not have found publication. This business house became the head-quarters of many movements, Mr. Holyoake's personal and social qualities, as well as his ability as an organizer of agitation, bringing him into constant demand. It was here that were held the ses-

---

*"The English Republic," Vol. I., March, 1853.

sions of the Anti-Conspiracy Committee formed to resist certain legislation proposed by Lord Palmerston. Before the Orsini attempt on the life of Louis Napoleon was made, England had always accorded the right of refuge to political offenders from other countries. After the Orsini plot, a great outcry was made in France against this policy. The demand made by the Imperial Government, though not as dictatorial in form, was in substance very much like that more recently made by the German Chancellor against the Belgian Government in the matter of an alleged ultramontane plot against Prince Bismarck. The French demand was aimed at the French exiles in the Channel Islands, and especially at Mazzini, whose extradition from London at the time and subsequently would have been regarded as a great triumph. The Italian Revolutionist was accused of participation in the attempted assassination or regicide. Those who knew him most intimately and possessed his confidence, emphatically deny this. The French exiles living in the Island of Jersey, Victor Hugo, Felix Pyat, since known as a communist leader, and others, were set upon by mobs; the inmates of Hauteville only escaping through the respect that even sycophancy could not help according to genius. George Julian Harney, now residing in Boston, but at the time editing a liberal newspaper in Jersey, was the only Englishman there brave enough to resist the tide of excitement. The committee of which Mr. Holyoake was secretary, and which met in his house, was composed of and sustained by some of the strongest men in England. Lord Palmerston's bill was defeated and with it, his ministry was overthrown. Mr. Holyoake was also the acting secretary of the Garibaldi Committee, by which the famous British Legion was organized and sent to the Italian Liberator. The officer in charge of that movement was an American brother of a distinguished admiral in our navy.

From the *Beehive* sketch, already referred to, the following personal facts are taken:

"When no one else could be found to publish the special unstamped newspapers, during the final agitation for repealing the taxes on knowledge, Mr. Holyoake undertook to do so, under the direction of Mr. C. D. Collet, the masterly secretary of that movement. The publication of the *War Chronicles*, devised during the Crimean war, involved Mr. Holyoake in fines of more than £600,000, which when called upon in the Court of Exchequer to pay, he was under the necessity of asking the Chancellor of the Exchequer to take weekly, not having the amount by him. The last warrant issued before the repeal of the acts was against Mr. Holyoake. In this matter, as all others in which he was concerned, Mr. Holyoake followed the rule of never putting himself forward to do the thing in hand; but, if no one else would do it, and it ought to be done, he did it.

" Mr. Holyoake's opinions have several times been quoted in Parliamentary debates. Under the encouragement of the late Mr. J. S. Mill, Mr. Holyoake became a candidate for the Tower Hamlets, in 1864, but ultimately resigned in favour of Mr. Ayrton. At the election before the last (1868) Mr. Holyoake addressed the electors of Birmingham, desiring if a working-class candidate was chosen, to represent his own town.

" Several public discussions, considered to have been

of influence in their day, have been held by Mr. Holyoake. Observing that reports had for many years been published by the Government on the state of commerce and manufactures abroad, for the use of merchants and manufacturers, Mr. Holyoake at length succeeded in inducing the Foreign Office, in the days of Lord Clarendon, to issue similar reports for the use of working men, from every country abroad where her Majesty had secretaries of embassy and legation.

"The plan of these reports was devised and furnished by Mr. Holyoake. They state what the purchasing power of money is in foreign countries compared with England, so that a workman may know, if he earns $2 per week at home or $4 a week abroad, whether he will be better or worse off ; what the state of the labor market is in foreign countries ; how workmen are hired and housed there ; what kind of habitations they would have to occupy ; what difficulty his family must have to exist in health ; what provision as to clothing they must make ; what is the character of workmen in countries abroad ; were they good craftsmen ; did they take pride in their work, and put their character into it? Such questions were never before put and never before answered ; and no books are more curious and valuable to working men than these publications of the Foreign Office. Lord Clarendon always said in the handsomest manner in his despatches that these reports were issued on the suggestion of Mr. Holyoake. After endeavours extending over twenty years, he mainly procured the passing of the Secular Affirmation Act, by which co-operative property was largely secured ; many of the most influential managers objecting, like Mr. Holyoake, to take the ordinary oath, not being able to do so in the sense required by the court."

Since the discontinuance of the *Reasoner*, Mr. Holyoake's time has been almost entirely occupied with co-operative work, and his journalistic labors. He has written extensively, and for several years past has been engaged on a "History of Co-operation," the first volume of which has recently been published by Trübner & Co. This work he regards as his *magnum opus*, and justly so. He reviews the curious out-of-the-way facts that belong to the pioneer period of the English movement, from 1812 to 1844.—now almost entirely forgotten. More than that, Mr. Holyoake's first volume is a decided contribution to the History of social science and civilization, as he links the present great practical efforts with the various preceding socialist schools and their leaders, bringing continuously before his readers the relations which they occupy to one another, and the points of difference as well as of similarity in their systems. It is full of scholarly information and "thumb-nail" sketches, so to speak, of men of the past fifty years, who have in their day and generation, been marked characters. No man can do such work better than Mr. Holyoake. Besides his pleasant graphic style, witty way, and thorough acquaintance with his themes, he can say with the pious Æneas—" all which I saw, and part of which I was."

Mr. Holyoake was married early in life. He has been a widower for several years. His two sons are both able men—one is an engraver of repute and the other is known in connection with art matters, as a good writer and critic, and also as an excellent restorer of pictures, by a process of his own invention. Mr. Holyoake has recently had two severe attacks of illness, one of which threatened his eye-sight so seriously that he has not yet recovered from its effects. His life has been so busily occupied in service to others, that the pleasant testimonial which his friends have been raising in his behalf will not be ungrateful or come before it is needed. A considerable amount has been collected. Among other sums was five thousand dollars raised by English weavers employed at Fall River, Mass. This fact speaks well for the esteem in which Mr. Holyoake is held by the class from which he sprung. There is now every hope that there will be years of useful literary life before him, if not of active agitation. He has long meditated a journey to the United States, and it is probable that he will carry this out soon after he is able to travel.

XVII.

JOSEPH ARCH.

THIS was a middle-aged strong-set man, with a powerful honest face and a powerful honest voice. He spoke with a slight country accent that was not disagreeable; on the contrary it seemed to give point and character to his sentences, as they came forth slowly and thoughtfully, true to their mark. It seemed to some of those who listened that it was not one man that was speaking; it was the voice of a whole generation of men and women who were telling the manner of their daily lives and of their daily wants. He spoke not very bitterly, but clearly and to the point;" it was evident too that he had "lived through it all himself and had felt hunger and biting cold, and seen his little children suffer," and while he was speaking "a sense of wrong had come to some of the poor fellows for the first time."

In these words Miss Thackeray, in one of her charming minor stories, sketches under the name of Budge the man who is now recognised as among the most notable public characters in Great Britain. Joseph Arch is indeed gifted with an honest face and voice, while animating both is a purpose so human, and so sincerely expressed, that it has made the almost unlettered peasant and humble hedge-side preacher capable of moulding the lowly and moving the gifted, into the servants of his mission. He is a man of middle stature, stout frame, heavy and plebeian in aspect, but not ungainly in his appearance; and slow of motion, as befits both his early pursuits and the gravity of his character. He dresses in plain and simple garments, bearing the appearance of an English yeoman of the humbler class. It is a face that when studied justifies his reputation. The head is large and well developed, high in the coronal and thinly covered with brown hair, now flecked with grey. Mr. Arch has a broad and moderately high forehead, deep bluish-grey eyes, heavy well arched eyebrows, large well shaped nose and full strong mouth, with wide flexible lips, which with a firm lower jaw, give an expression of will, force, kindliness and decision, such as his public life has shown him to possess. He wears his beard after the fashion of English farmers and workmen of middle age and beyond, trimmed close but full around his face, leaving the chin and mouth bare. It is a face full of character in the best sense. A simple, sincere man, but sagacious and wise. A man likely to be upheld and swayed by spiritual and moral insight—a dreamer of dreams, a man of visions, perhaps, but able to keep self-poised and self-contained. Joseph Arch could never betray a cause; he might become bewildered as the issues grew more complex, and men less sincere than himself came to fatten on its success. Yet, the very simplicity of his character would prove to be its strength, and in the end his wisdom would confound the self-seekers. This man is pre-eminently the leader and inspirer of a movement of which John Morley wrote when it began:—" The first current of a strange social agitation is passing over the land. At last, after generations of profound torpor, our eyes discern slow stirrings among the serfs of the field. The uncouth Caryatides who have for generations upborne the immense structure of civilization in which they have no lot, have at length made a sign. The huge dumb figure has tried to shift a little from a position of insufferable woe. Little may come of it. The current may soon spend itself; the monstrous burden soon settle pitilessly down again on the heavy unconquerable shoulders. The many are so weak, the few are so strong; the conditions of social organization shut effort so fast within an iron circle. However this may be, the attempt is being made by a company of poor men to win a few pence more for the week's toil, to raise the mere material conditions of life for their wives and their children a little further away from the level of the lives of brute beasts."*

This last statement embraced only the premonitory issues of demands more searching in their character than any of the radical agitations that have lately preceded them. Strangely enough, it is from these "uncouth Caryatides" that the romance of English political agitation has almost always proceeded. The Peasant wars of the fourteenth century have lent notable characters to dramatic literature, and the names of Wat Tyler, Jack Straw and

---

* *Fortnightly Review*, Sept. 1873. "The Struggle for National Education."

Jack Cade, with the memorable Friar John Ball, have lived in tradition and ballads, and animated many an English heart to life-long exertions in the People's cause. It was not for a day only that John Ball, the "mad priest" as he is still called, made household words of the rude but pithy distich:

> "When Adam delved and Eve span
> Who then was the gentleman?"

or condensed the whole philosophy of socialism into the words with which he is accredited— "Good people, things will never go well in England so long as goods be not in common, and so long as there be villains and gentlemen. By what right are they whom we call lords greater folks than we? on what ground have they deserved it; why do they hold us in serfage? If we all came of the same father and mother, of Adam and Eve, how can they say or prove that they are better than we, if it be not that they make us gain for them by our toil what they spend in their pride? * * * They have leisure and fine houses; we have pain and labor, the rain and the wind in the fields. Yet it is of us and our toil that these men hold their state." *

Joseph Arch, the Agitator, is the rightful heir of the protest and aspiration credited to Friar John Ball five centuries ago, carried through various outbursts and now being translated into the sober and practical, though radical demands, that properly fit in with modern English effort. It is difficult for a reader not thoroughly conver-

---

* "Green's History of the People of England."

sant with English social and industrial life to fully understand the importance of the movement of which Joseph Arch is the leader. The whole fabric of English caste and class is so built upon the system of Land Tenure and hereditary ownership of the soil by aristocratic families, that to assail it, either by an agitation for more wages and more rights, is certain to place the oligarchic control in danger. And the Agricultural Laborer's agitation has provoked a searching discussion of the feudal policy which animates every part of English land ownership.

Joseph Arch is now in his forty-ninth year. He was born and still lives in the village of Barford, Warwickshire, one of the loveliest counties in the west of England. If as Oliver Wendell Holmes wrote in "Elsie Venner," every man is an omnibus, whose inside passengers are his ancestors, it is not without significance that this man should have been born in a section of England where the old British stock has not been wholly obliterated by the Saxon, and from which sprung so large a proportion of the followers of Wycliffe and Lollard; among whom Alfred the Great a thousand years ago found shelter from hanging Northmen, where in latter centuries the followers of Hampden and Cromwell were largely recruited, and the Prince of Orange was welcomed when he came to reap a Kingdom from the overthrow of the Stuarts. Joseph Arch is the representative of one of those humbler yeoman families, now almost extinct in England, from which came so many of the early settlers of New England, and which on one side has given many recruits to the prosperous middle class, and on the other many more to the laboring poor who have so long occupied a "position of insufferable woe."

The father of Mr. Arch was, fortunately for his son, lifted one step above the condition of a day laborer, by being the owner of a tiny freehold only large enough for a garden patch, which with an humble cottage, has been retained by the President of the Agricultural Laborers' Union. He still resides there, in a style but little removed from that of the days of his severe manual labor. Born in 1826, it is said of his parents, that— "His father slaved and died, as most fathers do, without much hope and comfort in this world: but his mother, who felt and thought silently over the miseries of a poor man's home, and who, perhaps, had concluded that ignorance lay at the root of social misery, sent her son Joseph to school at the age of six, and kept him there till between eight and nine, and thus found him the key by which he afterwards succeeded in getting at some slight knowledge of the world beyond the bounds of the village in which he lived, and of seeing, in a dim way, those struggles of men in history which explain man's connection with his fellows in humanity, not only by the past history of life, but by the wonderful incitements of hope which carry forward the struggle in the direction of right, freedom, and justice." *

At nine years of age, Joseph Arch was taken from school, and hired out to a neighboring farmer at fourpence (eight cents) per day to scare birds from the growing crops. He was apt at work, and soon made himself useful at other and more important labor. His good mother died while he was still a youth, and his father ere long became incapable of hard labor. By dint of great exertions only was

---

* The *Beehive* " Labor Portrait Gallery," London, 1874.

the little freehold preserved intact. Early in his life, Mr. Arch married the daughter of a village mechanic, herself employed as a domestic servant in the houses of the neighboring gentry. As English peasant life goes, it was a good match for Mr. Arch, and as events have proved it was the most fortunate incident in his life. Mrs. Arch is evidently a woman of superior intelligence, spirit and ambition, and she was not content that her husband, in whom from the outset she recognized capacity beyond his class, should merely vegetate as a farm laborer. For some years his wages were but nine shillings or about $2.25 per week, out of which five persons were to be cared for—himself, wife, two children, son and daughter, and the decrepit father, " whose claim on the scant meal was never denied. * * The wife of Joseph Arch, however, in a sense of womanly affection, revolted against this, and told her husband that both of them must face the world and try if, by other labor —by anything, in fact, that might turn up—such misery as they and theirs had to suffer, could be prevented. This determination was carried out by the husband, and Joseph re-travelled and worked that the brood at home might be better fed. From one thing to another Arch got on, but not by any means to affluence. He read and studied, and respected his fellows too much to rise in the world by pressing them down. He read the newspapers and knew what was going on amongst the mechanics of the towns. The wrongs and the rights of labor are the same in kind all over England ; they only differ in degree." * In these struggles and endeavors, the skill of Mr. Arch in all farm

---

"Labor Portrait Gallery,"*Beehive*, London, 1874.

work, was his earlier mainstay. He was noted through the Midland and Western Counties as a "hedger"—at pruning and other garden and farm work, requiring more knowledge and experience than falls to the lot of the ordinary agricultural laborer. He became an authority among the farmers, and was greatly respected by them till his championship of the laborers' movement provoked an outburst of "bucolic" wrath, which would, if it had dared, have recked its first fury against the person of Joseph Arch. At the present time, however, he has very largely won their respect, as he most certainly has compelled their attention. He claims that in his efforts to elevate the laborers, he must necessarily benefit the tenant farmers, as a body. It should be borne in mind, that the farmers of England are very seldom owners of the land they cultivate. Some remnant of the freehold tenure still exists among the "statesmen" or "dalesmen" of Cumberland and Northumberland, while a few scattered families of yeomanry are yet found through the Western Counties. The tendency has been more and more marked for a century past, towards the absorption of the land into fewer hands. It would fill a volume to enter even into the mere outlines of the questions properly related to this agitation. Not only are the farmers as a class mere tenants on the land, but very few of them have any lease of their farms, or any control of them except at their landlord's will. This system of tenure, so injurious to enterprise and so depressing to the tenants, would have long since been overthrown in any country less conservative in its habits than England. Custom has made in this, as in so many other things, a fixity of tenure more equitable than the law itself. The rights of tenant farmers have long been a fruitful theme of debate at their clubs and market dinners, and by politicians seeking votes from among them. But until Joseph Arch compelled attention to the condition of the Agricultural Laborers these rights had, as a public issue, no significance whatever. Now, men of this class have elected one of their own number to the House of Commons, and a Conservative Ministry enrolls Mr. Clare Read, M. P. for one of the divisions of Norfolk, among its members, though in a subordinate position. Bills to regulate the tenure of land, more or less tentative in character, are pending, and economists like Professor Fawcett discuss the matter before great metropolitan constituencies. Progress in this direction may be traced directly to the agitation by the laborers, which the farmers as a body, at first by threats, often by acts of violence, and always with bitter denunciations and harsh actions, have sternly resisted. It was the wandering life of Joseph Arch that gave him that thorough acquaintance with agricultural life which enables him to talk to the laborers in a manner adapted to their local peculiarities, speech and mode of work. This must always prove one of the most essential qualities for success as a popular leader. But it is to his position as a local preacher among the Primitive Methodists, the sect to which he belongs, that much of his deeper power and insight is due. * * When a man of his class opens his mouth, if he has anything of true manhood really in him, he must soon make himself felt, not simply as a preacher in the pulpit, but as an utterer of truths that touch life on its practical side, and raise questions that involve, not God's justice only, but man's justice to man in the most ordinary concerns of the world."* The speeches of Joseph Arch show in every sentence how his thoughts and style have been moulded by the strong and simple Anglo-Saxon translation of the Hebrew Scriptures, which will always be the "well of English undefiled" to every one, layman or priest, who studies and masters it. Joseph Arch's speech is full of scriptural allusions, and his mind has much of the solemn fervor of the elder prophets. He is really an orator, and one too, of no mean pretensions. No writer, having to avail himself largely of the pen of others, he is, when standing before "his people," a man gifted with great powers.

The present Agricultural Laborers' movement dates back to the month of February, 1872, when Joseph Arch, then known only as a strong and fluent preacher of the sect to which he belongs, and as a man of strong sympathies with the class to which he is allied, was called to the leadership. No movement of importance among them had occurred for about thirty years, when the leaders of a Laborers' Union in Dorsetshire were tried under the unjust combination laws of that day and sentenced to several years penal transportation. The sentence was actually carried out, and the men served several years as convicts, and were finally pardoned and returned. Two of them are now living, and received quite an ovation at a mass meeting called for the purpose. During the Anti Corn Law League Agitation, meetings were held at which farm laborers participated. One of the most memorable of these was held on Salisbury Plain—the point of meeting being

---

* *Beehive* "Labor Portrait Gallery."

among the Druidical remains of Stonehenge. The time was night, and all England shuddered at the woe and misery the speeches conveyed. Men of middle-age, gaunt, grim, stalwart, told of their constant pinching,—how they and their children suffered from hunger,—and recited the fact that few of them were able to procure meat from one year's end to the other, with other facts not very gratifying to English pride. The Corn Laws were repealed soon after, and these significant meetings undoubtedly hastened that event. When this dumb giant does move under the English Etna, there are few statesmen hardy enough not to heed the sign. Since that event the agricultural laborer had remained silent in sullen acquiescence, until some of them at the village of Wellesbourne, near the fashionable summer resort of Leamington, Warwickshire, asked Joseph Arch to address them in the open air under the limbs of a great chestnut tree which spreads its branches over the common. Previous to this date, however, an effort at organizing a Union had been commenced in Lincolnshire. A great strike had been in progress at Newcastle, in the iron works, and discussion over this was the moving cause of the Lincolnshire attempt. The first meeting was held January 7th, 1873, and thereat, the following resolves were adopted :—

"(1.) That the agricultural laborers of England form themselves into a Union, having for its object the social redemption of the agricultural laborers of England generally.

(2.) That this meeting shall select from their number twelve of the most intelligent members to form a committee, a president, and a secretary.

(3.) That no member should strike work or ask his employer for a rise of wages, but should continue his employment the same as before.

(4.) That the Secretary and each member should do his utmost to augment the Union all over the country.

(5.) That this meeting assemble every fortnight to give in a verbal report of its proceedings and success.

(6.) That a meeting be held at the most central town of the county, on the first Monday in April, at which meeting each member shall pay 1s. entrance fee and 2d. per week subscription from this date.

(7.) All members to attend. A president, vice-president, executive committee, trustees, treasurer, and secretary, to be elected for the next six months; the result of this meeting only to be made public, and not those held previous.

(8.) That propositions be prepared and brought forward at this quarterly meeting, calculated to regulate the Union for the future."

Strikes were, it will be seen, forbidden, nor did the movers intend to make any public demonstrations. The fact however of the organization was published in a London paper, and Joseph Arch had his attention called to it by his neighbors.

The meeting at Wellesbourne was held. Mr. Vincent, Editor of *The Laborers' Union Chronicle*, who then published and edited a local paper at Leamington, gives the following account of the impression made by that meeting, and the result that followed so rapidly on its heels:

"Early in the month of February, 1872, an old man called at our newspaper office in Leamington, and asked us to send a reporter to Wellesbourne, to a meeting of agricultural laborers which was going to be held under the now famous chestnut tree, at which Joseph Arch, of Barford, would make a speech. We accordingly sent a reporter, who was astonished to find nearly 2000 people assembled. He was still more surprised at the speech made by Mr. Arch; and on reading the report of that meeting, we felt that in this man's impassioned yet thoughtful utterances there was a lever which would bring about a great moral and intellectual awakening among the downtrodden peasantry of England—a class hitherto supposed to be in such a hopelessly dormant state that the general progress of our country could scarcely affect it. That meeting at Wellesbourne was followed by similar gatherings in other Warwickshire villages, at each of which Joseph Arch, whom they had already enthusiastically accepted as their leader, spoke with unwearying eloquence and manly force the same deeply earnest words of encouragement and hopefulness for their future welfare. After some few weeks, during which we continued to report these gatherings in our local paper, the movement began to attract wider notice; it was everywhere hailed with surprise and satisfaction, and soon became the subject of comment and illustration by all the leading journals of the country. The movement in Warwickshire began early in February, and on the following Good Friday a monster meeting was held in one of the public halls of Leamington to inaugurate the establishment of a Union of agricultural laborers for this county. That gathering can never be forgotten by those who witnessed it. Crowds of laborers with their wives and little ones, often headed by the village drum and fife band, streamed into the fashionable spa; and the large hall of meeting could barely hold a third of the number of persons assembled. We may mention the kind encouragement and assistance rendered in the early progress of the movement by the Hon. Auberon Herbert and Mr. E. Jenkins, M. P.; and at the meeting on Good Friday, these gentlemen, together with Mr. Jesse Collings and Dr. Langford of Birmingham, were among the principal speakers. From that day, the Laborers' Union in Warwickshire became an accomplished fact. The effort made to suppress it on the part of landlords and farmers at Wellesbourne had been successfully resisted; public subscriptions in furtherance of the movement had been received to a large amount, the editor of this paper alone receiving about £400, including the handsome donation of £100 (announced amidst enthusiastic cheering at the Good Friday meeting) through Mr. Dixon, M. P., by a laborers' friend at Birmingham, accompanied by a brief note, which at once became the battle-cry of the movement: "The right to form the Union must be fought for to the death!" The laborers who had assembled on that memorable Good Friday evening, returned to their homes, many to the most distant villages of Warwickshire, with the firm conviction that they had laid the foundation-stone of a great movement for their elevation. For in very truth, the dry bones had begun to move, and the dumb mouths to speak."*

The next step was the publication by Mr. Vincent of the paper which he has since conducted, and of which it may be truthfully said, that no abler, wiser, or bolder labor organ has been or is now issued. That paper published a call for a National Congress which was held in May, 1872. In the meanwhile, the fierce opposition of the farmers had reacted vigorously in favor of the laborers. The weak and unmanly suggestion made in a public speech by the Bishop of Manchester, advising farm employees to put

---

* *Laborers' Union Chronicle*, June 5, 1875.

the Union organizers into the nearest horse ponds, had the effect of arousing the nonconforming hostility to the establishment, and of adding largely to the public sympathy. Many of the landed gentry joined with the farmers in their opposition to the movement. The unpaid magistracy swelled the chorus with stupid acts of injustice by imprisoning women and children who had hooted some men who were at work on the highways, while others were on strike. The radical party, through its leading men, at once made the laborers' cause its own. The Primitive Methodist ministry was made use of to circulate the call. The Chronicle says: * * * " We immediately issued two circulars, one addressed to every minister on the minute book of the denomination requesting him to put the other (which announced the Conference) into the hands of the most intelligent laborer in his district, and urge him to call a meeting of his fellows, and send a delegate to Leamington. We now began to prepare our programme, and to look into the causes of the degraded position of the laborer, and to consider what was required to assist him in the work of self-emancipation. With this view, we communicated with several well-known gentlemen, inviting them to contribute papers to the Conference, the same to form the basis of the future work of the National Agricultural Laborers' Union; the result being that the following subjects were most ably treated upon: The land laws, by the Hon. Auberon Herbert, M. P.; Garden and meadow allotments, by Sir Baldwin Leighton, Bart. (a Conservative landlord, by the way); Education, by Mr. Jesse Collings; Co-operative farming, by the Hon. and Rev. J. W. Leigh; The reclamation of waste lands, by

Mr. H. Brookes; Co-operative stores, by Mr. Butcher, of Banbury; Village clubs and reading rooms, by the Rev. H. Solly, etc., etc."

This programme was in reality too ambitious, and the work to be done was more immediate and practical. Though the Laborers' Association is by no means a mere Trades' Union, in the usual acceptation of that term, it had a great deal of similar work to do. To organize emigration was among the earliest aims. Much work was and is being done in that direction.

The work performed by Joseph Arch in travelling and speaking since that first meeting in February, 1872, has simply been prodigious in its extent. Up to the present date he has almost constantly spoken eight or ten times each week, at points far apart, and requiring a large amount of travelling in order to reach them. The only exceptions to this active agitation, was during his travels in Canada and the United States, in the winter of 1873-4, when, it will be remembered, he spoke in several American cities, the most notable demonstration being that held in Faneuil Hall, Boston, in which Wendell Phillips and Gen. B. F. Butler participated. This journey was undertaken for the purpose of facilitating the organization of their emigration movement, and was by previous understanding, confined chiefly to Canada. Mr. Arch has several times stated since, that he intended to re-visit and travel more fully through the United States, especially the western and southern portions.

In the spring of 1874, the farmers of Norfolk, one of the eastern counties, inaugurated a general lockout, which in its consequences embraced some 15,000 laborers. It resulted in an apparent victory to the employers, but in the end, the laborers have secured a large advance of wages. It continued for many weeks, and large contributions were made to support the men locked out, not by Trades' Unionists only, but by the liberals everywhere. Public meetings were held in all the large cities, at all of which Mr. Arch spoke. Mass meetings were held generally out of doors, among the laborers, and especially in the lock-out district. Mr. Arch was supported by men from the ranks, young and old, who have since developed much talent. The movement assumed something of the favor and excitement of a religious crusade. It went deeper and spread broader than a mere question of wages. The enclosures of common land, the relations of the state church to the people, the quality of the unpaid magistracy, the want of and demand for education, the tenure of the land, the feudal character of the law of entail, and the exclusion of the peasant from the franchise, were among the most prominent topics. But the thoroughness with which the branch Unions inquired into and made public the facts relating to the wages paid, the condition of cottages inhabited, the spirit displayed towards their movement, etc., by the leading public men and proprietors, had a more direct effect on the sentiment of their followers than all else. When they were told that the wages paid on the estates of the Queen and the Prince of Wales, did not exceed fourteen shillings (about $3.40) per week, and that this sum had been obtained only after persistent agitation in the neighborhood, it sensibly affected their loyalty, especially when it has been accompanied by very plain speaking and writing with regard to the cost and wealth of royalty, and the wasteful extravagance attributed to the heir apparent.

Mr. Arch himself, has shown in his speeches the same growth that has marked his followers' progress, but with him it has been accompanied by that deep sense of responsibility which necessarily precludes passionate expression or any tendency towards inflaming the minds of those who trust him. He has quite skilfully led them and their movement from one of personal amelioration to demands for reforms in legislation and legal position, which it must be evident will more permanently advance their interests. His speeches are notable for this sagacious comprehensiveness. In one, delivered May 13, 1875, in Norfolk, referring to previous reforms, he said :—

"That he believed the formation of the National Agricultural Union was one of these great reforms, and that in after years it would be seen to have saved the Protestantism of the country from putrefaction, to have saved the Government from going into excess, and to have saved agriculture from a landlord monopoly, which would, if not stopped, have laid the tenant farmers upon their backs. He asked whether it was right to offer opposition to such a movement—a movement which has for its end such noble aims and objects, and also a nation-saving design. He said 'nation-saving design,' because he felt satisfied that if the laborers had not moved in the matter, the tenant farmers would have been wrecked on the rocks of their own creation. Show him a country where agriculture is prosperous, then he would say that that country was safe; but show him a country where her laborers were becoming scarcer and scarcer, and where her bone and sinew were fast on their way to ruin, then he must say that that country was not safe. He claimed for this Union that it had been set on foot both for the benefit of the employer and the employed, and he was surprised to find that the tenant farmers were opposed to the movement.

* * * * * * * *

"He wanted that a privilege that was extended to one part of Her Majesty's subjects should be extended to all. The aim of the nobility and clergy had always been to keep the working-men of the country —the laborers—ignorant, and they said that this question was a social one. They had lost the sympathy of a great many of the clergy, because they dared attend public meetings and sign petitions; but he thought they could well dispense with the sympathy of the clergy, and they were determined to have their rights. Whether he wore a broadcloth coat or a smock frock, he claimed for them both an equal right, and that the one as well as the other could say, 'I am a man;' and as men they could claim the rights of men. They ought to say that, while they were called upon to pay taxes, they ought to have a voice, so as to be able to say how those taxes were to be spent, and they ought also to have a voice in the making of the laws which they had to obey, by sending men to Parliament who they thought would protect their interest.

Until the tenant farmers had got a fair sprinkling of their class into the House of Commons, their wrongs would not be redressed. It would seem rather strange to my Lords and the Squires, if one morning they found that the agricultural laborers had got enfranchised. Why, it would make them as wild as March hares to think that the wild agitator, Arch, had been there and done all this; but it was going to be done, and that speedily. There was not the slightest mistake about that. They never could expect justice from the landlords. The laborers of 1872 were not the laborers of to-day, for they grew more intelligent, more thoughtful and earnest about their own interests every week, and whereas some weeks ago they dared not to walk erect nor call their soul their own, now they walked erect, and were as intelligent as many of the farmers. And as this intelligence grew, so must they sell their labor at the best advantage, and if they could not get sufficient for it here, they must go somewhere else where they could." *

Mr. Arch has from the outset of the agitation been a

---

* Report of the *Laborers' Chronicle*, May, 1875.

strenuous advocate of emigration. In a speech made soon after returning from his Canadian journey, he said :—

> "In packing up and going to the Colonies the laboring man must not suppose that he is going to pick up dollars in the street or was going to wring a large fortune out of other people. * * If he intended to go to the Colonies, he must really mean to work, and to any industrious man who really meant manfully to work, the Colonies offered splendid advantages.
>
> They had 500 emigrants' letters at the League office, but not published. Throughout the whole of this country these letters are being sent, silently doing the work of emigration agents. * * He had received passes to travel over six States of America. Who was it that was sending for him? Not the Government, but the farmers of America who all wished him to go amongst them, and report as he had done of Canada. Could any one assert that his report of Canada was not a true one! No one could, and as he had truthfully reported of Canada so would he of America."

A considerable portion of the Union funds have been used to aid the emigration movement, and the English Colonial Agents have strenuously taken advantage of the interest aroused. Another policy pursued by the Laborers Union, and of which Mr. Arch was the mover, is that of an exchange of labor information, so that men may learn where employment is scarce or abundant, the wages paid, and other conditions. The constant drain which has been going on from the country to the towns, from England to the Colonies and elsewhere, and to the demand for the sturdier laborers, on railroads and other public works, has had a perceptible effect on the laborers' movement, by lessening competition. It appears by the last British census that "returns of farm laborers fell off in England and Wales from 958,000 in 1861, to 798,000 in 1871, or nearly 17 per cent.: and in Scotland, from 105,000 in 1861, to 93,000 in 1871, or nearly 12 per cent. Indoor farm servants, of whom about five-sixths are males, and many of whom probably are out of door laborers living in farm houses, numbered in England and Wales, 205,000 in 1861 and 159,000 in 1871, showing a decrease at the rate of 22 per cent. The large and increasing preponderance of the town over the country population in England and Wales, which was in the proportion of 62 to 38 per cent. in 1861, points to the probability of a continued decrease."

The Union itself, has not, of course, maintained the strength with which it started. The popular excitement at the time rapidly filled its ranks, but when it was evident that a long up-hill fight was before the organization, the membership fell off. Three annual congresses have been held, the last one at Birmingham, early in June, being largely attended. Moncure D. Conway, in a letter to the *Cincinnati Commercial*, wrote at the time that the laborers had "made a decidedly good impression on the country. They were able to point to wages substantially increased and hours of toil shortened by their movement; but better than either of these were the evidences given by the delegates to an awakened spirit of independence and intelligence throughout the nation in a class which, in all popular movements, had hitherto been counted out as abject serfs. It will be impossible to prevent the enfranchisement of these men very long."

The report made at the Birmingham Congress shows the condition of the Union to be as follows:—In the financial year of 1874 the number of members was computed at 86,000 in 37 districts and 1,480 branches, which was an increase on the year 1873 of 14,000 members. The number of members to the end of April, 1875, was 58,652 in 38 districts, with 1,368 branches. The total income from the branches to the districts in 1874 was £21,000; the amount in 1875 being £23,036, showing a greater return of contributions notwithstanding a decrease in numbers. The amount paid away for relief in cases of lock-outs and strikes in 1874 was £7,500. During 1875, on account of the great Eastern Counties' lock-out, it has reached the amount of £21,365. The amount paid away for migration was £2,630, and for emigration £3,367. Upwards of 1,600 adults have been assisted to New Zealand by free passages. 3,407 have also been sent to Ontario, Canada, and a considerable number have also gone to Queensland. In excess of the members' ordinary contributions, there was collected the sum of £5,595 in support of the lock-out, and contributions from the Trades' Unions, &c., and the general public amount to £21,613. The law expenses of the Union (including a libel suit against the editor of the *Laborers' Chronicle*, the liabilities of which the Union discharged), were £691. The entire cost of management, including lecturers, delegates, secretaries, and officers, amounts to £10,763. Cash on hand in 1874 was £2,148: in 1875 it was £4,200.*

A sharp dispute now prevails in the organization, which, while it may affect the original Union, will not injure the general movement. It grows out of a difficulty between the editor of the *Laborers' Chronicle* and the Gen-

---

* Condensed from the report of the *Laborers' Chronicle*, May 29th, and June 5th, 1875.

eral Secretary of the Union. The former has insisted that the effort was much more than a Trades' Union one, and that there must be a vigorous seeking after social advancement; that it was more desirable to organize for the control of land at home, than to remove labor abroad. Accusations of loose management by the executive officers, which, however, especially exclude Mr. Arch, have also been made. One result is the establishment of an official organ of the Union, and the organization by Mr. Vincent of another Union, embracing beneficial and co-operative objects. Mr. Arch appears to preserve the friendship of both sides. The *Chronicle*, speaking of him, said some time since :—

"This man in every way commands our warmest admiration. * * * * It is truly no insignificant fact that Joseph Arch is able to make himself understood by a simple-minded and reputed ignorant peasantry, as probably no man was ever able before to make himself understood who spoke the same great truths which this man speaks, and sustained the same wide bearing and statesmanlike argument which this man often sustains. The Earl of Kimberley, who, the other day, in the House of Lords, lamented his inability to explain to an agricultural laborer the nature and operation of the rural Education Act, might well take a lesson in the school of Joseph Arch and learn of him how to meet his fellow man face to face, and establish an interchange of thought with him. The secret of Joseph Arch's success is that he is, in truth and reality, still one of them, and not an outsider—a stranger, whose mode of thought, and language, and manners are not as theirs.

"It is education, and such unpurchaseable educational influences as those which Joseph Arch is now exerting amongst the laborers of England, by which such beneficent results must be achieved; an educational influence based on unquestionable love, and warmest good will and solicitude towards his fellow men; an influence which makes itself understood beyond the possibility of doubt, because it is a great active force which, being present, cannot help but make itself felt. Witness the hearty brotherly greetings which Joseph Arch receives when he presents himself before an assemblage of laborers in any part of England; see the smiles and almost frantic joy of the women, the warm pressing of hands and exclamations of grateful delight, as in the presence of a genuine hero and deliverer of a people from poverty and oppression."

"Joseph Arch is a true priest among his people—he still preaches voluntarily, and without fee or reward, two or three times on Sundays, in addition to his arduous work of the week; and when he meets them on these occasions it may be truly said that

> 'His ready smiles a parent's warmth express,
> Their welfare pleases and their cares distress.'

"It is impossible for any unprejudiced mind, whether it be animated with a lively faith in the progress of humanity or not, to listen to Joseph Arch, as we were privileged to listen to him   *   *   *   while addressing an assemblage of agricultural laborers, without being deeply impressed not only with his evident sincerity, his noble and generous sentiments, his strong, practical good sense, his intense love of freedom, and passionate hatred of oppression and meanness;—to see the sympathetic yet firm and uncompromising manner in which he admonishes and reproves the shortcomings of the class to which he belongs—the unaffected and manly pride with which he asserts and maintains the dignity of that class, and the clear sighted, yet simple and genuine spirit of brotherhood and loyal association with which he preserves his identity with it—the singleness and directnesss of purpose—the purity and exaltation of motive—the calm and equal manner with which he bears himself towards rich and poor alike—all these, and many more fine shades of character which we have not ventured to particularise, point to Joseph Arch not merely as one of the best talking and most talked of men of his time, but as one chosen in the providence of God to do a great work for humanity—to effect lasting and powerful results for good among the people with which he is especially identified, and to establish in England such a noble, self-dependent, moral, and intelligent peasant class as that in praise of which Burns, the ploughman poet of Scotland, breathed in prayerful melody his ardent patriotic soul, and on the existence and the native liberty-loving spirit of which Englishmen are largely dependant for their permanent continuance."

In the meanwhile the plain speaking and the agitation goes forward. Pages of extracts might be given to show how plain the speeches and how vigorous the agitation. Mr. Arch at Hungerford, Berkshire, illustrated both when, speaking of the House of Commons, he declared it to be a great "Trades' Union" of the "governing classes." Speaking of a criticism from a paper representing the farmers, he said that had it "been in existence when the great teacher of mankind travelled from village to village and town to town, it would have called him a roving agitator." When the laborers agitation began, "lips were sealed" he said, "by the hand of the oppressor; we were set down as ignoramuses; as men without feeling, to be treated as so many cattle, nay, worse than the cattle the farmer kept on his land—(Cheers,)—and yet when we began to speak the truth we were called roving agitators, demagogues, red republicans, and God knows what. (Cheers.) I don't know whether the statement I have just made may be questioned; but I have seen the farmer take the meat and give it to his dog while his laborer has sat close by in a shed without a mouthful to eat. ('That is true.') But the extra wages are not all the Union has accomplished. I venture to assert that the farm laborers never read in their lives as they read now—('never')—would never have thought so keenly, or had the liberty to speak so freely but for the Union. (Cheers.) If there was any gentleman who had any objection to raise let him raise it now and not twit him to-morrow before his laborers or next week in the local papers. (Hear, hear.) How many thousands of laborers has this movement taught to read, who would have lived and died without being able to read from the inspired book of God; and thousands, he was pleased to think of it, were now able to read that book of books for themselves. ('That is true.') But the movement in those counties where the men have remained true, has taught their employers a little bit of good behaviour. (Applause, and a voice: 'How to use their men.') And after giving the farmers two or three years more schooling they might send round the subscription boxes and ask them to pay for their education. (Applause.) I dare say there are plenty of laborers' wives who would have cheek enough to be collectors. (Laughter.) There was, beyond a doubt, a brighter future for the farm laborer of England, if the laborers were determined it should be so. (Cheers.) To shout hurrah merely will not make it bright; nor will spending your money in a public house; but sober, steady, unflinching perseverance, would not only make the future bright but prosperous. (Applause.) One of the bright hopes of that future was the possession of political power. This was a question a great many men in the country heartily wished had never been mentioned. ('True.') When I was first called out by my fellow laborers, and went from village to village, the clergy walked round patting me on the back, and said 'Now, look here, pray don't make this a political question, keep it purely social and you will be right.' (Laughter.) I ask, is there a class of men more jealous of their political power than are the clergy? ('None.') If every Bishop was drawn from the House of Lords, and every representative of the clergy turned out of the House of Commons, they would kick up a pretty dust over it. (Laughter.) If political power was good for the priest, it must be good for the people; and whether they say yea or nay, we think otherwise. (Hear.) I hold that the farm laborers of this country would not have been in the degraded condition they are if the rights of citizenship allowed their betters had been granted them. These rights have allowed our betters to steal away our commons, and make one law for the rich and one law for the poor. (Applause.) We are now rising up to a sense of our manhood, and are determined that we will have our rights as citizens. In the House of Commons the laborer can count on 175 votes in favor of his Bill; but the farmer can not lay his hand on a single vote in favor of the Tenant Right Bill. That Bill got the dirty kick out. (Laughter.) And what about the Tenant Right Bill in the House of Lords last night? If I read the speech of Lord Granville aright he represented the Tenant Right Bill to be like the colored bladders that men sell about the streets at a half-penny apiece—very pretty to the eye, going whichever way of the wind, but when opened there is nothing in them."

During the session of 1875, the bill extending the franchise to the agricultural laborers, introduced by Mr. Trevelyan and championed by all the advanced liberals was defeated by a vote of 268 to 166—102 majority against it. The London *Times* said next morning that they were "living in days when there is no political forecast," and intimated quite sharply that Mr. Disraeli was at fault in not acting favorably. John Bright presented a petition signed by 60,000 laborers, and in doing so, spoke with all of his old eloquence and earnestness in its favor. The Hon. Wm. E. Forster pressed the passage of the Trevelyan bill with all his skill, and paid a marked tribute to the movement out of which the demand has grown, in these words:

"The meetings of agricultural laborers show us a new class taking part in public affairs with great moderation and earnestness, and avowing that injustice will be done them if a settlement of the question is longer postponed;

and the petition presented to-day, signed by 60,000 laborers, is not a petition to be lightly treated. What do honerable members wish? Do they desire a repetition of the agitation which preceded the measures of 1830 and 1867? Here are a million householders who have not votes simply by reason of the accident that they live outside boroughs, some hundreds of thousands being agricultural laborers, a class which we acknowledge to have claims, and a class which is not represented in this House. These men have patiently, persistently and earnestly for years claimed that they should be treated in the same manner as urban householders. Hardly a member of this House, or any public man out of it, or any writer of the press, denies the justice of their claim; there is, in fact, no disagreement of opinion. No one doubts they ought to be voters. The demand made from these benches is met by the answer—We agree with you, only let us pass it at our convenience. It does not satisfy these men, nor ought it; they have reasonable ground for the belief that because they have no votes their interests are neglected in comparison with the interests of those who have. Is it not time for us to consider seriously how long we can with prudence persevere in a policy which would be absurd if it were not dangerous, the policy of excluding a million by treating their claim with indifference, almost contemptuous indifference, while we vie with each other in acknowledging its justice?"

The next general election will very probably see the laborer and agitator, Joseph Arch, elected to the English Parliament, the peer of the proudest man in that land. His career has been a remarkable one, and now with the consciousness of large abilities, the love and respect not only of his own class, but of the people generally, and in the full meridian of his powers, he has before him a career of influence to which it is difficult to assign limits.

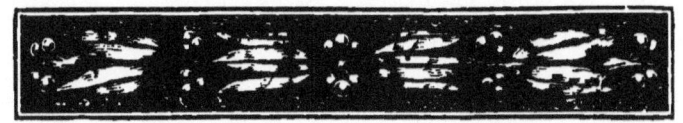

XVIII.

Charles Bradlaugh.

CHARLES BRADLAUGH was born September 26th, 1833, at Hoxton, an Eastern suburb of London. His father was a solicitor's clerk and law copyist. The son writes of him: "He was an extremely industrious man, and a splendid penman. I never had an opportunity of judging his tastes or thoughts, except in one respect, in which I have followed in his footsteps. He was passionately fond of angling." Mr. Bradlaugh's attendance on school began at seven and was completed before he was twelve, when he was employed as an errand boy in the solicitor's office, where his father was engaged. He left this office at the age of fourteen and became wharf clerk and cashier to a firm of coal dealers. Soon after commenced the life of agitation which Mr. Bradlaugh has since pursued. The Chartist movement was then at its height, intensified soon after by the revolutionary excitement of toppling thrones and fleeing kings, which the continental nations exhibited. Meetings were being constantly held in the neighborhood of young Bradlaugh's home. They were commonly held in the open air, and generally in the evening or on Sundays. Bishop Bourne's field was the favorite meeting place—then an open space in Eastern London, bearing historical associations in its name to every English ear, and close to a neighborhood that was most notable, and whose chief residents were and are the descendants of men and women who had occasion to remember the cruel ecclesiastic and the mistress he served—the "Bloody Queen" Mary Tudor, whose career Tennyson has freshly embalmed in the precious amber of his verse. The neighborhood referred to is that of Spitalfields, largely inhabited by weavers of the famous silk known by that name. These weavers are the descendants of Huguenot settlers, who fled to England after the revocation of the edict of Nantes. The narrow streets in which they then lived and worked appeared to a looker-on like a section of some French manufacturing town of the seventeenth century, slightly modernized, set down bodily in the poorer portion of London. There were dingy brick dwellings—three stories in height—the fronts of which, above the ground or store floors, were lit by narrow latticed casements with leaden frames and diamond shaped panes, running clear across the room-fronts, thus giving ample light to the workers at the Jacquard looms within. The principal business besides weaving seemed to be the rearing, buying and selling of song birds and fancy pigeons. Little shops, musical with the twitter and songs of birds, filled whole streets, giving space only to the necessary butcher, grocer, baker, and the "public," where both men and women met and discussed the birds, the flight and breed of their pigeons, the wages they received and the "Charter"—for the weavers were and are among the most ardent politicians in England. On the roof of nearly every dwelling could be seen the pigeon cots, and great numbers of the beautiful birds were continually being trained.

. Mr. Bradlaugh, then an ardent and studious boy of fifteen years, was far removed from the agitation into which he so soon developed. He attended an Episcopal church regularly with his parents, and was, he says, a teacher in the Sunday School attached thereto. This habit was however suddenly terminated in this wise,—to use Mr. Bradlaugh's own language.—

"The Bishop of London was announced to hold a confirmation in Bethnal Green. The incumbent of St. Peter's, Hackney Road, the district in which I resided, was one John Graham Packer, and he, desiring to make a good figure when the Bishop came, pressed me to prepare for confirmation, so as to answer any question the Bishop might put. I studied a little the Thirty-nine Articles of the Church of England, and the four Gospels, and came to the conclusion that they differed. I ventured to write the Rev. Mr. Packer a respectful letter, asking him for aid and explanation. All he did was to denounce my letter to my parents as Atheistical, although at that time I should have shuddered at the very notion of becoming an Atheist, and he suspended me for three months from my office as Sunday-school teacher. This left me my Sundays free, for I did not like to go to church while suspended from my teacher's duty, and I, instead, went to Bonner's Fields, at first to listen, but soon to take part in some of the discussions which were then always pending there."

As a polemist his first appearance was on the side of religion. But in 1849 he had become a "Freethinker," and a rupture with his father occurred. The Vicar instigated Mr. Bradlaugh, Sen., to demand the surrender of his son's opinions, coupling therewith a threat of loss of employment. The result of this was that the young man left his home, never more to return while his father lived. He began in earnest the life of a lecturer, following in the day whatever occupation he could obtain. During the previous year (1848) he had made his first political harangue at a large open air meeting held one Sunday in Bishop Bonner's fields,—a meeting which was violently assailed on breaking up by a body of armed police; and for speeches at which Ernest Jones, the eloquent barrister, brilliant writer, orator and poet, with one or two others, were subsequently arrested and sent to Tuthills·Penitentiary for two years, on account of the sedition which, it was charged, they advocated.

Charles Bradlaugh, the boy orator, soon became well known in the circles attracted to such discussions; first as a Deist, and later as an Atheist. At the same time he became connected with the "Secular" movement, which was just then shaping itself. From the time of leaving his Father's house in 1848, until December, 1850, his position was a severe one, full of arduous efforts at "making a living," and of attempts to obtain the knowledge to which preceding years had not been favorable. He wrote polemical pamphlets that attracted some attention; tried to do business as a coal dealer, but was not very successful; was very poor "and at the time" he says "was also very proud." He learned during these years, he says himself, "a little Hebrew and an imperfect smattering of other tongues." However imperfect were such acquisitions then, it is certain they have been so diligently used as to make his scholarship of accurate value to him in subsequent years of disputation. Mr. Bradlaugh's mastery of French is almost as complete as that of his mother tongue.

An event occurred at the time (1850) whose results have probably been quite marked on his character and career. Depressed by his penury, which had been brought home by a subscription raised and offered him by some freethinking friends, Mr. Bradlaugh in his nineteenth year enlisted as a private in the Seventh Dragoon Guards. He remained in the service for three years, being quartered during the whole of the time in Ireland. His father had died during this period, and receiving a small legacy from an aunt, Mr. Bradlaugh purchased his discharge and returned to London. No one familiar with the effects of military life can fail to detect them in the manner of the lecturer and agitator. His gestures are often as effective a part of his oratory as are his words. Those who have heard his vivid presentation of the French Revolution, or the other remarkable characterization and comparison of Cromwell and Washington, both of which were delivered in the United States as Lyceum lectures in the winter of 1874-5, will remember some of these gestures. One especially where he describes the unsheathing of the sword in the revolutionary period he portrayed, and during which he draws an imaginary weapon, bringing it apparently into the air with the rhythmical movement of the trained swordsman, must have strongly impressed his audiences. Another gesture, which indicated the drilled soldier, could be observed when in describing Cromwell, he pictured some trait as with a rapid dash of a brush on canvas, by swiftly throwing his hand to the left hip with the motion required in grasping a sword hilt.

On returning to civil life, Mr. Bradlaugh obtained employment as a clerk in the office of a Solicitor. At this time, in his writings, he assumed the signature of, "Iconoclast." The object was to veil his personality; but he could not have expressed it more perfectly. His employer, a Mr. Rogers, sturdily refused to interfere with his clerk's liberty of conscience or action, only requiring that he should not bring polemics into "chambers." Mr. Bradlaugh thus acquired a knowledge of common law and statutory enactments which bear upon the right of public meeting, printing, writing, petition and other conditions affecting his position as a radical agitator, that has been and still is of the greatest service to him in the part he plays and the place he strives to occupy. Many incidents could be given of his successful evasions of restraining law, and of the shrewd devices to carry his points, which have marked his twenty years of trenchant discussion. His skill in this way has been equalled only by that of the greatest agitator that has lived since the days of Peter the Hermit—Daniel O'Connell. The most notable illustration of this skill and the use he has put it to, may be found in his delivery of the famous "Impeachment of the House of Brunswick," a lecture which is the fiercest philippic and severest indictment of the reigning Royal family of Great Britain, ever made. It must be acknowledged to be an argument of remarkable vigor, research and directness. It raised a storm of fierce indignation, but the orator held his way without flinching, daring the government to arraign him, as was threatened, for treasonable utterances. His argument as to the legal right he claimed and has fully exercised, to agitate for the repeal of the "Acts of Settlement and Union," by which the electors of Hanover became monarchs of Britain, can be best stated in his own words: "It is of course assumed, as a point upon which all supporters of the present Royal Family will agree, that the right to deal with the throne is inalienably vested in the English people, to be exercised by them through their representatives in Parliament." He proceeds to affirm that "the right to succeed to the throne is a right accruing only from" the acts alluded to, and that therefore he has the same right to discuss the advisability of their repeal as he has of other laws. To deny this is to deny the fundamental right of control over the Executive power which he shows is historically to be the basis of the English system. Alluding to the precedents, he says,—evidently having in mind a living Heir apparent,—"The Convention which assembled at Westminster on January 22d, 1688, took away the crown from James II., and passed over his son, the then Prince of Wales, as if he had been non-existent. This convention was declared to have all the authority of Parliament—ergo Parliament has admitted the right to deprive a living King of his crown and to treat a Prince of Wales as having no claim to the succession."

After citing authorities in support of his position, Mr. Bradlaugh proceeds to arraign the Royal House on eight counts. He declares that with the exception of the present Queen, the policy of the family "has been hostile to the welfare of the mass of the people." In support of this he gives a formidable array of authorities, citing the personal and political offences of which the history of England has for a century and a half been full. He charges that fifteen-sixteenths of the National debt has been created in defence of a pro-German policy, and further that royal incompetency has during the Brunswick *régime* transferred the governing power to a few powerful families. A huge pension list has been created; national expenditures frightfully increased, America lost to Great Britain, Ireland made chronically discontented by bad government, and the burdens of taxation have been shifted from the land to the masses. He arraigns the Family as proven incapable, in that they have not initiated or encouraged wise legislation. The first George was a German, could not speak English, despised his new subjects and cared chiefly for what he made from them. The second George cared more for Hanover than England, and desired only the joint reputation of being a great general and a great libertine. The Third was often insane, "and in his officially lucid moments, his sanity was more dangerous to England than his madness." The Fourth George was a drunkard, debauchee, bad husband, unnatural son, false friend, unfaithful lover, corrupt regent and worse King. His successor William, was narrow-minded, obstinate, bigoted, timid, yielding when "continued resistance became dangerous." Mr. Bradlaugh's argument is carefully fortified by a long arrayed list of authorities and by a curious collection of the lampoon and satirical literature of the periods described.

Another illustration of his acquaintance with English laws and precedents, has reference to the allowance made the Duke of Edinburgh on the occasion of his marriage with the daughter of the Russian Czar. Some indiscreet radicals called a meeting in Trafalgar Square to discuss the pending measure. The proposed place of meeting is within a mile of the Palace of Westminster. It is forbidden to assemble for such purposes within that mile of Parliament while it is in session, and considering the proposition relating to which the meeting was to be called, Mr. Bradlaugh advised his friends they could not meet for such a purpose, and then headed a deputation to the Home Office, where he informed the Secretary that the meeting would be held. That functionary, in mild amazement at the audacity of his interlocutor, repeated the interdict which had already been made public. Mr. Bradlaugh's response was that the meeting would be held to petition Her Majesty the Queen to provide, in view of the burdens of the people, the marriage portion of the Duke from her own private purse. The Secretary still repeated his interdict, and Mr. Bradlaugh left with his deputation, declaring the call a legal one, and that the meeting would be held. He stated also very plainly that their legal right would be defended by resistance to any interference. The meeting was held and no interruption occurred. Still another illustration may be given of his ability. After several unsuccessful attempts to prevent the mass meetings in Hyde Park, which have been so common of late years, Mr. Ayrton, Commissioner in charge of Public Works and Parks, under the Gladstone administration of 1869, brought in a bill to effect that closing of the parks,—the inability to do which under then existing legislation had been clearly shown. The right of meeting was not so much involved, as a larger principle—that of whether or not the Crown Lands, of which the Parks are part, are personally seized to the reigning monarch; Mr. Bradlaugh and friends claiming that they always were public property, accessible to the people whenever they so desired. Finding the bill referred to was likely to slip through, Mr. Bradlaugh availed himself of a long disused privilege which he found in the books, and presented through Mr. Denman, now a leading judge, a petition to be heard at the Bar of the House, on the ground that his rights and privileges as a citizen were to be invaded by the act against which he desired to protest. The petition was not granted, but the Park measure was not pushed to a second reading.

The religious position of Mr. Bradlaugh has greatly obscured his political reputation with the general public, and has made the judgment of his opponents harsher than it would otherwise be. In part his extreme position is due to the logical directness which is a characteristic of his intellect, but the truculent and sometimes irreverent nature of his advocacy (for he is no respecter of persons) can be traced more directly to the bitter social and personal ostracism which followed, in his earlier years, the avowed advocacy of skeptical opinions. When to that advocacy was added attacks on existing institutions, especially vigorous ones on the church, marked according to popular rumor by want of taste and bitter assault, it must be acknowledged that the winning of recognition has been an arduous task indeed. To understand fully Mr. Bradlaugh's character, it must be also remembered, that in earlier manhood, the law made him a pariah, refusing his testimony in courts, holding him subject to pains and penalties as a "blasphemer," though this law has not been enforced since the imprisonment of George Jacob Holyoake, in 1844-5, on such a charge. Even now there are on the British statute books several acts, the enforcement of which would surely bring penalties and disabilities to those who are honestly heretical, or are openly known as "freethinkers." Mr. Bradlaugh himself, having been compelled by business misfortunes to become a bankrupt, was at first debarred from obtaining the benefit of the laws in such cases made and provided, and compelled at a large cost, to create public interest and agitation, sufficient to ensure attention for his petition to Parliament and secure a repeal of the disability. It should be stated to his credit that he has since, though not legally held, paid every dollar of the debts that were then compounded.

In the same way he had to fight, in 1870-71, an attempt to revive against his journal, the *National Reformer*, the penalties of a law long obsolete. He was convicted and a fine—a fine whose total would have beggared a millionaire—imposed for each copy published; from this decision he appealed, being his own lawyer, and practically gained a victory; the government breaking down at last on an attempt to fasten his connection with a certain issue and date. Here again his knowledge of law served him in good stead. The costs however amounted to about seven hundred pounds.

But in all probability, the animating impulse in the career of Mr. Bradlaugh as a skeptical writer and agitator, has been the political status of the established church, making it part of a system by which he considers the people oppressed and plundered. He once expressed this in a remarkable peroration to a lecture he delivered in reply to a book of the Bishop of Lincoln, when in defending himself from the charge of wantonly outraging religious beliefs and sentiments, he declared that such charge was false, affirming that he must express the truth as he understood it, and that he was compelled to resist institutions through which "the shadow of the Prelate's palace rotted the thatch on the Peasant's cottage."

In 1858, Mr. Bradlaugh became the President of the London Secular Society, in place of Mr. Holyoake, who was occupied with his general labor as a journalist and his special work on behalf of co-operation. When the Secularists formed a National Society, Mr. Bradlaugh became its President, a position he still fills. This remarkable movement requires some further reference, in order to a better understanding of the influences which sustain its leader. The National Association of "Secularists" in its declaration of principles, considers "the promotion of Human Improvement and Happiness" to be "the highest duty;" holds that current, theological teachings, are "obstructive" of the same; that in order to effectually promote both, every individual "ought to be well placed and instructed," and all of a suitable age "ought to be usefully employed for their own and the general good;" that civil and religious liberty are necessary, and that therefore every member must consider it a duty "to actively attack all barriers to equal freedom of thought and utterance for all, upon political and theological subjects." Among other objects it declares the following programme for political agitation: 1st. Secular education; 2d. Disestablishment and disendowment of the State Church; 3d. Improvement of the Agricultural Laborers condition; 4th. A change in the Land Laws, so as to secure for the laborer an interest in the soil he cultivates; 5th. Abolition of the hereditary House of Peers and substitution of a National Senate with life members; and 6th. Investigation of the causes of poverty in old countries; plans of amelioration proposed, with the laws governing the increase of population and produce, as well as the laws affecting the rise and fall of wages.

What is the general estimation of Secularism is thus stated by a recent author, himself a clergyman of the established church and vicar of Rochdale, John Bright's home. "Secularism is the study of promoting human welfare by material means, measuring human welfare by the utilitarian rules, and making the service of others a duty of life. Secularism relates to the present existence of man, and to action; the issues of which can be tested by the experience of this life; having for its object the development of the physical, moral, and intellectual nature of man to the highest perceivable point as the immediate duty of society; inculcating the practical sufficiency of natural morality apart from Atheism, Theism, or Christianity; engaging its adherents in the promotion of human improvement by material means, and making these agreements the ground of common unity for all who would regulate life by reason, and ennoble it by service. The secular is sacred in its influence on life; for by purity of material conditions the loftiest natures are best sustained, and the lower the most surely elevated. Secularism is a series of principles, intended for the guidance of those who find theology indefinite, or inadequate, or deem it unreliable. It replaces theology, which mainly regards life as a sinful necessity, as a scene of tribulation through which we pass to a better world. Secularism rejoices in this life and regards it as the sphere of those duties which educate men to fitness for any future and better life, should such transpire. Secularism is in fact the religion of doubt. It does not necessarily clash with other religions; it does not deny the existence of God or even the truth of Christianity: but it does not profess to believe in either one or the other."*

There are a considerable number of local societies, active or passive—the organization allowing both classes—and an active and skilful propaganda is maintained, the more especially since Mr. Bradlaugh has been enabled through its agency to create a respectable Republican agitation. Most of the secular Societies are also Republican Clubs. Mr. Bradlaugh is President of the principal one—that of London. Its objects are briefly defined in the secular publication already referred to, as being besides that of bringing together persons of the same opinions, "to promote (by intellectual, legal, and moral means only,) all efforts in Parliament, on platforms, and in the Press, in harmony with Republican principles; and to teach the best system of civil government amongst mankind." It affirms that "the word 'Republic' shall signify a commonwealth, a state, or a unity of states, in which public affairs are managed by persons appointed by the people; and in which the exercise of the Sovereign power is placed in

---

* Rev. W. M. Molesworth's "History of England from 1830 to 1874."

representatives freely elected by the people,"—and then declares its motto to be "Ballots, not Bullets." It is worthy of notice at this point, that in Mr. Bradlaugh's meetings, as in most connected with the Republican agitation of which he is recognized as leader, disturbances have come from those who sustain the existing order of things in the British Empire.

In connection with his political career, it may be stated that the charges of "Communism," "Red Republicanism" and "Revolutionist," which are freely made against him, are not sustained by his writings and speeches. In political economy he belongs to the Malthusian school, and at his best in that sense, is a strict disciple of John Stuart Mill. His land propositions are by no means as sweeping as those which the great Prussian statesman, Baron Stein, inagurated in 1814 for the lasting benefit of his own country. It is not until within the past three or four years that Mr. Bradlaugh has been in any way identified with the Labor movement, as strictly understood in England. Even that connection has been a political one. He does not hesitate to express a doubt whether combination can permanently raise the rate of wages, though he has always advocated the right to combine. The "Miners' National Union," and that of Northumberland, as well as the "Agricultural Laborers' Union" are those whose demonstrations Mr. Bradlaugh has attended,—and only there by invitation,—for as he has recently stated, it is not his desire to saddle them with such odium as rests upon himself in consequence of antagonism to the ordinary faiths.

As a politician Mr. Bradlaugh's activity did not fully begin until the civil war in the United States divided public opinion between the North and the South. During the ten years preceding, there had been no marked movement in radical politics, and most of the speeches made by him, bearing on other than his special topics, were in connection with the Italian movement, and in support of Mazzini and Garibaldi. During this time he first visited the continent and began to be intimately known to French radicals and republicans. Naturally Mr. Bradlaugh placed himself at the outset, on the side of the American Union. He also began to write and lecture upon the Labor and Church questions in Ireland, and when the Reform League of 1864–5 and–6, was organized under the presidency of Mr. Edmund Beales, he became one of the Vice Presidents and a member of the Executive Council.

From this date forward Mr. Bradlaugh's public career has been more essentially political, and his name has become known as that of a Republican leader. Allusion has been made to his trial for publishing the National Reformer, contrary to law. A brief autobiographical sketch thus details the circumstances:—

"In 1868 I entered into a contest with the Conservative Government which, having been continued by the Gladstone Government, finished in 1869 with a complete victory for myself. According to the then law every newspaper was required to give sureties to the extent of £800 against blasphemous or seditious libel. I had never offered to give these sureties, as they would have probably been liable to forfeiture about once a month. In March, 1868, the Disraeli Government insisted on my compliance with the law. I refused. The Government then required me to stop my paper. I printed on the next issue, 'Printed in Defiance of Her Majesty's Government.' I was then served with an Attorney-General's information, containing numerous counts, and seeking to recover enormous penalties. I determined to be my own barrister, and while availing myself, in consultation, of the best legal advice, I always argued my own case. The interlocutory hearings before the Judges in Chambers were numerous, for I took objection to nearly every step made by the government, and I nearly always succeeded. I also brought the matter before the Parliament, being specially backed in this by Mr. Milner Gibson, Mr. John Stuart Mill, and Mr. E. H. J. Crawfurd. When the information was called on for trial in a crowded court before Mr. Baron Martin, the Government backed out, and declined to make a jury; so the prosecution fell to the ground. Strange to say, it was renewed by the Gladstone Government, who had the coolness to offer me, by the mouth of Attorney-General Collier, that they would not enforce any penalties if I would stop the paper, and admit that I was in the wrong. This I declined, and the prosecution now came on for trial before Baron Bramwell and a special jury. Against me were the Attorney-General, Sir R. Collier, the Solicitor-General, Sir J. D. Coleridge, and Mr. Crompton Hutton. I found that these legal worthies were blundering in their conduct of the trial, and at *nisi prius* I let them obtain a verdict, which, however, I reversed on purely technical grounds, after a long argument, which I sustained before Lord Chief Baron Kelly and a full court sitting in Banco. Having miserably failed to enforce the law against me, the government repealed the statute, and I can boast that I got rid of the last shackle of the obnoxious English press laws. Mr. J. S. Mill wrote me: 'You have gained a very honorable success in obtaining a repeal of the mischevious Act by your persevering resistance.' The government, although beaten, refused to reimburse me any portion of the large outlay incurred in fighting them."

In 1868, Mr. Bradlaugh contested the Borough of Northampton, polling nearly a thousand votes. He has twice since then contested the same borough, receiving each time a larger vote. The last poll showed over 1700, and there is little doubt of his achieving his election ere long.

The canvasses as conducted by him have been quite characteristic. If assailed by his opponents, whether as to religious opinions or personal character, he at once retorted, not denying the first and replying to the latter. As most of these have been mere slanders, his retorts have been bitter and denunciatory. He recently refused to become the recognized Liberal candidate for Northampton at the next vacancy, unless it was arranged that the person who held that position at the last contest and who was guilty of making a libellous charge against himself, should be withdrawn from any further candidacy. It had been proposed to run them on the same ticket. Mr. Bradlaugh makes a practice of demanding retraction on entering a libel suit against any person or journal that make charges of a personal character.

During the latter part of the Franco-Prussian war, after *déchéance* had been proclaimed, Mr. Bradlaugh, with Dr. Congreve, Prof. Beesly, and other leading Positivists in England, organized a movement in sympathy with Republican France, for services in which he received from Tours a flattering letter signed by Leon Gambetta, Adolphe Crémieux, and Admiral Fourdichon, and endorsed by Emmanuel Arago. Since then his connection with the Continental Republican movements has been quite conspicuous, and in France his advice is sought for by persons of great prominence. He is among those who fully believe in the sincerity of the Republican declarations of Napoleon Joseph Bonaparte, the "Red Prince," as he is termed, with whom he is on terms of close intimacy.

In the summer of 1873, Mr. Bradlaugh visited Madrid, taking with him an address to the Spanish Republican leaders. He passed through a portion of Spain in which the Carlists were operating and was made a prisoner at a place where the train was stopped. Fortunately for him his person was unknown to them and they allowed him to pass unmolested, evidently believing him bearer of despatches to the English Minister or something equally important. At Madrid a banquet was given to him, and in a carefully arranged speech made in French, he defined a policy, surprising his hearers, and those who read it afterwards, by the moderate course he advocated for his own guidance. He there declared that Republics could not exist without Republicans, and that if he was able then to make a Republic in England he would not do it, because a course of political education not yet had, was absolutely essential to its permanence.

In his *National Reformer* of June 27, 1875, Mr. Bradlaugh, in a very severe castigation of the well-known Dr. Kenealy, growing out of an attack made first while the editor was lecturing in America and repeated after his return, both in Kenealy's paper, *The Englishman*, and before his constitutents, thus replies to a charge that he advocates a "Red Republic," one "of Blood," a "Republic to cut off the head of the Queen and the Prince of Wales," &c.

"I have never advocated a Republic of force, violence, or blood. I have never advocated any sort of vengeance against the Monarch or the Heir Apparent. While I have tried, and do try, to induce throughout England a Republican feeling and Republican hope, I have always, both here by tongue and pen, and in Spain by my tongue, and in France by my pen, and in America by tongue and pen—taught the doctrine that you can never make a Republic by killing a King, but that you must do it by gradually building up, through years of education, the brains and hopes of the people."

During the winters of 1873 and '74 Mr. Bradlaugh has become widely known to the American people. He was denounced at first by a few journals, one of them speaking of him, before he lectured in the city of its publication, as a "thorough-paced bully." Since then the same journal has complimented highly a lecture on the "Land and Labor" question, expressing editorial surprise at the moderation of the orator's views. In general his reception must have been satisfactory to himself, and the comments of the press are favorable. One journal describes him on the platform as having "not a particle of the peculiar English hesitation and embarrassment, his words flowing in a smooth, uninterrupted current with a promptness quite American, and with an eloquence and fervor quite inspiring. His diction, also, is that of a man of culture and study, though he says that he had no advantages of college education, and is, in fact, a poor man, rough and common — like the mass of the people from whom he sprang, and for whose rights he pleads." Another describes him as about "six feet high, of fine commanding figure, magnetic voice, and a hand that has a world of changeful expression in itself. Whatever may be said of Bradlaugh's sentiments, it cannot be denied that he has the charm and grace of the orator." Charles Sumner and Wendell Phillips have declared him to be of the most remarkable type of English speakers. A correspondent describes him in a Western paper, as an orator for "the out-of-door, with a voice that harmonizes with those of nature. It has a resonant ring in it, somewhat like the blare of the brass of which the German military instruments are made, the peculiar penetrating quality of which every one who has heard them will not fail to recall." Mr. Bradlaugh speaks naturally and with great ease, his *impromptus* being as finished as his prepared efforts. A little speech made in response to a call at a woman's suffrage meeting in Boston, exhibits this and will bear quoting in part. After saying that he only rose in response to the call, and would speak but briefly, Mr. Bradlaugh said :—

"There are only two grounds on which the exercise of individual suffrage can be claimed or denied. The first is that of right, the second that of expediency. I have long since eliminated the latter from my mind, and the former furnishes no sex distinctions. It is not a national question, it is a human one. All humanity have equal interest in its solution."

He then referred to the agitation in England, and said that he had always favored it on this ground :—

"That those who have to obey laws should have the opportunity of expressing consent to the legislation; on the ground urged by Pym and Hampden, and later by Chatham for yourselves, that a government has no right to put its hand in the pocket of a citizen who has no voice in its creation nor of control in its conduct. He was for woman's suffrage in no pretended spirit of chivalry or mockery of desire to assist a sex inferior in intellectual ability : he was in favor of it as a duty and a right. The sex which had its Hypatia, whose intellect and humanity stood out clear and bright in the world's then dark pages, need hardly even give as proofs of its efficiency the many brilliant stars which have so often shone, despite the clouds custom had hung to obscure woman's cause."

XIX.

GEORGE ODGER.

JUSTIN McCARTHY writing of "Republicanism in England,"* describes the meeting of sympathy for the French Republic held in Trafalgar Square, a place which, like Hyde Park, is often the scene of the great Radical gatherings that have of late years grown so common in England. McCarthy says: "The great political leaders never make their voices heard at Trafalgar Square; but Trafalgar Square makes its voice heard by all parties." He refers to this particular meeting at length, using it as a text by which to illustrate the growth of Republican ideas. "The meaning of the thing" he says "was plain, let who would pretend to ignore, or to deny, or to despise it." The meaning was that the vast majority of the intelligent working men of London are thoroughly, earnestly, and even passionately republican. Farther on he describes a small meeting held for

---

* The *Galaxy*, July, 1871.

deliberative purposes. Leaders of the working class were there, and so also were representative thinkers of the Positivist and other schools. " But the sentiment of the meeting was just the same as that of Trafalgar Square." It is not inappropriate, before proceeding to personal reference to Mr. Odger and his representative position, to give what Justin McCarthy says as to the ideas of Democracy entertained by the class of whom Mr. Odger may fairly be regarded as the most marked representative.

"The London artisan, always rather intelligent and always inclined to radicalism, is to-day a man well read in the politics of his time, highly practical in all his objects, well drilled into the discipline of co-operation and organization by his Trades' Unions, and as little inclined to rave of social contracts or demand re-distribution of property as Horace Greeley would be. He means what he says; he knows what he is talking about. When he throws up his hat for a republic, he has not the remotest expectation that a republic would make him rich or place the property of his wealthy neighbor at his disposal. But he has acquired a clear and strong conviction that a republican government is the fairest, the cheapest, and the best political system, and he sees plainly the real, not the imaginary defects and sins of the system which surrounds him." Of the "Trades' Union" to which Mr. McCarthy attributes a large degree of this republican spirit, he says; "Its own organization is essentially republican. It has been hitherto an association formed virtually outside the English constitution and with no protection from English law. It has looked royalty in the face, and seen there was nothing divine there; it has counted how much kings and queens cost, and found they were not worth the money. Of late, too, the London working man has discovered he counts for something. He has been called into council with the great political leader, or the great aristocrat, and he sees they are only men like himself. * * * By his brains and his own strength he fought his way upward."

Since these words were written, working men, as such, have entered the English House of Commons. The next general election, whether it comes soon, or shall be long delayed, will see a considerable increase in their number. It is quite probable that such a result may induce the "territorial" liberals, as the whig families have been named, to allow Mr. Disraeli a longer term of office than would otherwise be probable, on the principle of —"after us, the deluge."

One of the foremost men in bringing about the republican growth, which no impartial and clear-sighted observer can fail to see in England, is George Odger, a London shoemaker, and one who, were he ten or fifteen years younger than he is, might fairly see open before him prospects of marked honors in the future and more democratic life, on which his country is entering. Mr. Odger is spoken of "as one of the very ablest and best among the working-men leaders."* He is an avowed Republican, and shares with Mr. Bradlaugh the leadership of such movement in that direction as openly organizes itself. It might not be proper to say that Mr. Odger is the foremost

---

* Justin McCarthy, *Galaxy*, July, 1871.

leader; but it is certainly true that Mr. Bradlaugh's constituency would be small to-day, if he had not been preceded by George Jacob Holyoake in the organization of the Secularist movement, and by George Odger in the early federation and consolidation of the Trades' Societies, lifting them out of merely local and class importance into a distinct social, political and economical force. George Odger fairly represents the modern British artisan, in the same sense that Joseph Arch must be regarded as the representative of the agricultural Laborer, of whom Mr. McCarthy wrote in the same sketch from which quotations have already been made, that—" Of the mental condition of the English peasant, the laborer in the fields, who ought to be at least the peer of the artisan in the towns, I hesitate to speak in language which would seem to be adequate lest I should appear guilty of gross exaggeration. I doubt if any country in the civilized world has a class among its people so stupid, so ignorant, so debased in the passive sense, as the English agricultural laborer. * * * For the present the agricultural workers may be set down in politics simply as a torpid mass, as incapable either of individual or collective action, even in their own interests, as the pigs and the oxen who are their familiar companions." Yet this same class, within ten months of the publication of the foregoing, startled England with an organized movement as memorable in character and extent as any of the greatest popular efforts that preceded it. Within two years it commanded the voices of Francis Newman and Cardinal Manning; of Professor Fawcett and Charles Bradlaugh; of the Earl of Shaftesbury and John Bright; and in less than four years after Mr. McCarthy had written, that—"these men have no vote, and I hardly think the most ardent upholder of extended suffrage could find much cause to desire the immediate extension of the suffrage to them"—the bill to give them that suffrage was supported in the House of Commons by speeches from Trevelyan, Bright, Fawcett, Taylor, Dilke, Mundella, Lubbock, Brassey, Morley, Lord Montague and others, and received 167 votes in its favor. The rate of social progress is growing rapidly in England, and it is not safe to forecast without a clear apprehension of the conditions.

George Odger was born in 1829, at the little village of Roubro', lying between Plymouth and Tavistock, in the County of Devon, and is now in his fifty-fifth year. His father, John Odger, was a native of Cornwall and a miner. The son was born in penury, and habituated to toil from his earliest years. His boyish education was limited to the rustic "dame school" of his native hamlet, and hardly reached to the dignity of the "three R's—reading, 'riting and 'rithmetic." At about ten years of age, he began to learn the shoemaker's trade, and he continued to follow it regularly, until in his earlier manhood he became so noted a Trades' Leader, that employers marked him as a man not to be hired if it was possible to avoid it. This in the elementary days of the English labor agitation is reported to have been a favorite means of punishing workmen who became too conspicuous as leaders. There are a score of men now in radical politics there, who have been made prominent by the influence of such a policy. The craft Mr. Odger followed has always been noted for its tendency to produce strong and reflective men. Its sedentary character probably helps study and reflection, where the mind naturally turns that way. Certain it is, that Mr. Odger began early to read and study, and before he had arrived at manhood he became a local celebrity both as writer and speaker. He did not remain long in his native place, but travelled to the large towns, seeking and obtaining work, learning men and affairs, and at last settling in London, when about twenty years of age. He was soon known as an expert workman at his trade, and is to-day regarded as one of the very best in the English metropolis. Until very recently, at least, he worked quite regularly at his trade, though not entirely dependent upon it as a source of income. His extensive and accurate knowledge of English working life, and his power both as writer and speaker are generally sufficient to command all his time and return sufficient remuneration for his moderate habits,—enabling him also to serve the causes for which he has always struggled. The *Contemporary Review* of 1870 and 1871, published several able articles from his pen, on the Land question, the Labor Law, Representation, and similar topics.

It was in London that he first became prominent as a Trades' Unionist, but in a spirit more sagacious and liberal than generally prevailed at the time. The introduction of machinery into the cord-wainers' shops created, as is apt to be the case at first, violent opposition on the part of the operatives. Mr. Odger openly opposed this folly and was able to make his associates accept his views. He first became widely known by his active work in organizing the movements which dated from the great lock-out in 1851, by engineer and iron manufacturing firms of nearly or quite 30,000 workmen. This was in consequence of the determination of the Amalgamated Engineers, the strongest union of skilled artisans then or now in existence, to demand the abolition of piece-work and some other details. The result that followed was seen first in the consolidation of local societies or unions belonging to the same trade into general unions; next in the amalgamation of the trades belonging to a related group into a larger body. The Engineer Union already mentioned is an example. It is, as originally formed, one of eight or ten different Trades' Societies. Next came the effort towards federation, with which Mr. Odger has been most closely identified. It manifested itself first in efforts to form delegate councils in large towns and boroughs or other centers of industry, then in extending these till they embrace a whole district, like the potteries of Staffordshire or the collieries of Yorkshire and Durham. Then came the convening of an annual Trades Conference or Congress, and later still the remarkable organization known as "the International Working Men's Association." In both of these latter movements, Mr. Odger may fairly be regarded as a leading mind and organizing brain. He was connected with the "International" until when, after the close of the Paris commune rebellion, it felt itself obliged, on account of the position it had borne thereto, to assume the role of a political conspiracy instead of continuing as it had been, an open and avowed, but peaceful propaganda for social, economic and political changes, great in their scope and startling perhaps in their significance. George Odger appears from the first of the movements thus outlined, to have worked with a clear and definite apprehension of the end in view—that of organizing labor, so that it would not only demand more wages, but in the end require and compel the organization of a better economic system, through the operations of which a more equitable distribution of results should be attained. He also aimed at the political enfranchisement of his class, and to that end he has never failed to advise that their associations should, through their larger and delegated assemblies, take a decided political position. His speeches at the several Trades' Conferences and Congresses he has served in, from those at Sheffield and Preston sixteen years or so ago to the last, held in Liverpool, April, 1875, all advocate these views. A student of this remarkable phase of English radical politics, cannot fail to see that Mr. Odger's perceptions of the character of the force with which he was then dealing, as well as its relations to the general interests of the nation whereof he was a member, fairly entitled him to be regarded as possessing a great deal of philosophical and statesmanlike insight.

In 1859 he first became more generally known to the London artisans, by his service on a general committee appointed to aid the building-trades' workmen, then on strike to the number of 10,000, for a reduction of the hours from ten to nine per day. In any part of the United States, unless it might be Pennsylvania, it would be difficult for one to realise the sort of excitement that such an event could then produce in London and indirectly on the whole of England, the circumstance even assuming a political character. Great meetings were held in Hyde Park. The police were used to watch the strikers or to protect the "blacklegs," as those are called who work outside the Union movement. It was a common thing for men to be arrested for posting placards or distributing hand bills, while Parliament was besought to enact special legislation against the strikers. Mr. Odger was one of the active advisers of the latter class. His association with the Trades' Societies and the movement born of them has extended over nearly forty years. For many years he has been a member of the London Trades' Council, and until within a year or two has occupied the position of secretary.

It was this body, under the presidency of George Potter, editor of the London *Beehive*—who, like Mr. Odger, was also a member of the Executive Council of the Reform League—that induced the London Unions to abandon their policy of abstention from organized political agitations, and act on the advice of John Bright. They appeared in 1866 in a great street procession and meeting, 30,000 strong, in support of the popular demand for household suffrage. The effect of that demonstration was quite notable, and the London press for days after the procession had marched through the principal streets of the fashionable West End, teemed with half-frightened references to its military, aspect, good marching, admirable order, well closed column and complete discipline.

This energy and activity combined with his very. decided ability have kept Mr. Odger in the very front rank of agitation for at least a quarter of a century. During the decade between 1850 and 1860, when the English artisan was chiefly engaged in social and economic efforts, he was usually a member of delegations sent from bodies to petition or remonstrate with the Ministry in power on different measures that were pending. It is stated that Mr. Odger at one of these deputations strongly attracted ed the notice of Mr. Gladstone, then Chancellor of the Exechequer under Loid Palmerston's premiership. The occasion was a bill offered by the Government in regard to Friendly Societies. He was engaged in perfecting a series of fiscal and ameliorative measures, whose results have proven widely beneficial, especially to the working class. But every measure offered by the Palmerston Government was regarded by the working-men with suspicion, because of the fact that Lord Palmerston had promised a reform bill and then failed to fulfil his pledges. The particular bill which caused the sending of a deputation was designed to strengthen the societies, but some details were objectionable. Mr. Gladstone, who is reported to be much more friendly in his reception of such deputations than is common, took the opportunity of inquiring why such distrust prevailed of his own and colleagues, intentions, among those whom Mr. Odger represented. The Finance Minister was asked at once,—if he wanted a full and free answer? He replied affirmatively, of course. Mr. Odger replied—because the workmen had been betrayed. An animated discussion ensued. A few nights after Mr. Gladstone declared in the Commons in substance what the Radical Odger had affirmed—that it was the duty of those who keep the people out of the exercise of their right of representation, to give reasons for the wisdom and good policy of their acts. Mr. Gladstone spoke warmly and created some debate. It has been stated that Mr. Gladstone has since that day frequently had occasion to consult Mr. Odger, whose accurate knowledge of the working men's movements and wishes, has probably been of great value to the Liberal statesman.

Mr. Odger's connection with the "International Working Men's Association," began with the very first steps of that movement, in its organized form. The first proposition advanced for a general confederation of Labor, based on the assumption that its interests were necessarily at war with the current economic system, came from Dr. Karl Marx and Frederic Engel, two well-known German political refugees residing in London, who just before the outbreak of the French Revolution in 1848, issued an address setting forth their view of the historical-social development, and predicting that labor or production, as a controlling power, must take the place of the trading or commercial spirit. This document, a very remarkable one in its ability and purpose, was translated into English. No organization was made. Nothing was attempted until, in 1864, the leading English Unionists, of whom Mr. Odger was foremost, became converts to the plan long urged by Dr. Marx, who had returned to London after the Republican disasters of 1848, of organizing an International Society. The practical result at which the Englishmen aimed was, by arriving at a common understanding with Continental workmen, to prevent their being ignorantly used by English employers to replace their native workmen when a "strike" or "lockout" was in progress. This was the view first put forward by the English advocates. A meeting was convened at St. Martin's Hotel, September 28, 1864, at which Mr. Odger was a prominent speaker. It was at a time too, when a Polish agitation was in progress, and this lent some further interest to the movement. It is not necessary to follow the progress of this famous bug-bear, for such it was to the Conservative influences of the old world. The facts given as to its origin have been verified by original document, and personal knowledge. In England the movement always had, up to the outbreak of the Franco-Prussian wars a Trades' Union aspect. So also in Belgium to a certain extent. In France, Germany and elsewhere, repressive attempts made it political. Its platform made in 1865, at the first Congress it held in Geneva, expresses in simpler form than can be found elsewhere, the underlying ideas of the Democratic-Socialist movement, evidence of the deep seated character of which is everywhere visible in Europe —if not so plainly in the United States. The movement was an open one, though of course its policy and methods were not usually proclaimed. As George J. Eccarius, its able general Secretary for several years, once tersely said —"The people agitate; they do not conspire." Of course, he added—"We are the People." Mr. Odger remained a member of the general Council until 1872, when with most of the English sections and leaders he retired. Since then the "International" seems to have become almost as shadowy an affair as the famous Italian Carbonari. The English artisan has but little time for Utopian efforts, and those who lead them must not go so far in advance as to be lost in a mist.

During the American civil war, Mr. Odger was one of the most untiring advocates of the Union cause to be found in England. This fact and the exertions he made were of considerable benefit to the cause he espoused. The London artisans were more inclined than some of their provincial friends, to accept the theory that the Southern states were simply fighting for independence, and the Northern for empire. The agents of the South expended a great deal of money and labor in the effort to increase and spread this view, especially when, in the latter part of 1862, the policy of raising the Southern blockade by Great Britain for the purpose of obtaining cotton was persistently agitated and met with some favor. The plan of those interested was to obtain a demand from the working classes, on the score of the sufferings created among the mill operatives by the cotton famine. No class opposed this so bitterly and effectively as the operatives themselves. The allies of the South were never able to hold, in the cotton district, a free public meeting to advocate their policy—the workmen invariably taking control and passing Union resolutions. In London however they seemed to be making headway. Mr. Odger, Mr. George Howell, Mr. Thomas Mottershead, Mr. W. R. Cramer, and some others of the leading Trades' Unionists, devoted themselves to the work of opposing this policy. Their labors were great, and they were made at a sacrifice, as the advocates were poor. It was stated that at one time, the Southern agents, having bought the advocacy of one of the only two avowedly democratic weekly newspapers in London, had arranged the same purchase in the case of the other. Mr. Odger, who was a member of its Board of Directors, heard of the negotiations. There was an unpaid mortgage on the property. The facts were laid before Bazley Potter, M. P., and other friends of the Union; the money was found for Mr. Odger to take up the mortgage with, and at the business meeting called to consummate the bargain with the confederate agents, Mr. Odger announced that he held the controlling position. It was to this gentleman and his colleagues that the convening of the first public meeting of London workingmen in behalf of the Union was due. That meeting was the famous one held at St. James Hall, March 26, 1863, at which John Bright made one of the most memorable of the many remarkable speeches he delivered on the "American Question." This great meeting, practically turned the tide in the British House of Commons; — Mr. Bright followed up his address there, the very next night in the House, with a vigorous assault on the resolution of confederate recognition offered by Mr. Lindsay, which had been for some time pending, and practically caused its defeat. This broke the back of Southern sympathy in Great Britain. To Mr. Odger personally, who presided at St. James' Hall, very much of the success was due. He and his friends were but a small band—but they roused the Trades' Unions from indifference to active sympathy. It was the first public demonstration those bodies had ever collectively made on a question not related to their own affairs. So doubtful were Mr. Odger and his friends, that, as is related by one of them, they were almost afraid when within a few blocks of the Hall, to go on. They dreaded lest it should be a failure, or should prove to be in the hands of an hostile crowd. But to their great pleasure they found the large hall filled to overflowing, and enough unable to enter, to make a goodly out-of-door meeting. The expenses of this meeting were all advanced by these poor men, though they were afterwards reimbursed.

Such incidents and facts illustrate the character of Mr. Odger's work and position as a public man. Soon after the cessation of the Reform League agitation, he identified himself with an avowed Republican movement, in support of which he then made an extended lecturing tour. His speeches have followed the same general lines that Mr. Bradlaugh's pursue, and are always within the law. He was however set upon by Conservative mobs and at one place was severely beaten, suffering injuries that confined him for some time. He is an excellent speaker with a strong, steady presence, good voice, and clear grasp, of his subject. He is a man of short stature, but of a massive frame, deep chested, broad shouldered, with great girth. His limbs are rather short for his trunk. The head is very large, and full in every respect. The forehead rises dome-like above the deep set greyish eyes that have a keen, humorous and questioning look in them. The features are large and rather heavy, the nose being full, the mouth large and mobile, the lower jaw heavy and firm. The general expression is kindly and sagacious, thoughtful and quiet. He is the peer in native ability of the most promising public men in England, and had he been endowed with the culture of a Gladstone or Derby, or had he been possessed of a fair pecuniary independence, there can be little doubt that George Odger would long since have been in Parliament, and would have sat in more than one British Cabinet. He is married, and his family now consists of his wife and two sons, one of whom has served in the British army.

Mr. Odger has become widely known from his unsuccessful canvasses for a seat in the House of Commons. He was the first distinctive representative of his class who offered himself as a candidate. He stood the first time for the borough of Chelsea,—now in part represented by Sir Charles Dilke. This borough was a new one—created by the Reform bill of 1867. Mr. Odger says of his candidature, that "I went to Chelsea at the invitation of a thousand electors, and the cry was then raised that I was dividing the Liberal interest, and in deference to a great principle, in order that I might not jeopardize Mr. Gladstone's power in Parliament with reference to the Irish church question, I, at the request of the working-men, who said there was a principle at stake, accepted arbitration, which being against me, I left Chelsea."*

In June, 1869, he contested the Borough of Stafford, now represented by Mr. Macdonald, President of the National Miners Union. The population consists largely of shoemakers. Four Liberal candidates (including himself) were in the field. The Tories had but two—the number to be elected. The other Liberals were Mr. W. J. Evans, and Mr. Benjamin Whitworth, both of whom had been in the House, and Mr. Edward Jenkins, author of "Ginx's baby." A biographical sketch of Mr. Odger gives the following facts in relation to this and subsequent efforts: "Mr. Odger declared his willingness that a preliminary ballot should decide which two of the three were to go to the poll; at the same time not concealing his opinion, that, since he came forward distinctly as the workingman's candidate, he ought to have been adopted, and the preliminary ballot confined to the other three. Moreover, he contended that it would have been better to give each elector but one vote in the ballot and to extend it to the whole constituency instead of confining it to such as voted for the Liberal candidate at the preceding election. The ballot, however, was taken with the following result:

---

* "Labor Portrait Gallery," *Beehive*, London, 1873.

Whitworth, 720 votes; Evans, 519; George Odger, 375; Jenkins, 182. But when the election came on, the two Liberals were rejected, and the two Tories (Salt and Talbot) were returned—a result for which George Odger, at all events, was in no way responsible.

"Not daunted by the want of success in one of the centres of his own craft, George Odger presented himself, in February, 1870, to the notice of the borough of Southwark. The constituency, always one of advanced opinions, had, by the extension of the franchise, become increasingly favorable to candidates of that stamp. It may have been warrantable also to expect that the tanners and curriers of Bermondsey would look kindly upon a candidate connected with the manufacture of shoe-leather. In fact, had George Odger been simply pitted against Colonel Beresford, there is not the least doubt that he would at this moment have been sitting as Member for Southwark. We are sorry to have to charge a gentleman deservedly so popular on other grounds as the last Lord Mayor of London, with the contrary result. Yet it cannot be doubted that Sir Sydney Waterlow insisted upon going to the poll when it was known that his chance was doubtful; and although he withdrew in favor of George Odger, he did not take the step until he had brought up a sufficient number of Liberal voters to the poll to make it quite certain the Tory must win. Beresford was encouraged to come forward by Waterlow's persistence in going to the poll in competition with George Odger; and was encouraged to persevere by the large number of votes thrown away upon the Alderman. Had the latter retired when the three Liberal members consulted first advised him, George Odger would have got in; but Sir Sydney gave to the Tory the full benefit of another hour, and Colonel Beresford the seat. The numbers were, for Beresford, 4,686; for George Odger, 4,382; for Waterlow, 2,966.

"These figures indicated so clearly the favor of the borough towards George Odger, that, when, in the following month he offered himself for Bristol, the wisdom of the step was called in question by some of his sincerest and most earnest friends. Here, as at Stafford, the Liberal to be selected as candidate for the seat vacated by the decease of Mr. Henry Berkeley was made the subject of a preliminary test ballot. Those excepted who had plumped for Mr. Miles, Tory candidate at the preceding election, each elector received a perforated card bearing in different colors the names of the three candidates, Robinson, Hodgson, and George Odger. The balloting was then carried out with admirable order under the superintendence of Mr. Crossley, of Manchester, and of Mr. Charles Godwin. The result was for Robinson, 4,558; for Hodgson, 2,761; for George Odger, 1,361."*

At the last general election Mr. Odger redeemed his promise to stand for Southwark again, but under the reaction that took place he was unsuccessful—the Liberal vote being again divided.

Mr. Odger has naturally been a leading spirit in the "Labor Representation Society." He has also served for the last four years on the Parliamentary Committee of the Trades' Union Congress, a body charged with watching and resisting class legislation in the British Parliament. The Positivist writers Frederic Harrison and Henry Comp-

---

* "Labor Portrait Gallery."

ton, with others, have served as advisory members of the same committee. Mr. Odger's is a well known figure in the lobbies of the House of Commons ; and he is there treated with uniform respect. His ability is admitted and his influence courted or feared. At a great meeting called at Hyde Park, in the summer of 1873, in regard to the so-called Labor Laws then under consideration, Mr. Odger made a speech which is spoken of as " a fair example of the manner· and spirit in which he handles the most exciting topics of common interest of the working classes. For them he claimed a full share of credit as to the high place that England occupies in the eyes of the world ; and for them also, he resented the indignity by which they had been repaid in home-made laws dooming them to a position of injury and degradation worse than they had ever known before. If Englishmen feel a law to be harsh and oppressive, they openly proclaim the fact, and, by rational discussion among themselves, lead each other along the safe and open path of manifest reason. Why, asked George Odger, should a workman be sent to prison for the violation of a contract with the master, and the master be allowed at pleasure to break his engagement with him? And there must be many, even in the master class itself, who see plainly that without any further extension or more equal distribution of the franchise these cruel and one-sided laws cannot long be kept on the Statute Book."*

The last sentence was almost prophetic ; within two years these laws have been rescinded. The London *Beehive* of August 7, 1875, contains a very clear presentation from the pen of Frederic Harrison of the legislation which the Disraeli ministry have carried. He says that it is—

"1. General abolition of special legislation against workmen as a class.

"2. Redress of the ancient rule that breach of contract by a working man is a crime.

"3. Practical as well as nominal equality between the employer and the employed as to their contracts.

"4. Redress of specific enforcement of a workman's contract as carried out by the Act of 1857.

"5. Reform in the application of the doctrine of conspiracy to all disputes between employer and employed.

"6. Repeal of the special Criminal Law Amendment Act applying to workmen.

"7. Specific legalization of attending (*i. e.*, picketing) when done in order merely to obtain or communicate information."

Mr. Harrison adds "the principles contained in the two new Bills virtually exhaust all the points for which the workmen have long contended. I am far from saying that all of these have been carried out in a way that excludes all possible evil; but it is clear that in principle every one of them has been distinctly affirmed. There has been, one must say, a scrupulous, indeed as between the rival parties, at times a jealous and most pharisaical eagerness to abolish the very shadow or semblance of partiality from the statute-book. But this very anxiety testifies to the genuine desire of the Home Office to remove every symbol of offence. It is most significant that the phrase 'employers and workmen' take the place of 'master and servant.' * * * 'This marks the opening of a new era and a new spirit in the governing class."

---

* "Labor Portrait Gallery."

Emphatic praise is accorded to Mr. Mundella for his "untiring and almost single-handed labors * * for many years, and also for the tact and patience with which he * * managed the protracted transformations through which the two Bills passed before they became law." On this side of the Atlantic it is hardly possible to appreciate the experiences and feelings of men, who, like George Odger, have for so many years fought an apparently almost hopeless fight against class rules and social oppression and political disability, as they see their cause growing daily, and feel that, one after another, the barriers in the path of "government of the people, by the people, and for the people," are being swept away forever.

XX.

JOSEPH CHAMBERLAIN.

THE Mayor of Birmingham is regarded by all parties in England as a man of marked promise, though his future value is to be best estimated by the opinions of those who differ from him. A representative man in the best sense of the well-to-do English middle-class, Mr. Chamberlain has already achieved, without any fortuitous aids, a position of considerable influence. It is not too much to say that his opinions are largely instrumental in moulding the demands of advanced Radical or Liberal politics in Great Britain.

Born in London, July, 1836, Mr. Chamberlain has at the age of thirty-nine, achieved a prominence unusual in Great Britain for a man heretofore comparatively unknown and, without those advantages of birth or liberal culture which tell so forcibly there. He was educated at an Academy School, connected with the London University from which it is named. He is a leading lay member of the Unitarian denomination — a fact which in itself has had a considerable influence on his public career. At twenty years of age Mr. Chamberlain made his permanent residence in Birmingham, becoming a partner in the firm of Nettlefold & Chamberlain, screw manufacturers. From this establishment, after a prosperous career, he recently retired in 1875, with independent means, to expend thenceforward his time and energies in the public service.

Devoting himself to business with strictness and aptitude, Mr. Chamberlain did not enter political life until 1868, at the age of 32, though he had been known before that as a man of large reading and close application, and moreover as a good public speaker, clear-headed thinker, and forcible writer. He became conspicuous at a time when a vigorous effort was being made to secure a Conservative triumph in the famous borough of which he is now the chief executive officer. But he was more widely known in the two following years from his connection with the National Education League, as the Chairman of its Executive Committee. Since then no Radical movement is counted complete without the name of Mr. Chamberlain as one of its prominent friends and advocates. He is in person rather tall, and sinewy, with a long head and face, bold, high forehead, strong features, fresh complexion, clear bright eyes, and light brown hair, and the impression that he makes is that of being a younger man than he is in reality; while before an audience his cheery aspect, readiness and ease, as well as a good voice and a wit that never deserts him, makes his presence attractive and his speech influential.

The bare facts of his public life, so far, can be briefly stated. From 1868 to 1873, his position has been that of an agitator, chiefly in support of a system of National Education entirely free from denominational control.

He is known also for the bold expression of advanced politics — to the extent even of being regarded by many as a supporter of Charles Bradlaugh and his Republican agitation. So generally did this opinion prevail, that when on the 3rd of November, 1874, it became necessary for Mr. Chamberlain as Mayor of Birmingham to officially welcome the Prince of Wales to that borough, as well as to act the host at a banquet in his honor, there was a degree of curiosity aroused, almost national in its extent, as to how he would demean himself. His speech was not Republican in character, nor did it fail in those general expressions of loyalty which form part of the paraphernalia of official life in Great Britain, though as far removed from the adulation common among municipal officials when in the presence of Royalty. In fact the Mayor's speech was a genial and manly recognition of the gentleman whose dignities and position, as the Heir to the Crown of Great Britain, demanded at least the outward respect that was paid. Some criticism was made of Mr. Chamberlain's attitude. He himself seems to have felt the necessity of correcting the wide spread belief that he was an avowed Republican in principle. A short time before the Royal reception he made a brief speech at a dinner held in his honor, and in defining his position he said he had no objection to admit that he was a Republican, if they would allow him to state what a Republican was. If it meant faith in representative institutions, and a government in which merit is preferred to birth, then he, in common with nearly all the greatest thinkers of the country, held it to be the best, at least in theory for a free and intelligent people. But, he continued, "I have never, in public or in private, advocated Republicanism for this country. We may be tending in that direction, but I hold that the time has not arrived yet, even if it ever arrives; and I hold also that Radicals and Liberals have quite enough practical reform to strive after without wasting their time in what seems to me a very remote speculation."

A leading Republican C. C. Cattell of Birmingham, in commenting on this declaration, thinks that it settles Mr. Chamberlain's position and adds: "If at any time he has befriended the Republican side, as a matter of justice, that is only what he has done to many other movements, the general principles and intentions of which he may or may not have approved. No doubt the Republican party would gain strength by having Mr. Chamberlain on their side; but it is only a matter of decency that they should wait till he so declares himself. For the present they should treat him as a possible future friend."

In 1873 he was unanimously elected President of the Birmingham School Board,—next to that of London, the most important in Great Britain. At the following municipal Election he was chosen Mayor of Birmingham by a large majority, and at the general Election of 1874, he contested with Messrs. Mundella and Roebuck the borough of Sheffield. In announcing his candidature he made a vigorous speech, remarkable for the bold liberal programme he advocated, and also for the directness with which he ranged himself on the side of Labor. This speech gave rise to extended discussion and criticism, which was not lessened by the tone of several notably trenchant articles published in the *Fortnightly Review* of about the same period. Mr. Chamberlain gave expression in these to what he regarded as the issues on which the Liberal party should be recognized, and the rallying cries under which it should be led to battle again. Among other critics was the venerable Earl Russell, who in discussing the cause of Mr. Gladstone's defeat, and the demands of the Radical politicians, says :—

* " Mr. Chamberlain, who is a leading apostle of this school, reminds me, with his notions of progress, of Tony Lumpkin, in the play of 'She Stoops to Conquer.' I will copy part of a dialogue from that play, in which Tony Lumpkin and his mother represent tolerably well Mr. Chamberlain and John Bull. When asked to describe his journey, Tony answers,—

'*Tony.* You shall hear. I first took them down Featherbed Lane, where we stuck fast in the mud. I then rattled them crack over the stones of Up-and-down Hill. I then introduced them to the gibbet on Heavy-tree Heath ; and from that, with a circumbendibus, fairly lodged them in the horse-pond at the bottom of the garden.

'*Hast.* But no accident, I hope ?

'*Tony.* No, no, only mother is confoundedly frightened.'

" So in this case, no harm, no accident has happened, but John Bull was 'confoundedly frightened.' In fact, he has been more frightened than hurt by the threats of the advanced Liberals."

---

* " Recollections and Suggestions," pages 343-4.

The Mayor of Birmingham was unsuccessful at Sheffield, standing third in the poll, receiving 11,124 votes against Roebuck's 14,193,—Mr. Mundella having 12,911 votes. The large vote given Mr. Chamberlain in a borough where Mr. Roebuck's popularity is so great as to insure his election against any new aspirant, may be regarded as an evidence that under more favorable conditions, the National Education League and its friends will be gratified by seeing one of its most vigorous leaders seated in the House of Commons. The work it has undertaken is of great importance, and all the energy of its Executive officers are in demand. The activity has been greatly increased since 1869, while the object of the League can be most readily understood by quoting its own declaration, which is "the establishment of a system which shall secure the education of every child in the country."

The means proposed to accomplish this, are, that—

" 1.—Local authorities shall be compelled by law to see that sufficient school accommodation is provided for every child in their district.

" 2.—The cost of founding and maintaining such schools as may be required shall be provided for by Local Rates, supplemented by Government grants.

" 3.—All schools, aided by Local Rates, shall be under the management of the Local authorities, and subject to Government inspection.

" 4.—All schools aided by Local Rates shall be unsectarian.

5.—To all schools aided by Local Rates, admission shall be free.

" 6.—School accommodation being provided, the Local

authorities or the Government, shall have power to compel the attendance of children of a suitable age, not otherwise provided for."

Perhaps nothing will more clearly show the radical nature of the foregoing propositions, than a brief statement of the present position of Education in England and of legislation thereon.

The first general attempt at the education of the masses began by the organization in 1805 of the British and Foreign School Society. This is within the fold of the Church of England. In 1811, the National School Society was formed by the dissenting or non-conforming sects. Both societies, in the absence of state machinery, have been of great service. It was not until 1833 that the first step was taken by the British Government, in the appointment of a committee of Education from the Privy Council and an appropriation of £20,000 to the schools of the two associations. The same year saw the adoption of a Factory Bill, reducing the hours of labor for children, which was the first of a series of steps of great importance in this general direction. In 1842 another act was passed forbidding the employment of children in coal and other mines, and requiring those of the permitted age to attend school for a certain part of the time. It was common before the passage of this act for children of seven and five years, and even four, to work underground from twelve to sixteen hours out of each twenty-four. In 1843, the Educational Grant was increased to £30,000. At the time, it is stated in Molesworth's "History of England from 1830 to 1874," that there were 1,014,193 children growing up completely illiterate. Another measure was then adopted compelling the education of pauper children and those employed in factories—the latter being brought about by fines and penalties imposed on the employers who hired children without the proper certificates of school attendance, or worked them so as to render them unable to attend the necessary hours. In 1844, another factory act required two and a half hours of daily school attendance in summer and three hours in winter for all children between the ages of eight and thirteen, employed in mill work. Interest gradually increased in the subject of popular education, and this increase became more rapid after the International Exhibition of 1851. For the next fifteen years the largest advance was made in the direction of scientific and technical instruction. This increased interest is shown by the following statement:

"The annual parliamentary grants to popular education in Great Britain, which amounted to £30,000 in 1840, rose to £83,406 in 1848; to £189,110 in 1850; to £326,436 in 1854; to £668,873 in 1858; to £774,743 in 1862; in 1863, the grant was reduced to £721,386; in 1864, to £655,036; in 1865, to £636,306; in 1866, to £649,006; in 1867, to £682,201; and in 1868, to £680,429; while in 1869 it was raised again to £840,711; in 1870, to £914,721; in 1871, to £1,038,624: and in 1872 to £1,551,560. The total grants for the financial year 1873-4 amounted to £2,472,780, and for 1874-5 to £2,577,389.

"In the distribution of the * * grants * * about seven-tenths were given in recent years for examination and attendance of pupils, two-tenths as stipends and salaries to teachers, and one-tenth spent in administration and for building schools. The income from the fees paid by the children in the elementary schools amounted, on the average of the last five years, to less than a sixth of the sums voted by Parliament."*

When the first national education act was passed, the cost of the Elementary schools in England, aided by Government grants, was £1,483,472. They numbered 8,281, with accommodations for 1,878,584 pupils, and showed an average daily attendance of 1,152,389. By the act for Public Elementary Education it is ordered that there shall " be provided for every school district a sufficient amount of accommodation in public elementary schools available for all the children resident in such district, for whose elementary education efficient and suitable provision is not otherwise made. It is enacted further that all children attending these 'public elementary schools', whose parents are unable, from poverty, to pay anything towards their education, shall be admitted free, and the expenses so incurred be discharged from local rates. The new schools are placed in each district under ' School Boards', invested with great powers, among others that of making it compulsory upon parents to give all children between the ages of five and thirteen the advantages of education."†

The general control of this system is under the Committee of Education of the Privy Council ; Lord Sandon being Vice-President under the Disraeli Ministry, as was the Right Hon. W. E. Forster, M. P., under Mr. Gladstone's Premiership. This department determines the accommodation required. It apportions the grants ; approves or rejects the resolution of the Local School Board to enforce a compulsory rule ; directs the times, etc., of election for

---

* Martin's Year Book, 1875, pp. 212–213.   † Id., p. 212.

members of such Board; determines where they are necessary, which is to be judged by the deficiency existing and wishes of the rate-payers. The Boards are elected for three years. The cumulative vote is applied in the Elections and no restrictions provided, as to the candidacy of either ladies or non-residents. The Boards have power to determine the amount of school fees or remit them altogether, for a period not exceeding six months; it may in some cases aid in feeding the poorer children: it has the general maintenance of the schools, can purchase sites and erect buildings. How rapid has been the growth of these elementary schools may be seen from the following facts:

In 1871–2, the schools under government inspection numbered 9,854; the children in them, 1,336,000; School Boards 82.

In 1872–3, the schools numbered 11,094; the children 1,482,000; the School Boards 520; children at schools where compulsory attendance was enforced, 70,000.

In 1873–4, schools 12,246, children 1,679,000; School Boards 838; pupils under compulsory attendance 138,000.

In August 1874, the Inspectors' reports showed that there were 1,727,275 pupils in attendance at the Elementary Schools. The number of School Boards in October of that year was 854. It is estimated there will be, at the end of the school year 1875–6, not less than 2,057,567 pupils under the new educational policy, in England and Wales alone. In Scotland, the number of scholars is stated at 342,847, and in Ireland, there were on the 31st of December, 1874, 7,257 schools with an enrolment of 1,006,511 pupils, and an average daily attendance of 395,390. It was stated by Lord Sandon that, before the year 1875 closed, accomodation would have been provided for every child of school age in the United Kingdom. This would, it is estimated, give 2,500,000 places in schools receiving government grants; in others, not receiving such grants, but inspected and passed as efficent, 1,000,000; in Board Schools, 500,000. This supply would be ample, and without the enforcement of compulsory attendance, it is estimated, one-third of those seats would be daily unoccupied. The battle is really turning on this point,—the anti-denominational issue, though discussed, not being as vigorously pressed. Out of a total population of 22,712,266 in England, only 10,818,825 are included within the jurisdiction of School Boards; and of these the number to whom by-laws for enforcing school attendance apply is 9,538,971. Compulsion is now the law for rather less than forty-two per cent. of the entire population, and for about seventy-nine per cent. of the town population. In many places Boards have been formed for no other purpose than to enforce the attendance of children in schools of which the supply was already sufficient. It is regarded however as very costly machinery for the purpose.

Mr. Chamberlain represents very forcibly, in his speeches and writings, the hostility roused at the compromise made by Mr. Forster, in the act of 1872,—a compromise which, it is declared, largely tended to accelerate the retirement of the Gladstone ministry. To sum up then, the present situation in Great Britain on the subject of national education, leaves three parties,—the first of which insists on distinct dogmatic teaching, the second contends for Bible reading only (Earl Russell and Liberals of his school would be contented therewith), and the third wants instruction to be made secular. The other issues are whether the school system shall continue as now, to be supported by a mixed plan of government grants, local rates and tuition fees, or by the local rates only. The latter is the demand of the League, of which Mr. Chamberlain is an active leader. The difference may be seen by the position and requirements of the legislation now in existence. Under the present system, schools are maintained by means of voluntary contributions and tuition fees, supplemented by local rates and government grants. The rates are applied only in School Board districts. The schools aided by government grants may be under public or private control, but must be, as to instruction, up to the parliamentary standard. Government inspection is enforced, not voluntary. Denominational schools are permitted, but the system is not extended. Religious instruction can be given, but the government grants or local rates are not to be used in support thereof. Children are not compelled to be in attendance if their parents object. Inspection, as such, by the church or other denomination, is not permitted. The Privy Council committee of education do not aim to control or direct, but only to supervise and inspect. Compulsory attendance can be enforced only by the by-laws of the several Local Boards, first approved by the Privy Council. These are the salient features of the plan now in operation.

Mr. Chamberlain's activity is felt in many directions. Like other prominent Liberals, whose practical knowledge rendered them available for the service, he has been engaged as arbitrator in Labor disputes. A notable case of this kind was the settlement through him, of a long strike in 1873-4, between the employers and coal-miners of South Staffordshire, over a question of reducing wages. Mr. Chamberlain's decision substituted a sliding scale for a fixed rate; the scale to be determined by the price list issued by Earl Dudley, the largest operator in the district. The principle is the same as that which the anthracite miners of Pennsylvania have sought to maintain, and against the overthrow of which they were on strike for several months of 1875.

Mr. Chamberlain has also been an early and liberal contributor to the "Agricultural Laborers Union" agitation, and he is regarded by its journal, the "Laborers' Union Chronicle," as one of their best friends. He gives his support and presence to the aid of co-operative efforts and meetings. At a public meeting held in the Birmingham Town Hall, November 25th, 1874, to urge a plan of productive co-operation, the Mayor presided, and declared in his speech, that such experiments were desirable quite as much in the interests of employers, as in the interests of the employed. If working-men could really successfully conduct on their own account complicated manufactures, they would learn on the one hand to appreciate the difficulties which frequently beset employers, and the objects by which capitalists were trammelled; and on the other hand, they would do a great deal towards settling the vexed question of what was the fair proportion in which profit should be divided between labor and capital. He held however that the right principle of co-operation as applied to manufacture, was that when a fair market wage had been paid to the laborers, and when a fair market interest had been paid to those who found the capital, whether they were working men, or capitalists, or anything else, all surplus should be equally divided between both classes.

There were two advantages which would follow this, and they were practical advantages: In the first place, the working people in such a concern were not tied down by any hard and fast line called the rule of supply and demand, since there was no limit to the wages they might possibly earn; but they would depend in a great measure upon their own exertions,—they could earn something above the fixed rate, if they gave their minds to it. In the second place, inasmuch as all the work-people in such a concern would be partners in it, every man among them would have a direct interest in its success, and each, in his own way, would do something to secure it. In making such an experiment, there were three conditions which he thought necessary to success. In the first place, they must choose their ablest, their best men, as their managers. They must bear in mind that a man might be a capital workman, and a clever fellow, and yet might not possess the peculiar talent which they called business capacity, and which, he believed, was just as much a special gift as the taste for music or the taste for drawing.

When they had foud their good managers, it was no use attempting to get them below the market price; and if they were ungenerous in this respect, they might be sure that they would not rivet the interests of those men to theirs, and they would be certain to be deprived of their services just when they were becoming most useful to them. And lastly when they had got a good manager and paid him well, they must give him their full and complete confidence. They must be prepared for bad times, for there were fluctuations even in the most successful business ; and must express and show always a generous and loyal confidence in those whom they had selected to guide their councils and to manage their business.

The political opinions and character of Mr. Chamberlain have, however, become most widely known in England through the vigorous articles prepared by him and published in the *Fortnightly Review* of 1873. It is these papers which have aroused the most admiration and criticism, according as the reader's opinions were or were not in harmony with the writer's. That they were not regarded as politic or wise by the more moderate Liberals, or approved by oldtime and honored leaders like Mr. Bright, was evident from the letters of the accomplished correspondent of the New York *Tribune*, Mr. G. W. Smalley, who represents more closely even than English writers do, the opinions held by the persons indicated.

But the articles themselves stamp Mr. Chamberlain as a man of unusual force, and their appearance was opportune, as the Liberal party had practically broken to pieces for want of salient policy. In the place of compromise and temporizing, which is the usual course pursued by English statesmen, it had been found that the Conservative party, under Mr. Disraeli's leadership, was capable of making almost as rapid strides as the Liberals under Mr. Gladstone, and that when so moving of late years, they have been more successful, in that they could utilize all the arduous preparatory labors of their opponents to help their eleventh-hour efforts. Mr. Chamberlain urged the need of decisive action ; pointed out issues, and formulated new rallying cries. The paper, under the title of "The Liberal party and its leaders," appeared in the *Fortnightly* of September, 1873, and the second under the caption of "The next page of the Liberal programme," appeared in October of the same year.

The first paper was, as its title indicates, a review of Liberal measures and men. After showing the internal causes of party dissatisfaction and emphasizing the services of the Gladstone ministry, the foremost of which were stated to be the pacification of Ireland and the disestablishment of the Irish State Church, Mr. Chamberlain proceeded to show the reasons for the grave discontent, which he declared to exist in the party. These are the failure to rectify unjust working class legislation; to extend the county franchise, and the paltry compromise on the matter of education. With regard to these issues, Mr. Chamberlain said in his first article, that—

"Of one thing we may be certain—that if we continue much longer to flaunt our wealth and luxury in the face of a vast population, whose homes would disgrace a barbarous country, whose lack of culture and education leaves them a prey to merely animal instincts, and who find it difficult, and often impossible, to procure the barest necessaries of life, we shall be startled some day by the abrupt and possibly inconvenient accomplishment of reforms which will throw into the shade the splendid achievements of a Ministry that now confines itself to preparing bills which are meant to be withdrawn, and which pass into the limbo of unaccomplished legislation, unwept, unhonored, and unsung."

He then referred to optimistic views that were broadly put forth on the hustings and said in reply—

"It is impossible to say with certainty what will be the exact form of this protest against the ever-recurring assumption that the time has come when statesmen may rest from their labors and parties be at peace, but it must include some or all of the following ideas which have been exercising a growing attraction for political thinkers, and which are summed up in the sentence which may perhaps form the motto of the new party—*Free Church, Free Land, Free Schools, and Free Labor.*"

Following this attractive and alliterative rallying cry—one which seems to have taken hold of the Radical masses—the writer proceeded to define in detail what is to be aimed at under each division of the motto he shaped, and what are the forces that will rally around the new Liberalism he advocates. That of a "Free Church," will unite the divided Non-Conformists, and the working class—the latter having however no sympathy with the theological phase which will attract the former. A demand will be made that disendowment shall accompany disestablishment, and the claim will be eagerly put forth that in "the nation as a whole the control and management of the vast funds which have been monopolized and misappropriated by an ecclesiastical organization"—shall hereafter be vested. "Free land," writes Mr. Chamberlain,

"Involving the reform of laws, passed admittedly in the supposed interest of a very limited class, and operating, notwithstanding, to their injury, while materially diminishing the happiness and the prosperity of the rest of the population, will have to be contended for at the same time and wrested from the same political opponents."

He speaks of "wealthy legislators, acred up to their eyes" who are also "stolid defenders" of the establishment, expecting to find in "that Church the most zealous upholders of their privileges and monopoly." He declares that:—

"The English land system has no parallel in the world. It makes proprietorship a luxury, attainable only by a few, and seems ingeniously designed to discourage profitable investment in the soil, and involve landlord and tenant alike in a suicidal struggle to exhaust the land, during the existence of their limited interests."

"Free Schools may possibly," he thinks, "have to wait longer for their general acceptance and development, although the progress of compulsory education is certain to create and stimulate the demand for them." It is just that education should be a national charge borne equally by all the people. There is a fashionable political economy "very popular in the parliament of the rich, which has made the discovery that such a wide distribution of a charge which is to secure a universal benefit, is calculated to degrade and pauperize those whom it relieves from a heavy and onerous payment, levied at a time when they are least able to support it." This is "the gospel of selfishness," and teaches that philanthropy has performed its duty "when it buttons up the breeches pocket." The "superfine philosophy" involved, will however be "repudiated as suddenly as it has been accepted by the great body of politicians who obtain their opinions ready-made, and change them as soon as they discover they do not fit the humor of the majority."

Mr. Chamberlain's judgment is vindicated by later events in England, when he declared that :—

"Free Labor—the last position named in the Quadrilateral which the Irreconcilables attack—will probably be the first to be gained by them. The questions involved admit of only one possible solution. * *

The legislative changes sought by the workmen are surely moderate enough. They seem to be confined to three points :—the amendment of the law of conspiracy, the operation of which has been generally admitted to be unjust ;—the alteration of those clauses of the Criminal

Law Amendment Act which wound the self-respect and offend the common sense of the men by creating new crimes which are incapable of clear definition, while at the same time they are of no real value to employers in any serious struggle;—and the abolition of imprisonment for breach of contract where no malicious injury is intended to person or property. It can hardly be worth while to perpetuate ill-feeling and irritation for the sake of defending such a paltry stake as this."

During the Parliamentary session of 1875, the Conservative ministry has utilized, for its own advantage, the long discussion of these questions; and, under the leadership of Mr. Cross, Secretary of State for Home affairs, has succeeded in perfecting a measure which almost entirely sets at rest the mooted points indicated in the foregoing. Mr. Chamberlain's second paper was published after the general election of 1874 had resulted in returning a Conservative majority to the House of Commons. In it he is even more outspoken. The following extract will illustrate the style and directness of this new aspirant in the field of political polemics. As to the causes of the Liberal defeat he says:

"There are two popular theories on the subject. The Tories claim pardonably enough, that what their merits alone might have been unable to effect was achieved through the misdeeds of their opponents. According to this explanation, the nation, tired of the plundering and blundering of a tyrannical faction, roused itself to throw off the yoke, and flung itself with a sigh of relief into the arms of the Tories. The Liberal view is still more simple. Aristides was ostracized because he was just, and the Gladstone ministry fell by its own virtues. There is some truth in both these statements. It is certain that the late Government was thoroughly unpopular at the time of its fall; and, on the other hand, it must be admitted that it performed much useful work, and that its chief measures were called for by Liberal opinion, and if not perfect exponents of the wishes of its constituents, were, at least, in the desired direction. It may be said broadly, however, that the ministry had offended every one to whom change was objectionable, and that it made no bid for the support of those who conceived that further change was necessary. It must be granted that the English are naturally a Conservative people. We cling fondly to

> 'Custom, which all mankind to slavery brings,
> That dull excuse for doing silly things,'

and we are slow to appreciate and assimilate new ideas. Above all, we are impatient of small changes, and intolerant of infinitesimal reforms. It would be easier to disestablish the English Church than to clothe the Blue-coat boys in decent ordinary costume, while it would almost be safer to proclaim a republic than to meddle with certain ignoble petty interests, as, for instance, the control and management of their funds by some of the City companies. It was the evil genius of the late Government which somehow prompted their interference in a hundred minor matters which involve no game worth the candle, but which deeply interested the prejudices of various members of the community. Every class and every section of the population have had reason to be annoyed during the last few years, and have felt perhaps their wound was great because it was so small. There has been too much 'nagging' in legislation; and the Imperial Parliament, which, like the elephant's trunk, can pick up pins or rend an oak, has gathered pins enough to fill a lady's reticule."

Mr. Chamberlain's future is in his own hands, and that which has been so well begun, may be expected to develop in usefulness and power.

www.ingramcontent.com/pod-product-compliance
Lightning Source LLC
Chambersburg PA
CBHW020319240426
43673CB00039B/858